T0265677

THE THEOLOGY OF THE BOOK OF SAMUEL

The Old Testament book of Samuel is an intriguing narrative that offers an account of the origin of the monarchy in Israel. It also deals at length with the fascinating stories of Saul and David. In this volume, John Goldingay works through the book, exploring the main theological ideas as they emerge in the narratives about Samuel, Saul, and David, as well as in the stories of characters such as Hannah, Michal, Bathsheba, and Tamar. Goldingay brings out the key ideas about God and God's involvement in the lives of people, and their involvement with him through prayer and worship. He also delves into the mystery and complexity of human persons and their roles in events. Goldingay's study traces how God pursues his purpose for Israel and, ultimately, for the world in these narratives. It shows how this pursuit is interwoven with the realities of family, monarchy, war, love, ambition, loss, failure, and politics.

John Goldingay is an Anglican priest and former Principal of St. John's Theological College, Nottingham, and Emeritus David Allan Hubbard Professor of Old Testament at Fuller Theological Seminary in Pasadena, California. He is the author of *Old Testament Theology* and commentaries on a number of biblical books.

OLD TESTAMENT THEOLOGY

GENERAL EDITORS

Brent A. Strawn
D. Moody Smith Distinguished Professor of Old Testament and Professor of Law
Duke University

Stephen B. Chapman
Associate Professor of Old Testament
Duke University

Patrick D. Miller[†]
Charles T. Haley Professor of Old Testament Theology, Emeritus
Princeton Theological Seminary

This series aims to remedy the deficiency of available published material on the theological concerns of the Old Testament books. Here, specialists explore the theological richness of a given book at greater length than is usually possible in the introductions to commentaries or as part of other Old Testament theologies. They are also able to investigate the theological themes and issues of their chosen books without being tied to a commentary format or to a thematic structure provided from elsewhere. When complete, the series will cover all the Old Testament writings and will thus provide an attractive, and timely, range of short texts around which courses can be developed.

PUBLISHED VOLUMES

The Theology of the Books of Nahum, Habakkuk, and Zephaniah,
Daniel C. Timmer

The Theology of the Book of Proverbs, Katharine J. Dell

The Theology of the Books of Haggai and Zechariah, Robert L. Foster

The Theology of the Book of Kings, Keith Bodner

The Theology of the Book of Amos, John Barton

The Theology of the Book of Genesis, R. W. L. Moberly

The Theology of the Book of Jeremiah, Walter Brueggemann

THE THEOLOGY OF THE
BOOK OF SAMUEL

JOHN GOLDINGAY

Fuller Theological Seminary

CAMBRIDGE
UNIVERSITY PRESS

CAMBRIDGE
UNIVERSITY PRESS

Shaftesbury Road, Cambridge CB2 8EA, United Kingdom

One Liberty Plaza, 20th Floor, New York, NY 10006, USA

477 Williamstown Road, Port Melbourne, VIC 3207, Australia

314–321, 3rd Floor, Plot 3, Splendor Forum, Jasola District Centre,
New Delhi – 110025, India

103 Penang Road, #05–06/07, Visioncrest Commercial, Singapore 238467

Cambridge University Press is part of Cambridge University Press & Assessment,
a department of the University of Cambridge.

We share the University's mission to contribute to society through the pursuit of
education, learning and research at the highest international levels of excellence.

www.cambridge.org
Information on this title: www.cambridge.org/9781009519748

DOI: 10.1017/9781009519762

First published 2024

A catalogue record for this publication is available from the British Library

Library of Congress Cataloging-in-Publication Data
NAMES: Goldingay, John, author.
TITLE: The theology of the book of Samuel / John Goldingay.
DESCRIPTION: 1. | Cambridge, United Kingdom ; New York : Cambridge
University Press, 2024. | Series: Old Testament theology | Includes
bibliographical references and index.
IDENTIFIERS: LCCN 2024000031 (print) | LCCN 2024000032 (ebook) |
ISBN 9781009519748 (hardback) | ISBN 9781009519762 (ebook)
SUBJECTS: LCSH: Bible. Samuel, 1st – Theology. | Bible. Samuel, 1st – Criticism,
interpretation, etc. | Jews – Kings and rulers. | Kings and rulers – Biblical teaching. | Monarchy.
CLASSIFICATION: LCC BS1325.52 .G64 2024 (print) | LCC BS1325.52 (ebook) |
DDC 222/.406–dc23/eng/20240216
LC record available at https://lccn.loc.gov/2024000031
LC ebook record available at https://lccn.loc.gov/2024000032

ISBN 978-1-009-51974-8 Hardback
ISBN 978-1-009-51973-1 Paperback

Contents

General Editors' Preface

Some years ago, Cambridge University Press, under the editorship of James D. G. Dunn, initiated a series entitled New Testament Theology. The first volumes appeared in 1991 and the series was brought to completion in 2003. For whatever reason, a companion series that would focus on the Old Testament/Hebrew Bible was never planned or executed. The present series, Old Testament Theology, is intended to rectify this need.

The reasons for publishing Old Testament Theology are not, however, confined solely to a desire to match New Testament Theology. Instead, the reasons delineated by Dunn that justified the publication of New Testament Theology continue to hold true for Old Testament Theology. These include, among other things, the facts that (1) given faculty and curricular structures in many schools, the theological study of individual Old Testament writings is often spotty at best; (2) most exegetical approaches (and commentaries) proceed verse by verse such that theological interests are in competition with, if not completely eclipsed by, other important issues, whether historical, grammatical, or literary; and (3) commentaries often confine their discussion of a book's theology to just a few pages in the introduction. The dearth of materials focused exclusively on a particular book's theology may be seen as a result of factors like these; or, perhaps, it is the cause of such factors. Regardless, as Dunn concluded, without adequate theological resources, there is little incentive for teachers or students to engage the theology of specific books; they must be content with what are mostly general overviews. Perhaps the most serious problem resulting from all this is that students are at a disadvantage, even incapacitated, when it comes to the matter of integrating their study of the Bible with other courses in religion and theology. There is, therefore, an urgent need for a series to bridge the gap between the too-slim theological précis and the too-full commentary where theological concerns are lost among many others.

All of these factors commend the publication of Old Testament Theology now, just as they did for New Testament Theology more than two decades ago. Like its sister series, Old Testament Theology is a place where Old Testament scholars can write at greater length on the theology of individual biblical books and may do so without being tied to the linear, verse-by-verse format of the commentary genre or a thematic structure of some sort imposed on the text from outside. Each volume in the series seeks to describe the biblical book's theology as well as to engage the book theologically – that is, each volume intends to *do* theology through and with the biblical book under discussion, as well as delineate the theology contained within it. Among other things, theological engagement with the composition includes paying attention to its contribution to the canon and appraising its influence on and reception by later communities of faith. In these ways, Old Testament Theology seeks to emulate its New Testament counterpart.

In the intervening years since New Testament Theology was first conceived, however, developments have taken place in the field that provide still further reasons for the existence of Old Testament Theology; these have impact on how the series is envisioned and implemented and also serve to distinguish it, however slightly, from its companion series. Three developments in particular are noteworthy:

1. *The present hermeneutical climate*, often identified (rightly or wrongly) as "postmodern," is rife with possibility and potential for new ways of theologizing about scripture and its constituent parts. Theologizing in this new climate will of necessity look (and be) different from how it has ever looked (or been) before.

2. *The ethos change in the study of religion, broadly, and in biblical studies in particular.* No longer are the leading scholars in the field only Christian clergy, whether Catholic priests or mainline Protestant ministers. Jewish scholars and scholars of other Christian traditions are every bit as prominent, as are scholars of non- or even anti-confessional stripe. In short, now is a time when "Old Testament Theology" must be conducted without the benefits of many of the old consensuses and certainties, even the most basic ones relating to epistemological framework and agreed-upon interpretative communities along with their respective traditions.

3. Finally, recent years have witnessed *a long-overdue rapprochement among biblical scholars, ethicists, and systematic theologians.* Interdisciplinary studies between these groups are now regularly published, thus furthering and facilitating the need for books that make the theology of scripture widely available for diverse publics.

In brief, the time is ripe for a series of books that will engage the theology of specific books of the Old Testament in a new climate for a new day. The result will not be programmatic, settled, or altogether certain. Despite that – or, in some ways, *because* of that – it is hoped that Old Testament Theology will contain highly useful volumes that are ideally poised to make significant contributions on a number of fronts including (a) the ongoing discussion of biblical theology in confessional and nonconfessional mode as well as in postmodern and canonical contexts, (b) the theological exchange between Old Testament scholars and those working in cognate and disparate disciplines, and (c) the always-pressing task of introducing students to the theology of the discrete canonical unit: the biblical books themselves.

Brent A. Strawn
D. Moody Smith Distinguished Professor of Old Testament and Professor of Law, Duke University

Stephen B. Chapman
Associate Professor of Old Testament Duke University

Patrick D. Miller[†]
Charles T. Haley Professor of Old Testament Theology, Emeritus Princeton Theological Seminary

Abbreviations

1QSam, 4QSam	Fragmentary manuscripts of Samuel from Qumran Cave 1 and Cave 4
AB	The Anchor Bible
b.	*Babylonian Talmud* (followed by the name of a tractate)
BibInt	*Biblical Interpretation*
BZAW	Beihefte zur Zeitschrift für die alttestamentliche Wissenschaft
CBQ	*Catholic Biblical Quarterly*
CEB	Common English Bible
Diss.	Dissertation
FOTL	The Forms of the Old Testament Literature
JBL	*Journal of Biblical Literature*
JSOT	*Journal for the Study of the Old Testament*
JSOTSup	Journal for the Study of the Old Testament Supplement
KJV	King James Version (Authorized Version)
LHBOTS	Library of Hebrew Bible/Old Testament Studies
LXX	Septuagint

MT	Masoretic Text
NPNF	Nicene and Post-Nicene Fathers
NICOT	New International Commentary on the Old Testament
NIV	New International Version
NJPS	New Jewish Publication Society Translation
NRSV	New Revised Standard Version
OTL	Old Testament Library
TDOT	*Theological Dictionary of the Old Testament*
Tg	Targum
Vg	Vulgate
VT	*Vetus Testamentum*
VTSup	Vetus Testamentum Supplement
WBC	Word Biblical Commentary
ZAW	*Zeitschrift für die alttestamentliche Wissenschaft*

English translations and printed Hebrew Bibles have different versions of the chapter divisions in the Scriptures, which were introduced into the text in the medieval period. Where necessary, I give the English reference first, then in square brackets the equivalent in a printed Hebrew Bible: for example, 2 Sam 19:3[4]. All biblical and other translations are my own unless otherwise indicated.

CHAPTER 1

Introduction

First and Second Samuel tell the story of a crucial century early in Israel's life. After introducing Samuel himself, they relate how Saul became king and failed as king, and how David became king and also then went through crises. The story takes the Israelites from being a loose collection of clans living in homesteads, villages, and small townships to being a state with a capital and a central government, with a king whose son will succeed him and with prophets who support him and/or confront him. The Israelites share a relationship with their God who lives among them. At the beginning of the story he is living above the "covenant chest" (the "ark") in a sanctuary at Shiloh; by the end of the story the sanctuary has come to be located in the capital city and their king is planning to build a temple there. At the beginning of the story they are under pressure from the Philistines to the west and north; at the end of the story they are in control of an area corresponding to the modern bounds of Israel and Palestine along with much of what is now Jordan and Syria. These epoch-making developments take place over a period of a few decades, the reign of two kings, maybe from about 1070 BC to about 970 BC. The focus of the story does not lie simply on these developments but on the human and family processes and events associated with them – the family origins of the first prophet, Samuel, the conflicts between the first

1

king, Saul, and his apparent rival, and the family conflicts of this
rival, David, when he becomes the second king.

Three related theological paradoxes emerge from this process
and constitute central features of the theology of Samuel. Yahweh
is ambivalent about the introduction of a monarchy that made
this development possible. Events involve Yahweh's activity and
also human initiative. And both the first two kings whom Yahweh
chose were religiously and morally ambiguous characters.

Whereas First and Second Samuel appear as two books in
modern Hebrew and English Bibles, the Babylonian Talmud
(*Baba Batra* 14b) refers to Samuel as one book, and it is one book
in Hebrew manuscripts, including the Masoretic Text. First
Samuel is a coherent unit with a proper beginning (Samuel's
birth) and a meaningful end (Saul's death), "but when read
together with 2 Samuel these elements increasingly appear in
retrospect to have been a tragic episode en route to something
else."[1] If one were to attach a single name to the entire work as its
subject, it would be David.[2] This volume thus studies "Samuel"
as a whole; the context should make clear when Samuel refers to
the book and when it refers to the prophet Samuel. The division
between Samuel and Kings is slightly odd, since it is 1 Kings 1–2
that brings the David story to an end. Kings thus leads seam-
lessly on from Samuel, and the Septuagint is onto something
when it describes Samuel-Kings as the "Four Books of Reigns."
But 2 Samuel does come to a conclusion of its own, and 1 Kings

---

[1] Stephen B. Chapman, *1 Samuel as Christian Scripture: A Theological
Commentary* (Grand Rapids, MI: Eerdmans, 2016), 46.

[2] A. Graeme Auld, *I & II Samuel: A Commentary*, OTL (Louisville, KY:
Westminster John Knox, 2011), 1–2; Robert Alter's title for his study is *The
David Story: A Translation with Commentary of 1 and 2 Samuel* (New York:
Norton, 1999).

1–2 is the beginning of Solomon's story as well as the end of David's.

Like most of the Scriptures, Samuel is anonymous, and we can only make informed guesses about the process whereby it came into being.

- The Talmud (*Baba Batra* 15a) goes on to name Samuel as the book's author, but it then qualifies that statement by adding that Gad and Nathan completed the work after Samuel's death. Samuel is indeed a key figure in the book, as the person who anoints first Saul and then David. There is hard information in the book that would need to go back to the time of David and Solomon, and one can imagine that people in that time would be interested in having an account of how the monarchy came into being and how David and Solomon came to the throne.[3] Scholarly theories have inferred that from that time there were indeed accounts of Samuel, of the adventures of the covenant chest, of the rise of David, and of the story of David's family that was background to Solomon's succeeding him, accounts that were incorporated into the book as we have it.
- The nearest thing within Samuel to a concrete clue about its origin lies in its references to things that remain true "now" or

---

[3] See, for example, David Toshio Tsumura, *The First Book of Samuel*, NICOT (Grand Rapids, MI: Eerdmans, 2007); Moshe Garsiel, "The Book of Samuel: Its Composition, Structure and Significance as a Historiographical Source," *Journal of Hebrew Scriptures* 10/5 (2010); Andrew Knapp, *Royal Apologetic in the Ancient Near East*, Writings from the Ancient World 4 (Atlanta, GA: SBL, 2015), 161–248; Lester L. Grabbe, "Mighty Men of Israel: 1–2 Samuel and Historicity," in W. Dietrich, ed., *The Books of Samuel: Stories–History–Reception History*, Bibliotheca Ephemeridum Theologicarum Lovaniensium 84 (Leuven: Peeters, 2016), 83–104.

"today" (1 Sam 5:5; 6:18; 9:9; 27:6; 30:25; 2 Sam 4:3; 6:8; 18:18), but they do not indicate when "now" or "today" is, except in one reference to the kings of Judah (1 Sam 27:6). This note, then, comes from a time following the split between Ephraim and Judah after Solomon's day, and before the end of the Judahite monarchy in 587. Theologians with a "prophetic" outlook in the time of Isaiah or Jeremiah might have generated a version of the story of the monarchy that incorporated those earlier materials.[4] In Jewish thinking, Samuel is part of "The Former Prophets," while an influential scholarly theory links a first edition of the narrative as a whole with the time of King Josiah, the late seventh century.[5]

- The next nearest thing to a clue is the narrative's raising the question of who will succeed David and build the temple, but not answering the question, and leaving David's story hanging in midair. Other points of connection suggest that Samuel is written in a way that makes links with what will follow in Kings. The Septuagint's seeing Samuel and Kings as the four books of Reigns coheres with the possibility of seeing Samuel and Kings as a two-part work telling the story of the monarchic period as a whole from its beginnings to its caesura in 587 BC. Perhaps the books originally belonged

---

[4] See, for example, Antony F. Campbell, *Of Prophets and Kings: A Late Ninth-Century Document (1 Samuel 1–2 Kings 10)*, CBQ Monograph Series 17 (Washington, DC: CBA, 1986); P. Kyle McCarter, *I Samuel: A New Translation with Introduction, Notes and Commentary*, AB 8 (Garden City, NY: Doubleday, 1980), 18–23 – he emphasizes the northern background of the story.

[5] See, for example, Richard D. Nelson, *The Double Redaction of the Deuteronomistic History*, JSOTSup 18 (Sheffield: JSOT Press, 1981); P. Kyle McCarter, "The Books of Samuel," in Steven L. McKenzie and M. Patrick Graham, ed., *The History of Israel's Traditions: The Heritage of Martin Noth*, JSOTSup 182 (Sheffield: Sheffield Academic Press, 1994), 260–80.

together like Exodus–Leviticus–Numbers, and like them they were subdivided for convenience, as Samuel itself was subdivided later. Samuel, then, more or less as we have it belongs in the time after 587 BC.[6]

- There is more than average difference between the versions of Samuel in MT, in the Septuagint, and in the fragmentary manuscripts among the Qumran scrolls.[7] The marginal notes in modern translations indicate that they often follow these other versions of the book; I have usually stayed with MT. The existence of these slightly different versions indicates that Jewish teachers were still working on the book in the Persian and Hellenistic periods, perhaps in different contexts in Judah, Egypt, and Babylon. Indeed, as an aspect of scholarly inclination to ask whether the First Testament as a whole largely comes from the Second Temple era, it has been suggested that this period was the key one in which Samuel came into existence.[8]

Different groups of modern scholars are more inclined to focus on one or other of these periods as fundamental to an

---

[6] According to traditional critical theories, it then forms part of the Deuteronomistic History: on which see, for example, Cynthia Edenburg and Juha Pakkala, ed., *Is Samuel Among the Deuteronomists? Current Views on the Place of Samuel in a Deuteronomistic History*, Ancient Israel and Its Literature 16 (Atlanta, GA: SBL, 2013).

[7] See, for example, Philippe Hugo and Adrian Schenker, ed., *Archaeology of the Books of Samuel: The Entangling of the Textual and Literary History*, VTSup 132 (Leiden: Brill, 2010); Philippe Hugo, "1–2 Kingdoms (1–2 Samuel)," in *The T&T Clark Companion to the Septuagint*, ed. James K. Aitken (London: T&T Clark, 2015), 127–46; Frank Moore Cross et al., *Qumran Cave 4.XII: 1–2 Samuel*, Discoveries in the Judaean Desert 17 (Oxford: Clarendon Press, 2005); Ariel Feldman, *The Dead Sea Scrolls Rewriting Samuel and Kings: Texts and Commentary*, BZAW 469 (Berlin: de Gruyter, 2015).

[8] See, for example, John Van Seters, *The Biblical Saga of King David* (Winona Lake, IN: Eisenbrauns, 2009).

understanding of the book, and I will occasionally draw attention to the way the story might have come home in different periods. My own hunch regarding the process is that the second of the four stages above is the key one; the crucial creative work on the book happened in Jerusalem sometime during the divided monarchy. With any narrative, it can be worth asking what is the key question it seeks to answer, and a key question in Samuel might then be, "How did we come to have kings, anyway?" The vagaries of the Judahite monarchy could make this a natural question. More specifically the question might be, "Who was this David, who continues to be so important to us?" David's significance as the first great king, as the recipient of Yahweh's promise, and as the benchmark by which Judahite monarchs are measured in Kings, would also make this question natural.

An understanding of Shakespeare's plays (for instance) benefits from a knowledge of the period in which they were written, yet they make sense, stand, and speak independently of such knowledge. Likewise, the Samuel narrative makes sense, stands, and speaks independently of our being sure which period it comes from. Like other works from the ancient world such as the Iliad, it needs to be understood against the broad historical background of its culture, but within that broad context, more insight emerges from reading it in its own right as a narrative than from focusing on questions about precise historical background.

While the book does not reveal its author's identity, then, we can infer what kind of person it was. He or she

- had research access to state records and existent accounts of events in the time of Samuel, Saul and David;
- had the skill and education to write a work of some length – in other words, he or she was a scribe, and someone who would be at home in the circles of the "wise";

- was gifted with the literary ability to paint a creative portrait of events, to imagine conversations that people had, and to work out what they would be thinking;
- had a prophetic sensitivity to what Yahweh was doing in this sequence of events and to what Yahweh thought of events as they developed;
- knew that Yahweh was at work in them but also knew that he mostly works behind the scenes through or despite the actions of human beings;
- had a prophetic perspective in emphasizing faithfulness, proper government, commitment, and truthfulness (*ṣədāqâ, mišpāṭ, ḥesed, 'ĕmet/'ĕmûnâ*) and the need for kings to heed prophets;
- affirmed a commitment to the worship of Yahweh in the sanctuaries and eventually in the temple in Jerusalem but did not work with a specifically priestly perspective;
- was broad-minded, confident, and fearless in painting a portrait of people such as Eli, Samuel, Saul, David, and Joab;
- yet was then confident enough to leave the story's audience to come to their own assessment of these individuals in their complexity;
- emphasized the role of significant women, beginning with Hannah, almost ending with Rizpah, and including Abigail, Michal, Bathsheba, Tamar, and the smart woman in 2 Samuel 14;[9]
- and was fervently pro-Israel over against nations such as Moab and Ammon, but open-minded in relation to foreigners such as Uriah and Araunah.

[9] Cf. Susan M. Pigott, "Wives, Witches and Wise Women: Prophetic Heralds of Kingship in 1 and 2 Samuel," *Review and Expositor* 99 (2002): 145–73.

If one wanted a figure to whom one might attach the work in one's imagination, then it might be Huldah (2 Kgs 22:14–20).

While Samuel opens in a way that could constitute an absolute beginning (it compares with the beginning to Ruth), it can be seen as continuing from Joshua and Judges, which link forward to it. Broadly it is thus part of the much longer story that runs from Joshua to Kings (the "Former Prophets") or from Deuteronomy to Kings (the "Deuteronomistic History") or from Genesis to Kings (the "First History"). In Chronicles-Ezra-Nehemiah (the "Second History"), Chronicles then retells the story from the end of Saul's life onwards in an account of David that focuses on his preparations for the building of the temple and reflects its context in the Second Temple period. Samuel, then, forms part of Israel's story from its origins to the end of the monarchy, and in relating the story of the monarchy's origins, it has an important place in that narrative.

To understand the working of the sequence of scrolls from Genesis to Kings, an illuminating model is a sequence of television series. As Series Eight in the sequence that runs from Genesis to Kings, Samuel picks up issues left unresolved in Series Seven, tells its own story, and closes with unresolved questions that make the audience continue into Series Nine.

Like many television series and movies, Samuel is not simply history, but neither is it historical fiction. It is dramatized, visionary history, not chronological, objective history. While it concerns itself with things that happened, it uses imagination to discern what sort of thing people could appropriately have said, felt, and thought, and what will help the audience understand the significance of what was happening.

In the First Testament, there are works that are close to chronological history (e.g., parts of 2 Kings) and works that are close to fiction (e.g., Jonah), and scholarly views on Samuel's historical value vary. Whereas figures in Kings such as Omri and Hezekiah feature in other Middle Eastern documents, we have no mention of Saul or David, though an inscription from Tel Dan does refer to "the house of David." The book covers a period when Assyria and Egypt were in decline, which could make David freer to assert himself in the region than would have been possible at some other times. Other peoples such as the Aramaeans, the Ammonites, and the Philistines were doing the same. In this sense, David's story is historically plausible. But intensive scholarly research over two centuries has not generated progress in agreement on Samuel's historical value. It surely never will. There are scholars who believe that the narrative is simply factual and scholars who believe it is pure fiction. While my working assumption is that it is something in between, I do not know which pole it is nearer to. On one hand, I assume that people such as Hannah, Eli, Saul, David, Abigail, Mephiboshet, and Bathsheba indeed lived in Israel in the eleventh and tenth centuries and lived the kind of lives that Samuel relates. In this sense they are like people such as Jehoiachin, Zedekiah, and Gedaliah in 2 Kings. While the Christian description of Joshua to Nehemiah as "The Historical Books" may give readers a narrow or thin perspective, it is not totally inappropriate.[10] But in telling these people's stories, Samuel uses the techniques of the story of Jonah in imagining their lives, thinking, and conversations. It sits between Homer and Herodotus as a work that relates a historical story in an imaginative way.

Studying the Samuel narrative is then again comparable with studying Shakespeare's "historical" plays. One can investigate

---

[10] See further Rachelle Gilmour, *Representing the Past: A Literary Analysis of Narrative Historiography in the Book of Samuel*, VTSup 143 (Leiden: Brill, 2011).

their sources and the historical events to which they refer, and/or study the plays themselves and their theology or ethics or ideology. The forms of study have different aims. In this volume we are concerned with "the plays." Actually, "you wouldn't go to *Macbeth* to learn about the history of Scotland – you go to it to learn what a man feels like after he has gained a kingdom and lost his soul."[11]

Samuel has a further parallel with (post)modern drama. It is quite common for individual episodes in a television series to jump forward and backward, and to make such jumps within an episode. So it is with Samuel. First Samuel 13–15 comprises two accounts of Yahweh's decision to terminate Saul's reign or not allow him to be the beginning of a dynasty. These accounts directly follow on his accession as king and they are but the beginning of an account of his reign. They function to tell the auditors where the story is going. But their message is not presupposed by the chapters that follow, which tell the auditors how Saul's story eventually reached this denouement. Samuel's own story constitutes a series of snapshots from his birth, his summons maybe twenty years later, his challenge to turn to Yahweh another twenty years later, and his old age (though he then takes fifteen chapters to die). In David's story, the sequence of material in 2 Samuel 2–10 is as much thematic as chronological, though 2 Samuel 11–20 follows a more connected chronological sequence. The closing chapters, 2 Samuel 21–24, then comprise a collection of songs of praise, lists, and stories from different periods, to bring the book to an end. Thus the order of the book is often dramatic rather than chronological.

Further, several writers, directors, and producers of a television series may contribute different episodes. The Samuel scroll brings

---

[11] Northrop Frye, *The Educated Imagination* (Bloomington: Indiana University Press, 1964), 64; cf. Chapman, *1 Samuel as Christian Scripture*, 92.

together material of various kinds from various origins, with less concern for smoothness than normally obtains in television. The material includes:

- An account of Samuel's origins (1 Sam 1–4:1a).
- Within it, Hannah's thanksgiving in 2:1–10 stands out as a separable unit.
- A narrative about the covenant chest (4:1b–7:1).
- An account of how Saul came to be king (7:2–12:25).
- More positive and more negative accounts of the idea of having a king.[12]
- A narrative about how Samuel rejected Saul (13:1–16:13).
- Two stories about Yahweh's dismissal of Saul, which opens the way for David.
- A substantial narrative about how David comes to succeed Saul (1 Sam 16:14–2 Sam 4:12). It includes several examples of where two stories go over the same ground: two about David's introduction to Saul (16:14–23; 17:1–40), two about the Ziphites betraying David to Saul (23:19–28; 26:1–5), and two about David refraining from killing Saul when he has the chance (24:1–22[2–23]; 26:6–25).
- An account of David's actually becoming king and his success as king (2 Sam 5:1–10:19).
- A substantial narrative about the great failures of David's life and the consequences regarding the question of who will succeed him (11:1–20:25).
- Some closing footnotes to David's story (21:1–24:25).

[12] See Marsha White, "'The History of Saul's Rise': Saulide State Propaganda in 1 Samuel 1–14," in Saul M. Olyan and Robert C. Culley, ed., *A Wise and Discerning Mind: Essays in Honor of Burke O. Long*, Brown Judaic Studies (Providence, RI: Brown University, 2020), 271–92.

While the broad structure and plot of the work is clear, it does not provide explicit markers of a structure, so any structure of the kind just outlined comes in part from the imagination of the reader; other commentators lay it out differently.[13]

There are many ways to do Old or New Testament theology, as is revealed by a glance at the volumes in the series to which this volume belongs and its companion series on the New Testament. Different approaches allow different insights to emerge from the text. Samuel is a narrative book, which makes for a distinctive approach to doing theology and has distinctive implications for reflection on its theological significance. This fact is more obvious since the "literary turn" in the Humanities during the last decades of the twentieth century, which affected biblical studies and issued in a number of illuminating studies of Samuel.[14] These literary studies have especially worked with the regular focuses of literary study, particularly the human characters; in this volume we work more with the theological implications of the narrative.

The characteristics of Samuel's theological approach as a narrative need not be unique to a narrative book, but they come out particularly clearly in a narrative book.

- It focuses more on something that God did do, once, than on general statements about what God always does. It thus invites readers to live in a world in which God did this thing once.
- Yet it also speaks about things that God and people recurrently do. It thus invites people to live in a world in which these things recur.

[13] See the survey in Michael Avioz, "The Literary Structure of the Books of Samuel: Setting the Stage for a Coherent Reading," *Currents in Biblical Research* 16 (2017): 8–33.

[14] See David G. Firth, "Some Reflections on Current Narrative Research on the Book of Samuel," *Southeastern Theological Review* 10 (2019): 3–31.

- It can incorporate statements that stand in tension with each other. God relented; God does not relent.
- It can thus leave irresolvable enigmas unresolved: What is the relationship between God's grace and human commitment to God?
- It can tell its readers the facts without necessarily telling them how to interpret them.
- It can leave questions open. Did God forgive David for his affair with Bathsheba and his having Uriah killed?

In discussing Samuel's theology, one might proceed by writing chapters on its understanding of God, of Israel, of prophecy, of monarchy, and so on, or one might proceed by writing a chapter-by-chapter theological exposition of the text. I have done something in between, in dividing the book into six parts, working through the parts one by one, and looking from a theological perspective at topics as they arise. Sometimes these topics are explicitly theological (e.g., God, his activity in the world, and his relationships with people). Sometimes they are more general (e.g., family or monarchy), and the chapters consider their significance in the context of human life lived before God.

Doing such theological study can then seek to confine itself to teasing out the theological implications of the Scriptures themselves, or it can allow for evaluating their theology in light of convictions one brings to them. My focus lies on the first of these alternatives. Where the theology of the text goes against my convictions or convictions that are common in my culture, I seek to let the text confront them.

CHAPTER 2

Yahweh Who Prepares the Way for a King
(1 Samuel 1:1–4:1a)

The overarching theological theme in 1 Samuel 1–12 is Yahweh as one who designates a king. There are two stages to the process whereby that designation happens. First, Yahweh brings into being and summons a prophet who will do the designating of this first king, and of the second one (the third will emerge without divine intervention). Then this prophet does the actual designating, summoning, and anointing of the king. The exposition of the overarching theological theme and its implications concerning the nature of God and the nature of monarchy incidentally allows other themes to develop: something about the nature of family, about prayer, about ministry, about vocation, and about being the people of God.

In the Septuagint and thus in most English Bibles, Samuel follows Ruth, and shares the dynamics of that story. Ruth is a story about a family that suggests a theology of family, a story about individuals that suggests a theology of the individual, and a story about women that suggests a theology of womanhood. It implies that Yahweh is active in its story, though only once does it explicitly speak of his acting, in a way that parallels Samuel: "Yahweh enabled her to get pregnant" (Ruth 4:13). The close of Ruth then relates it to the broader narrative of Yahweh's involvement with the story of the monarchy. In connection with the anticipatory element in 1 Samuel 1, the parallel with the end of Ruth is especially significant: The Ruth story looks on to David, the Hannah story to Saul.

Samuel links in a related way with Judges, which precedes Samuel in the Torah, the Prophets, and the Writings. "In those days there was no king in Israel – an individual would do what was upright in his eyes" (Judg 21:25) makes an appropriate conclusion to an unsavory story. The Israelites have slaughtered most of the Benjaminite clan. They have given 400 Gileadite girls as wives to the surviving Benjaminites. And they have directed the rest of the survivors to the annual festival at Shiloh where girls would be joining in the festival, so as to get some of the girls to go off with them. Samuel begins with a more seemly story about such a festival. The story anticipates a time when there will be kings in Israel who might constrain such waywardness.

Notwithstanding their faults, maybe Saul and David do. Before they appear, 1 Samuel begins as an account of Yahweh's bringing into being and summoning a prophet who will designate both those kings. It opens as a story about a family and about its individual members, and about their relationship with Yahweh and Yahweh's relationship with them.

THE GOD OF HANNAH

The God of Samuel is Yahweh. The book makes nothing of the possible etymological meaning of this name any more than it does of the names Eli, Elqanah, Hannah, or Peninnah (Samuel's own name will be a different matter). Like most names, its significance lies in what it refers to. Yahweh is "simply" the name of the God of Israel. Eli blesses Hannah in the name of "the God of Israel" (1:17) and subsequently a prophet-type figure speaks in the name of "Yahweh, the God of Israel" (2:30; cf. 10:18; 14:41; 20:12; 23:10, 11; 25:32, 34; 2 Sam 12:7). The title "God of Israel" recurs on the Philistines' lips (1 Sam 5:7–6:5) and on David's lips (2 Sam 7:27; 23:3).

Near the beginning of 1 Samuel (2:1–10) there comes a song of praise that makes key theological affirmations concerning who this Yahweh is. It glorifies Yahweh in three respects:

> Yahweh is the all-powerful God
> Yahweh turns things upside down
> Yahweh will give strength to his king.[1]

It is Hannah, Samuel's mother, who proclaims this song of praise, as Yahweh has enabled her to move from barrenness to birth. That move is complemented by a movement from protest to praise.[2] The content of her praise does not relate to the particularities of her experience. By implication, that experience assists her to articulate broader truths about Yahweh.

First, Yahweh is the crag onto which his people can climb, and it is in this way that Yahweh is unique as the holy one (2:2). Hannah's description of Yahweh as holy is almost the first such description in the First Testament story (Josh 24:19 precedes it) and almost the only occasion when Samuel describes Yahweh as holy (1 Sam 6:20 is the other example). It does bear comparison with the description of Yahweh in Exodus 15 as majestic in holiness. If "there is no holy one like Yahweh," however, there are evidently lots of holy ones, as the First Testament does not mind presupposing that there are lots of *'ĕlōhîm*, of gods. The word "holy" applies to any supernatural beings. It denotes the metaphysical distinction

---

[1] Adapted from Tsumura, *The First Book of Samuel*, 68.
[2] Cf. Walter Brueggemann, "1 Samuel 1: A Sense of a Beginning," *ZAW* 102 (1990): 33–48 (39).

between them and human beings. But there is variety among the holy beings, as there is among *'ĕlōhîm*. Yahweh is supreme over other holy ones and is the source of their life. They can die, he does not. The First Testament is not concerned to declare that Yahweh is the only being who can properly be described as *'ĕlōhîm* – it is not very interested in monotheism. It is interested in declaring that Yahweh is more powerful than all other *'ĕlōhîm*, than all other holy ones. If Hebrew could distinguish orthographically between God and a god, then this ability would help it to make the point. Its declaration is that Yahweh is uniquely formidable as his people's protector. Therefore, human beings should not pretend to an impressiveness that they lack. Their self-deception and willfulness will be exposed. Yahweh is the God who must be acknowledged and cannot be put right (2:3). "The song of Hannah emerges as a study in power."[3]

Second, Yahweh is therefore capable of turning things upside down, and bringing about a reversal whereby people who looked strong collapse and feeble people become mysteriously strong, the well-endowed must seek jobs and the hungry have plenty, the childless are fertile and the fertile are bereaved, the alive die and the dying recover, the haves and have-nots and the insignificant and powerful change places (2:4–8a).[4] In some ways Hannah's psalm anticipates motifs within Samuel: Yahweh will deliver, he will prove to be a crag on which someone may find safety, he will silence the arrogant, he will break the bows of the mighty. In other ways her affirmation does not describe the activity Yahweh undertakes within Samuel, and people would need to think about it (for

---

[3] J. P. Fokkelman, *Narrative Art and Poetry in the Books of Samuel, Volume IV: Vow and Desire (I Sam. 1–12)* (Assen: van Gorcum, 1993), 105.

[4] Cf. Gale A. Yee, "The Silenced Speak: Hannah, Mary, and Global Poverty," *Feminist Theology* 21 (2012): 41–57 (42–47).

instance) after 587.[5] The affirmation also relates backwards to the deprivations and afflictions described in Judges.[6]

Hannah returns more plainly to speak of power the other side of her study of reversal, making explicit that it is Yahweh's possession of power that makes possible the imposition of reversal. Yahweh has this capacity because he is the one who established the world with stability (2:8b). Whereas the first two themes in the song concern the strong and the weak and then the haves and the have-nots, with little implicit religious or ethical slant, this part of the song adds that other dimension. Yahweh protects people who are committed to him, whereas the faithless go silent into the darkness of death (2:9a). It is the people who assert themselves against Yahweh that he shatters (2:9b–10aα). He makes decisions about the entire world (2:10aβγ). In the opening cola of her song, Hannah opened her mouth wide; in the final strophe God himself does.[7]

Hannah's song resembles a psalm, and it would fit in the Psalter, which helps to clarify its meaning and significance. It implies that what Yahweh has done for Hannah is an expression of his activity on the widest canvas, like many songs of praise in the Psalms (e.g., Ps 113). Yahweh's blessing of Hannah leads her into an act of praise that acclaims the entire breadth of Yahweh's activity. A psalm of protest will sometimes end with such an act of praise, and so may a thanksgiving psalm (e.g., Pss 22; 30). When Yahweh delivers an individual or a community, it issues in praise in general terms, because Yahweh's act gives expression to who he always is. While

---

[5] Randall C. Bailey, "The Redemption of Yhwh: A Literary Critical Function of the Songs of Hannah and David," *BibInt* 3 (1995): 213–31 (217–19).

[6] Francesca Aran Murphy, *1 Samuel*, Brazos Theological Commentary on the Bible (Grand Rapids, MI: Brazos, 2010), 19.

[7] Fokkelman, *Narrative Art and Poetry* 4:99.

one can make direct links with Hannah's story by seeing Peninnah behind the reference to enemies and seeing Hannah as the mother of seven, the points of connection are weak. "She sings not just as the mother of Samuel but as a mother of Israel."[8] The pattern suggested by the Psalms is that one protests to Yahweh, gives thanks for Yahweh's answer, and praises Yahweh for who he is and for his characteristic acts that have been (partially) embodied in his response to the protest. Here Hannah jumps straight to the last component.[9]

The third way in which the song glorifies Yahweh also parallels some psalms, in particular Psalm 18 which also appears at the other end of Samuel as 2 Samuel 22. Hannah prays "in a prophetic spirit" (Tg), like Zechariah (Luke 1:67).[10] Her song speaks about the king for whom her story prepares the way:

> He gives vigor to his king,
> lifts up the horn of his anointed one. (2:10)

When animals such as bulls fight, their horn is their key expression of strength. Breaking a horn signifies defeat; elevating one's horn signifies victory. Yahweh ensures that his anointed does hold

---

[8] Bruce C. Birch, "The First and Second Books of Samuel: Introduction, Commentary and Reflections," in *The New Interpreter's Bible* (Nashville, TN: Abingdon, 1998) 2:947–1383 (980); cf. Fokkelman, *Narrative Art and Poetry* 4:40.

[9] Whether or not the poem is a later addition to the story, it is the product of a creative author imagining what Hannah might appropriately be pictured as saying, like the account of conversations in 1 Sam 1.

[10] Tg sees Hannah as prophesying of Assyria, Babylon, Persia, Greece, and Rome. Augustine (*City of God* 17:4) sees her as looking beyond David to Jesus, in keeping with messianic interpretation in *Liber antiquitatum biblicarum*: see Hannes Bezzel, "Hannah's Prayer(s) in 1 Samuel 1–2 and in Pseudo-Philo's Liber antiquitatum biblicarum," in Susanne Gillmayr-Bucher and Maria Häusl, eds., *Prayers and the Construction of Israelite Identity* (Atlanta, GA: SBL, 2019), 147–64.

his horn high. The close of the song also clarifies the significance
of its beginning:

> My heart has exulted in Yahweh,
>> my horn has lifted high through Yahweh.
> My mouth has opened wide at my enemies,
>> because I have rejoiced in your deliverance. (2:1)

While Hannah speaks here, she does not speak for herself. The voice
is "the triumphant voice of the Lord's Anointed."[11] The language of
enemies, deliverance, horn, rock, strength, Sheol, exalting, silence,
and thunder resounds again on David's lips when Psalm 18 recurs
as 2 Samuel 22. The close of the psalm thus answers the question
"Who speaks?" that is raised at the beginning, and makes clear
that it begins with the king speaking: "Yahweh is my crag." But it
goes on to speak about the king, declaring that Yahweh is "a tower
of deliverance to his king and one who acts in commitment to his
anointed, to David and to his offspring for all time." Psalms 61 and
63 are other examples of movement between speaking as the king
and for the king. In Psalm 18, a psalmist wrote that way for the king;
and here a psalmist makes Hannah the mouthpiece for such an act
of praise. She speaks as if she were the king at the beginning and
she speaks of the king at the end. In the psalm she "pleaded" (2:1),
and a midrash neatly has her praying for Peninnah.[12] Actually, her
whole psalm is spoken for the (second) king whom her son will
anoint. He is the one who looks open-mouthed at his defeated
enemies and rejoices in Yahweh's deliverance.

---

[11] Francisco O. García-Treto, "A Mother's Paean, a Warrior's Dirge: Reflections
on the Use of Poetic Inclusions in the Books of Samuel," *Shofar* 11/2 (1993):
51–64 (56).

[12] Leila L. Bronner, "Hannah's Prayer: Rabbinic Ambivalence," *Shofar* 17/2
(1999): 36–48 (43–44).

Admittedly it is not clear that Saul or David facilitates the reversals Hannah describes. While she belongs in a sequence of feisty women such as Rebekah and Deborah in the First Testament, it is not clear that kings generally facilitate the self-fulfillment of the women associated with them. If anything, the stories of women function to expose the abuse of power in the David story.[13] And so do the stories of men.

THE GOD OF SHILOH

In due course, then, Samuel will tell of Yahweh's involvement in the beginnings of Israel's monarchy. One might say that theologically Yahweh's action is the framework round the entire story and is theologically prior to the human action. One might further assume that a divine purpose is finding fulfillment in this story. But neither of these convictions forms the book's starting point. Further, the narrative may presuppose a divine sovereignty such as ensures that human actions do not get out of hand and that in the end Yahweh's overall aim is kept on track. But it describes human initiatives to which Yahweh responds, as well as divine initiatives to which human beings respond. It would be a converse oversimplification to say that Samuel adopts Qohelet's "under the sun" perspective, portraying things only as they can be seen with ordinary eyes, and implying no claim to supernatural illumination. Samuel will tell its auditors things about Yahweh's specific intentions, actions, and reactions (e.g., 1 Sam 1:5, 6, 19; 2:21, 25; 3:4, 6, 8, 10, 11, 19, 21), though on other occasions it will simply relate things that happen and make no comment. Samuel assumes that

[13] See April Westbrook, "And He Will Take Your Daughters": Woman Story as Didactic Narrative in the Biblical Account of King David (Diss., Claremont, 2010).

Yahweh is pursuing a purpose in Israel's story, but much of the
time he lets it unfold by its own dynamic.

So the story opens with a human initiative, Elqanah's taking
his family to Shiloh for a festival. It may be a set annual occasion
(presumably Sukkot, the main harvest festival). It would also be a
response to a divine initiative, both in the sense that it celebrates
what Yahweh has done and in the sense that the Torah has expectations of such celebrations. It also recalls the annual occasion at
Shiloh to which the close of Judges refers.

Israel's ancestors were frequently on the move, and God would
meet with them on their travels, wherever they were. But Israel is
now a settled people, Yahweh is settled with them, and he has a
house (1:7) – maybe more than one, though the covenant chest's
presence (4:3) would make the one at Shiloh especially important.
But families living further away would go to other sanctuaries, and
Shiloh may not have been the nearest sanctuary to Elqanah's family's home.

Actually, Yahweh's house is a palace (hêkāl, 1:9; cf. Jer 7:4).
English translations have "temple," but Hebrew has no word for
"temple" in the sense of a sacred building, and Samuel uses the
word for a king's dwelling, which fits Yahweh's being the divine
king. It need not imply a palatial structure, or indeed a structure
at all (the reference to a doorpost might be an anachronism). It
is still a tent sanctuary (2:22), as David's plan to build a "proper"
dwelling for Yahweh implies (2 Sam 7:1–6). As a tent sanctuary
it can still be moved around (in Josh 8 it is at Shechem and in
Judg 20:26–28 at Bethel). The point is that Yahweh lives there, and
someone can go to see him there, as they can go to see the human
king (e.g., 1 Kgs 3:16). It is a portal, to Yahweh's heavenly palace
(2 Sam 22:7). In principle there are no restrictions on access,
though Eli's position and action outside the actual holy place hints

that its staff would have some responsibility for ensuring that no one improper defiled it.

At the beginning of Samuel, the name of the God whom the family go to worship at Shiloh is nuanced as Yahweh Armies or Yahweh of Armies (*yhwh ṣabāôt*; 1 Sam 1:3). Hannah uses this title in addressing God (1 Sam 1:11) and it recurs later (4:4; 15:2; 17:45; 2 Sam 5:10; 6:2, 18; 7:8, 26, 27). It is prominent in Isaiah, Jeremiah, Haggai, Zechariah, and Malachi. In this title, the name Yahweh is followed by the ordinary Hebrew word for armies. NRSV and NJPS have "LORD of hosts," following the Vulgate in taking the title as a construct (genitive) expression which would mean more literally "Yahweh of Armies." The Septuagint takes it the same way in 2 Samuel 6:2, 18. But a rendering such as "Lord of armies" masks the oddness of the Hebrew expression. "Lord" replaces the name Yahweh, and proper nouns such as Yahweh cannot generally be used thus in construct expressions. "Yahweh Armies" would therefore be a more plausible understanding of the phrase. NIV's "LORD Almighty" follows the Septuagint's translation in 2 Samuel 5:10; 7:8, 26, 27, taking the noun as an abstract plural. Elsewhere In 1 Samuel, the Septuagint throws up its hands and simply transliterates the word for "Armies" as Sabaōth.

The title does imply that Yahweh is one who controls all combative power in the heavens and/or on the earth; he is indeed a king. He has the power to attack anyone or defend his people. The use of the title suggests the theology associated with his presence at Shiloh. He sits (by implication, enthroned) above the covenant chest (1 Sam 4:3–4), which is more likely his footstool than his throne. The title has not appeared earlier in the First Testament narrative, which may suggest that its distinctive background lies in Shiloh. Shiloh had a sanctuary before the Israelites arrived, and the title would likely reflect the theology of the people who already worshiped there. The Israelites' adoption of this designation compares with their adoption of 'Elyon, "One On High," whom Melchizedek worshiped (Gen 14:18). The title's thrust presupposes that it is Yahweh who is the (real) Almighty/Lord of Armies, as the combined title *yhwh 'elyôn* (e.g., Ps 47:2[3]) asserts that "Yahweh is the (real) One On High."

The designation also compares with the designation *šadday*, which also makes the Septuagint throw up its hands and decline to translate it, in Genesis. Elsewhere, the Septuagint often has "Almighty," the word it also uses for *ṣəbāôt*. The First Testament use of *šadday* (almost exclusively in Genesis and Job) implies that it, too, is not an originally Israelite designation and that it is simply a name of whose meaning Israelites might not be conscious. Curiously and strikingly, both these two designations can suggest the personal commitment of the powerful God to his people and to the individual. The Septuagint's translation of *'ēl šadday* as "your/my God" in Genesis points in that direction; so does Hannah's appeal to *yhwh ṣəbāôt*, which compares with the expression's recurrence in Psalms 80 and 84. Yahweh Armies is the real God, the powerful God, and the God on whom his people can therefore rely.

In a paradoxical way, those facts about Yahweh emerge in the references to his relationship to Hannah in connection with her inability to have children. Samuel repeats that "Yahweh had closed her womb" (1:5, 6). It is but the first in a series of statements about Yahweh doing tough things in Samuel.[14] There will soon be a frightening comment on Eli's exchange with his sons, who "did not listen

---

[14] See Marti J. Steussy, "The Problematic God of Samuel," in David Penchansky and Paul L. Redditt, eds., *Shall Not the Judge of All the Earth Do What Is Right? Studies on the Nature of God in Tribute to James L. Crenshaw* (Winona Lake, IN: Eisenbrauns, 2000), 127–61.

to their father's voice because Yahweh wanted to put them to death" (2:25). It is "the first hint in Samuel of the theme of divine dangerousness" (cf. 6:19–20; 2 Sam 6:6),[15] though the declaration hardly means they cannot turn, as is suggested by his not yet actually putting them to death. And in Hannah's story, Yahweh is subsequently the subject of two more promising verbs: He gives, he is mindful (1 Sam 1:17, 19).

Difficulty over getting pregnant is a recurrent issue in the First Testament, and sometimes Yahweh causes it (e.g., Gen 16:2; 30:2), but it is never said to be a punishment for wrongdoing (Gen 20:18 is a special case). The First Testament can conversely refer to Yahweh opening the womb of someone who cannot conceive (e.g., Gen 29:31; 30:22) and enabling someone to get pregnant without this implication in the background (Ruth 4:13). Theologically, one might say that Yahweh is always the one who opens and closes wombs, but using this language on particular occasions suggests a special divine deliberateness or a special significance attaching to a particular woman's infertility and pregnancy. While pregnancy may just concern one individual or family, record of it in the Scriptures commonly relates to Yahweh's broader purpose – as is the case with Hezekiah's healing at the other end of Samuel-Kings (2 Kgs 20). We will discover that this note about Hannah relates to the link between her eventual pregnancy and the theme of kingship in Samuel, like the note about Ruth's pregnancy.

FAMILY

Samuel begins with a scene from family life. "Samuel most resembles Genesis in its preoccupation with founding families and in

---

[15] Ellen F. Davis, *Opening Israel's Scriptures* (New York: Oxford University Press, 2019), 177.

its positioning of these representative households at the fulcrum of historical change."[16] The scene illustrates the First Testament's vision of family, tempered by realism about how life is. Whereas one might have expected "family" to imply three or four generations, this story speaks only of two generations, and thus in effect of a nuclear family. We hear nothing of Elqanah's siblings or parents beyond the mention of his father in the list of his ancestors. The family is evidently enjoying the blessing that the Torah promises, in that it has produce to share and to offer to Yahweh, and it can "go up" to the sanctuary, making pilgrimage for a celebration each year. "In a world in which God is the primary reality, worship is the primary activity."[17] The story goes from infertility plus worship to birth plus worship (1 Sam 1:2–3, 27–28).

The family bears Elqanah's name. It is "he" who goes up to the festival to worship and offer sacrifice, and who presides at the family celebration. But the family are full participants; it is not just for the men. Peninnah's daughters share in it as much as her sons (1:4), as Deuteronomy emphasizes daughters, wives, and mothers as well as sons, husbands, and fathers. The family is presumably patrilocal: When a woman marries, she joins her husband's extended family. It is patrilinear: It traces its genealogical line via the husband, and its male line has responsibility for the family assets. The story thus works with an order in which the husband has formal primacy, and its opening suggests that Elqanah will be its hero or subject. Yet he is not.[18] The family is apparently not

---

[16] Joel Rosenberg, "I and 2 Samuel," in Robert Alter and Frank Kermode, eds., *The Literary Guide to the Bible* (Cambridge, MA: Harvard University Press, 1987), 122–45 (123).

[17] Eugene H. Peterson, *First and Second Samuel* (Louisville, KY: Westminster John Knox, 1999), 21.

[18] Fokkelman, *Narrative Art and Poetry* 4:7.

patriarchal, any more than the First Testament generally thinks Israelite marriages should be.[19] Elqanah loves Hannah, and she is "his woman," but he is also "her man" (1 Sam 1:8, 19; Hebrew regularly uses the ordinary words for "man" and "woman" to denote "husband" and "wife"). After the festival, together they get up early, together they worship, and together they go home (1:19).[20] Hannah negotiates on an equal basis with Elqanah over going to the festival next time and about giving her baby to Yahweh. Elqanah's "do what is good in your eyes" (1:23) contrasts with the "do what was upright in his eyes" at the end of Judges. Hannah can then stay home while Elqanah takes the family to make the regular sacrifice and an extra sacrifice he has promised (1:21), perhaps one made by the household relating to the harvest or the family or Hannah's baby. It seems that they subsequently go together to surrender Samuel. The narrative says that Hannah went up with Samuel, but "they" slaughtered the sacrifice and brought Samuel to Eli, and it makes sense if "they" then worshiped there (1:28).[21]

It is Hannah who names her baby. In the First Testament, naming a baby can be the task of father or mother or both, another indication of a difference between the father's formal power in relation to the world outside the family and the power within the family. The husband does not have authority to make decisions for the family, nor do his wives have to submit to their husband's authority. Nor does the First Testament suggest that a wife's main

---

[19] See Carol L. Meyers, "Was Ancient Israel a Patriarchal Society?" *JBL* 133 (2014): 8–27.

[20] Fokkelman, *Narrative Art and Poetry* 4:53.

[21] *Wayištaḥû* (missing in LXX and NRSV) can be understood as singular (Eli?) or plural. In 1:19 *wayištaḥăwû* was unambiguous, but Vg and Syr have a plural here, and for the plural at Gen 43:28 K has *wyštḥw* and Q *wayištaḥăwû*. Tg has singular.

role is to have children. Proverbs 31:10–31 indicates how being a mother is not the only way a woman can be significant. Both for a woman and for a man the family is where they find their significance and work. Like other women in the First Testament story such as Rebekah, Hannah assumes freedom to approach Yahweh. She does not need a priest's mediation. She is also free to negotiate with Eli and be glad of his blessing. The stories of Abraham and Sarah, Isaac and Rebekah, and Jacob and Rachel and Leah show how in Israel as in Western societies, often it is the women who have the effective power, and the Hannah story "is, if anything, a matriarchal story."[22] While a husband might exercise authoritarian and oppressive power over the family, the First Testament does not tell of families having that problem, and its main block of family stories in Genesis portray wives behaving in at least as feisty a way as Hannah. Her story illustrates how behind the great man there is often a great woman (cf. Exod 1–2; Luke 1–2).

The story does not idealize the family. Families in the Scriptures are usually dysfunctional, and so is this one. It is a locus of conflict, and grievously its worship and celebration is a context in which conflict emerges. While this occasion was potentially one that expressed and strengthened the family bond, "for Hannah, it became a nightmare."[23] The story does not pass judgment on the family in that connection. It is what it is. Nor does the story pass judgment on its individual members. It is tempting for readers to critique Elqanah as clueless and/or narcissistic in his attempts to reassure Hannah about not being able to have children, to critique Eli for being judgmental of Hannah in his baseless accusation

---

[22] Robert Alter, *The Art of Biblical Narrative* (New York: Bantam, 1981), 82.
[23] Koowon Kim, *Incubation as a Type-Scene in the Aqhatu, Kirta, and Hannah Stories*, VTSup 145 (Leiden: Brill, 2011), 279.

of her, to critique Peninnah, the "wicked stepsister,"[24] for being resentful of Hannah, vexing her, and making her thunder, or to excuse her because Elqahanah did not love her, or to critique Hannah for not standing up to Elqanah or Penninah like Sarah or to commend her for her silence, to commend or critique her for being "bitter in her entire being" and "tough-spirited" (1 Sam 1:10, 15). Such interpretations miss the point, impose Western concerns, and apply Western assumptions. The story does not focus on the feelings of Elqanah, Peninnah, Eli, or even Hannah, or imply an evaluation of them.[25] Its comments on Eli's sons (2:12–36) work differently: It does make comments on them.

The specific realism about the negative way family can work stems from Hannah's inability to have children. In a Western context, a man and a woman may feel that love is essential to marriage, but also feel that they are not complete if they cannot have children. For men and women, having children is often important to their sense of being fully human, though it may be more intrinsic to womanhood. The First Testament may also assume that love is essential to marriage, and this story notes Elqanah's love for Hannah. But it also assumes that a family needs children, for practical as well as personal and theological reasons. In a traditional society, having children is economically important. The man and the woman need children to work on the farm and in the house, they need daughters as well as sons to pass on to other families as part of the arrangement whereby other families generate wives for their sons, they will need their sons and their wives more as they themselves get older, and they will need them

---

[24] David Jobling, *1 Samuel,* Berit Olam: Studies in Hebrew Narrative and Poetry (Collegeville, MN: Liturgical Press, 1998), 182.
[25] Murphy, *1 Samuel,* 7.

to pass the farm onto. Hannah would be insecure if Elqanah dies. Given that having children is intrinsic to being human and given the practical importance of children to a family's viability, having children conveys a sense of honor (Ps 127:5). Both for personal and practical reasons, then, being unable to have children is indeed generally a massive deprivation for a man or a woman,[26] and it threatens to be a cause of shame. The idea of children is built into the idea of family.

When a wife cannot get pregnant, the First Testament implicitly assumes that the problem lies with the wife, and the husband may marry a second wife. A story such as this one supports that assumption. And Peninnah has no trouble getting pregnant. While Genesis 1–4 pictures the first marriages as involving one man and one woman who form a family unit with their children, it also tells of an unhappy exception to that rule. In general, the First Testament implies the ideal of one man and one woman together for life in the setting of an extended family. But it recognizes that divorce happens and that extended families split up, and a wife's infertility might count as grounds for divorce. But the First Testament has no actual accounts of divorce, and several of its stories relate how a man rather marries a second wife. Polygamy in itself can be harmonious, but the First Testament portrays it commonly issuing in conflict, with the capacity to get pregnant being a cause of the conflict. And there were aspects of the festival celebration that drew attention to the disparity between Hannah and Peninnah. While Peninnah is a full second wife and not a servant wife like Hagar, she may know that Hannah is Elqanah's

---

[26] Solomon O. Ademiluka, "Interpreting the Hannah Narrative (1 Sm 1:1–20) in Light of the Attitude of the Church in Nigeria towards Childlessness," *Verbum et Ecclesia* 40/1 (2019): 1–10 (4–5).

real love. Does Elqanah love Peninnah, or is she just there to bear children?[27] The dynamics recall the stories of Jacob, Rachel, and Leah, as well as Abraham, Sarah, and Hagar, though Elqanah values Hannah for who she is and not what she can produce, and wishes she could value herself on that basis.

The story of Eli and his sons is quite different, and grievous. One may guess that Eli and Ms. Eli have done their best in bringing up their sons, and Eli has one last attempt to turn them back to the right way, but they do not listen (1 Sam 2:22–25). And an emissary from Yahweh comes to confront him about their wrongdoing, in which Eli is also implicated, and to announce the catastrophe that will come on the entire family (2:27–36).

PRAYER AND PROMISE

The Scriptures include several other stories about God telling a woman she will have a baby, apart from Hannah's. The most detailed are the ones about Samson's mother and Jesus's mother. "Hannah's prayers and spirituality set the context for what follows, much as Mary's do for the Gospels."[28] Lectionaries pair Hannah's story with Luke 2:41–52: Mary will have to give up Jesus too.[29] Both stories relate announcements that come by divine initiative and by means of a supernatural agent. In Hannah's story, the messenger is human and the message comes as a result of Hannah's prayer. While taking a second wife who could have children solves the practical problem in Elqanah's family, it does

---

[27] Johanna W. H. van Wijk-Bos, *A People and a Land 2: The Road to Kingship* (Grand Rapids, MI: Eerdmans, 2020), 26.

[28] Peterson, *First and Second Samuel*, 9.

[29] Murphy, *1 Samuel*, 16.

not solve the personal problem of the person who cannot conceive and whose position in the family is marginal. So the story suggests insights about a theology of the individual as well as a theology of the family. It raises the question "how we might conceive of the community for all without losing the spirit of emancipation hermeneutics" and whether "marginality can be redefined as having power to transform self, community and society."[30]

Whereas infertility leads to conflict in other stories, for her part Hannah avoids the conflict by praying.[31] She does not respond to either Peninnah or Elqanah but to the one to whom the festival draws attention. Perhaps in theory she should have been able to accept Elqanah's reassurance that he will look after her if she has no sons to do so (1 Sam 1:8), and to come to terms with her infertility and with the possibility that there are other forms of fruitfulness, of "capacity to touch hearts and to give life."[32] But fortunately for the story that will unfold, she is not prepared to do so. She anticipates the woman who would not accept "No" from Jesus (Matt 15:21–28) and the woman who would not accept "No" from an unjust judge (Luke 18:1–8).

Neither the festival, with the prayer that would accompany the sacrifices, nor the well-meaning words of Elqanah helped Hannah. Maybe they made them worse.[33] Yet the festival and the offering of sacrifice is also a natural occasion for personal prayer. An Israelite

---

[30] Yung Suk Kim, "The Story of Hannah (1 Sam 1:1–2:11) from a Perspective of Han," *The Bible and Critical Theory* 4/2 (2008): 26.1–9 (1, 2).

[31] Joan E. Cook, *Hannah's Desire, God's Design: Early Interpretations of the Story of Hannah*, JSOTSup 282 (Sheffield: Sheffield Academic Press, 1999), 49–51.

[32] Jean Vanier, *Man and Woman He Made Them* (London: DLT, 1985), 141.

[33] See Yairah Amit, "'Am I Not More Devoted to You Than Ten Sons?' (1 Samuel 1.8): Male and Female Interpretations," in Athalya Brenner, ed., *A Feminist Companion to Samuel-Kings* (Sheffield: Sheffield Academic Press, 1994), 68–76.

can have a strong, frank, confident relationship with Yahweh,
such as Jesus has with his Father, and Hannah prays in the way
that Yahweh invites any Israelite to, the way the Psalms embody.
She goes to the sanctuary and takes her stand in the sanctuary
courtyard in front of the holy place. She is thus before Yahweh
(1 Sam 1:12), not just physically in the sanctuary.[34] She wants to be
seen,[35] and there Yahweh can "actually look at your maidservant's
lowliness" (1:11); "actually look" represents an idiom whereby one
juxtaposes two forms of the same verb for emphasis, "with looking
you look." Her "lowliness" (*ŏnî*) means she speaks as an ordinary
person without power, significance, or influence within the people
or the clan. She "has nothing in her power, nothing in her free will,
no presumptive claims…; all things here are entirely in the hands
of God."[36] Appeal to being an ordinary person without power is
a feature of prayers in the Psalms (e.g., 25:18; 88:9[10]; 119:50). It
means calling on Yahweh as someone who has the capacity to look
at people in need. And what one has to do is get him to look. He
will surely then be unable to resist using his power to act on one's
behalf. The appeal is thus to "be mindful," and not to "put out
of mind" (*zākar, šākaḥ*). Yahweh has many things and people to
think about, so Hannah needs to get him to focus on her.

Like Naomi (Ruth 1:20), Hannah "was bitter in her being, and
she pleaded with Yahweh" (1 Sam 1:10). Hannah "pleads" (*pālal*
hitpael) more than anyone else in the First Testament (1:10, 12, 26,

---

[34] Kim, *Incubation*, 299.
[35] Barbara Green, *How Are the Mighty Fallen: A Dialogical Study of King Saul in 1 Samuel*, JSOTSup 365 (London: Sheffield Academic Press, 2003), 100.
[36] Johannes Bugenhagen, *Annotationes … in Deuteronomium. In Samuelem prophetam, id est, duos libros Regum* (Nuremberg: Petri, 1524), 187, as translated in Derek Cooper and Martin J. Lohrmann, eds., *1–2 Samuel, 1–2 Kings, 1–2 Chronicles*, Reformation Commentary on Scripture: Old Testament 5 (Downers Grove, IL: InterVarsity, 2016), 6.

27; 2:1). More broadly, Samuel has more references to "pleading" than any other First Testament book, all but one of them in 1 Samuel 1–12. The default English translation of this verb is "pray," which is a usefully but also pusillanimously vague verb that can cover any kind of speech or non-speech in a relationship with God (or no such relationship, as in the contemporary expression "our prayers are with you"). But "pleading" means asking for something for oneself or for someone else. It means supplicating or interceding. The word has a legal background. And it implies being desperate and powerless, with no other recourse, no other direction to turn. Prayer was not a means of getting to feel better but of getting God to act. And Hannah's prayer and promise changed what Yahweh was doing and resulted in the birth of Samuel, the reform of the priesthood, and the birth of the monarchy.[37] Eli warns his sons of there being no one to pray for them (2:25), and they die. Prayer was the key that opened Hannah's closed womb.[38]

She also "cried and cried" (1:10 again juxtaposes two forms of a single verb, "with crying she cried"). Even if the gates of the sanctuary are locked, "the gates of tears are not locked" (b. Berakhot 32b). Only here does someone pray "towards" or "with" Yahweh; usually one prays "to" Yahweh, as Hannah later says she did (1:26). This preposition ('al) has more aggressive connotations. It fits with Hannah's being called "bitter in her being" and "tough in spirit" (1:15).

An odd thing about her prayer is that it was silent (1:13), which is not the nature of prayer in the Scriptures. But silence is one

---

[37] Cook, *Hannah's Desire*, 21.

[38] Lancelot Andrew[e]s, *Apospasmatia Sacra: Or A Collection of Posthumous and Orphan Lectures* (London: Moseley, 1657), 567; cf. Cooper and Lohrmann, *1–2 Samuel, 1–2 Kings, 1–2 Chronicles*, 7.

of Hannah's characteristics.[39] "Prayer is … converse with God. Though whispering, consequently, and not opening the lips, we speak in silence, yet we cry inwardly. For God hears continually all the inward converse."[40] Hannah's praying silently does anticipate Jesus's later bidding to pray secretly (Matt 6:5–6). On the other hand, it was no brief prayer: As well as "crying and crying" (1 Sam 1:10), she was "profuse in her pleading" (1:12), like the people Isaiah and Jesus critique (Isa 1:15; Matt 6:7–8)!

A further link with prayer in the Psalms is that Hannah goes on to make a promise to Yahweh that she will fulfill if he answers her prayer. While prayer means asking God to do things or to give you things, it also implies a commitment. "If you will give your maidservant offspring, I will give him to Yahweh all the days of his life, and a razor will not come upon his head" (1 Sam 1:11). While one could read her promise as a questionable attempt to bribe Yahweh and/or a questionable imposition on her son, the story implicitly sees it as an aspect of a reciprocal relationship with Yahweh and a proper gesture of thankfulness to Yahweh. "Truly here was a daughter of Abraham. He gave when it was demanded of him. She offers even before it is demanded."[41]

The nature of her plea makes her promise paradoxical. Giving the child to Yahweh would imply giving him to serve at Shiloh, as it does happen, so Hannah is not focusing on having someone

[39] Jenni Williams, "Hannah: A Woman Deeply Troubled," in Keith Bodner and Benjamin J. M. Johnson, eds., *Characters and Characterization in the Book of Samuel*, LHBOTS 669 (London: T&T Clark, 2020), 42–58 (56).

[40] Clement of Alexandria, *Stromata* 7:7 (cf. John R. Franke, *Joshua, Judges, Ruth, 1–2 Samuel*, Ancient Christian Commentary on Scripture 4 [Downers Grove, IL: InterVarsity, 2005], 199).

[41] John Chrysostom, commenting on Eph 6:18, *Homilies on the Epistle of St. Paul the Apostle to the Ephesians*, NPNF I, 13 (reprinted Peabody, MA: Hendrickson, 1995), 170 (cf. Franke, *Joshua, Judges, Ruth, 1–2 Samuel*, 197).

who will look after her in her old age. Will simply having a baby mean her humanly, womanly life is complete and her shame removed, so she can then happily give him up? Might she pray in a way that Eli couldn't hear because she wants a son in the service of Yahweh through whom she can vicariously have the ministerial position that is not open to her as a woman?![42] But "offspring" (*zera' 'ănāšîm*) is literally "seed of human beings," which neither designates the sex,[43] nor limits the offspring to one; "seed" has plural reference in 2:20 and mostly elsewhere. It would make sense to assume she envisages her womb remaining open, which is what happens (2:21), and envisages surrendering her first child while expecting she would have more.

Letting one's hair grow can be a sign of spending a short period as someone "consecrated" (*nāzîr*). So it is in Numbers 6, with no explanation of the practice, though that consecration also involves abstaining from alcohol and avoiding the defilement that comes through contact with a corpse. Hannah's promise is that her son will have a lifelong obligation, but just to the commitment about hair.[44]

An amusing hiccup follows when Eli reacts to Hannah's prayer, though John Chrysostom, after encouraging members of his congregation, "You, then, woman, ... appeal to the priest to join in making intercession for you,"[45] rather notes the pathos of the

[42] Jobling, *1 Samuel*, 132.
[43] Tsumura, *The First Book of Samuel*, 116.
[44] LXX, 4QSam[a] refer to his being someone "consecrated" and mention abstaining from alcohol.
[45] John Chrysostom, *Sermones V de Anna*, Patrologia Graeca 54, 631–76 (658); cf. Robert C. Hill, "St. John Chrysostom's Homilies on Hannah," *St Vladimir's Theological Quarterly* 45 (2011): 319–38 (328). Hill notes that Chrysostom does not imply that Hannah is an example only for women.

scene. "At home her rival mocked her. She went into the temple, …
and the priest upbraided her. She fled the storm at home, entered
port and still ran into turbulence."[46] Eli is a tragically ambiguous
figure, and here "we are already alerted that this is a priesthood in
decline."[47] Hannah being beside herself, Eli takes her for a drunk,
not an unlikely inference at the festival when the wine flows. And
it is "after the eating at Shiloh and after the drinking" (1:9) that she
goes to the sanctuary. But she hasn't been drinking. She is not a
"daughter of Belial," which might etymologically suggest a worthless woman, comparable to some people close to Eli (2:12) and to
some people opposed to Saul's designation as king (10:27) and to
someone who later tried to oust David (2 Sam 20:1).

Eli's misjudgment and Hannah's response further highlight her
modeling the nature of a relationship with Yahweh. The positive
side to Eli is that he can see where he needs to change his mind,
and that his eventual response to Hannah models what it means
to be a priest. While the narrative presupposes that Hannah can go
straight to God without going via a priest, it rejoices in Eli's eventually supporting her. "Go, with things being well," he says, *ləkî
ləšālôm* (1 Sam 1:17). He hardly means "go in peace" in the sense of
going home with a sense of peace; *šālôm* implies not peacefulness
but well-being. That meaning especially fits, given that Eli literally
urges Hannah to go *into* well-being, which sounds more dynamic
than going *in* well-being. The birth of a baby will mean things will
indeed be good for her. Eli spells out the implications when he
adds, "The God of Israel – he will give you [or may he give you]

[46] John Chrysostom, *Old Testament Homilies* Volume 1 (Brookline, MA: Holy
    Cross Orthodox Press, 2003), 2 (as quoted in Franke, *Joshua, Judges, Ruth, 1–2
    Samuel*, 199).
[47] Rosenberg, "I and 2 Samuel," 124.

what you asked of him."[48] How did Eli know to issue this promise (or how did he know that a wish was appropriate, if that alternative understanding of his words is right)? Perhaps it is simply a priest's job to know what Yahweh is saying to a suppliant. The Psalms may again imply as much. Perhaps a priest has to have prophetic gifts as well as the authority that comes from heredity and ordination.

The dynamics of what follows again match those implied by the Psalms. They presuppose two stages to the answering of prayer. Stage One is Yahweh saying, "I have heard, I will do as you say." Stage Two is Yahweh doing it. The expression of thanks and trust that often closes a protest psalm (e.g., Ps 22) responds to an awareness of the Stage One answer. After the Stage Two answer, a thanksgiving/testimony psalm is appropriate. In 1 Samuel 1, having received the Stage One answer, Hannah went back to the family, had something to eat, "and her face was no more" (no more distraught, presumably, as LXX, Tg make explicit). The family went home and Elqanah and Hannah made love (the other infertility stories do not have this feature). Yahweh was mindful of Hannah, and she got pregnant and gave birth, and thus received the Stage Two answer (1:19–20). If the celebration was the Sukkot festival, it marked the end of a year, and she gave birth towards the end of the next year. When the family went up to Shiloh for the festival this time, she and her newborn did not go, but the family went and Elqanah fulfilled its promise, and in due course she went.

Hannah calls her baby Samuel (1:20). Her explanation raises eyebrows. The name (*šəmûʾēl*) sounds like a cross between something such as "Heard by El" and "His Name is El" or "The Name of El." But Hannah says she called him Samuel because "it was

---

[48] LXX and Vg take *yittēn* as jussive rather than *yiqtol*, but this makes less sense in the context.

from Yahweh that I asked for him" (*myhwh šā'altîw*). Now, explanations of names often involve paronomasia rather than etymology; "Abraham" does not mean "father of a multitude" (Gen 17:5), but it could sound like an expression with that meaning. Here, Eli has already spoken of Yahweh giving Hannah "the asking that she asked" (1 Sam 1:17). Hannah emphasizes the point when she takes Samuel to Shiloh: "Yahweh gave me the asking that I asked" (1:27). Eli takes up that phrase again later (2:20); it occurs only three other times in the First Testament. Hannah further develops the point in using this same verb in an unusual way, or two unusual ways (1:28). She is giving Samuel back to Yahweh as something she asked for, or as if he were something he asked for (*hiš'iltihû*), and she is doing so because he is "asked in connection with Yahweh" (*šā'ûl lyhwh*; 1:28).[49] There is subtlety there, because *šā'ûl* is the name of the king whom Samuel will anoint when the people "ask" for a king and "ask" who it should be (8:10; 10:22; then acerbically, 12:13, 17, 19). Looking back to Hannah's words after Saul's designation reveals their hint that the family story and the woman's story are also a story about the origin of the monarchy. In asking for Samuel, Hannah has asked for the prophet who will be Yahweh's means of designating Saul. Unwittingly she has asked for Saul, who will be the one for whom people ask. Notwithstanding the unhappy way Saul's story will unfold, Hannah was not drunk in asking for Saul.

MINISTRY

Accompanying the transition to being a settled people, with God having a more settled home in their midst, was a transition to

---

[49] CEB's "give back/given" is as near as one can get with a translation; contrast KJV "lend/lent."

having a body of ministers who worked at that more settled home. To judge from the Torah and from the Jerusalem temple, the Shiloh sanctuary would have a regular daily worship program, while the Hannah story indicates that it would also host the annual festivals and visits from people bringing sacrifices for personal reasons – for instance, in connection with prayers for healing or for a baby, or thanksgiving for healing or a birth. Portions of such offerings would be given to Yahweh, by being turned to smoke. Portions would be shared by the family. Portions would be shared with the priests for whom it was part of their livelihood, for themselves and their families. Leviticus incorporates rules for sharing out the offerings, though one cannot infer from them the rules that would apply at Shiloh, in theory or in practice.

Many modern and traditional cultures assume the practice of having people whose full-time occupation is caring for the community's religious life. It was not an aspect of Israel's ancestors' life as Genesis describes it. For them, the family's father figure functions as its priest, though ordinary individuals such as Abraham's servant or Rebekah can also take the initiative in approaching God about questions that matter to them (Gen 24:12; 25:22). One could say that the entire people is a priestly kingdom, a holy nation (Exod 19:6). But the chapter making that affirmation also presupposes the presence of priests among the people (Exod 19:22, 24), and the Torah lays down copious rules for their work. Perhaps priesthood, like kingship, is an institution that Yahweh eventually adopts because it corresponds to a human instinct, and/or it is a gift of God to humanity as a whole that he then also gives to Israel. But like kingship (and for that matter prophecy), priesthood works out with some ambiguity.

The priests have two roles. Eli's sons offer sacrifices, and facilitate people making their own sacrifices (1 Sam 2:28). It would be

physically tough but straightforward work that might be appropriate for younger men, which could link with the rule that men
should retire from regular priestly service when they were fifty
(e.g., Num 4). The problem is that while Eli was evidently capable
of failing in his work, his sons were comprehensively wayward in
theirs.

Eli himself is fulfilling an aspect of the second role, as he is
engaged in keeping watch at the sanctuary, sitting on a throne outside Yahweh's palace (English translations have him sitting on a
"seat," but there are virtually no other places where *kissē'* refers to
an ordinary seat; cf. 1 Sam 2:8). Eli is in effect the next-to-last of the
"judges" (cf. 4:18), the nearest thing to an authority figure in Israel.
He is the first Israelite ever to sit on a throne, but he will soon fall
off it (4:13, 18). He is in a position of authority in the courtyard of
the meeting tent, watching for people who should not come too
near – for instance, because they are having too good a time at
festival parties. Priests on this duty might also advise people on
whether they should come to the sanctuary if they might have skin
disease or be otherwise unclean. In other words, they need to be
able to make proper distinctions between holy and common and
between clean and unclean, and to teach people about proprieties
related to worship and other aspects of life (Lev 10:10–11). Eli's
misjudgment of Hannah does not take away from the importance
of this role, as the story of Uzzah (2 Sam 6) will shortly demon-
strate in its way, like the stories of Nadab and Abihu (Lev 10) and
Jeroboam (1 Kgs 13). The importance of the gatekeepers of the
Jerusalem temple (e.g., 1 Chr 9:17–27) will also reflect its importance. But Leviticus and the rest of the First Testament assume
that propriety does not concern only matters of bodily fitness (see
Pss 15; 24), and the critique of the Shiloh priests focuses on the
broader realm. In addition, Eli "carries" – rather than "wears" – a

chasuble (*'ēpôd*, conventionally transliterated "ephod"; 1 Sam
2:28), an object containing the means of consulting Yahweh about
questions and telling people how Yahweh responds to them (1:17).
Priests thus fulfill the role of prophets as well as priests; Eli challenges his sons like a prophet (2:23–25).

Young Samuel himself engages in "ministering" to Yahweh
(*šārat* piel; 2:11), which usually denotes priestly work. For a "boy"
(*na'ar*), it suggests practical work by way of assisting the priests.
Wearing a linen chasuble (2:18), he looks like a trainee priest, ready
to replace the current priests. He is under the eye of Eli (2:11), train-
ing for both the sacrificial and the instructional roles – at least, he
will fulfill both later. Eli's sons, too, have "boys" they have trained
(2:13, 15, 17). It will be as well if Samuel learns from Eli rather
than from them.[50] They were indeed "sons of Belial." The cynical
manner of their overseeing sacrifices indicated that they did not
acknowledge Yahweh (2:12–17). While being priests may not have
been a full-time job and they may have also worked the land, like
Jerusalem priests, their priestly work did entitle them to a share
in sacrifices, and through the boy who assisted them they insisted
on a cut that was other than was allowed by the "rule" for priests.
We do not know what the rule at Shiloh would have been, nor is it
clear what they insisted on, but their claim evidently ignored the
sacrifices' significance for the people who brought them and also
signified that "they treated Yahweh's offerings with contempt"
(cf. 2:28–29) and were "slighting God" (3:13).[51] In addition, they were

[50] Serge Frolov, *The Turn of the Cycle: 1 Samuel 1–8 in Synchronic and Diachronic Perspectives*, BZAW 342 (Berlin: de Gruyter, 2002), 102–3.

[51] This translation assumes that MT's text, which excludes the reference to God, reflects a *tiqqun sopherim* censoring the direct reference to slighting God; see Carmel McCarthy, *The Tiqqune Sopherim and Other Theological Corrections in the Masoretic Text of the Old Testament*, Orbis Biblicus et Orientalis 36 (Göttingen: Vandenhoeck, 1981), 77–79.

involved in sexual relationships with women ministers on duty at the meeting tent entrance (2:22), apparently people with roles like those of the Levites.

They were thus involved in two common ministerial failings. Their ministry became something in which they engaged for their own benefit. And they were in these sexual relationships with people who worked with them, specifically with people who had less power than them. When people's offspring follow their parents in ministry, it may work well, but it has risks attached. The parents may have a hard time disciplining their offspring and may take risks with and for them. Engagement in ministry is dangerous in its temptations and in its penalties, and ministers run greater risks than laypeople. Eli makes the point in an abstruse way, but the idea is clear. Someone who offends against another human being can get Yahweh to plead for them, but someone who offends against Yahweh has no one who can help them (2:25). Eli may imply that "ordinary" sexual wrongdoing is one thing, but sexual sin in the context of the service of Yahweh is a whole other level of wrongdoing.

Eli knew his sons were slighting God and he did not "restrain" them (3:13). He had tried, but failed (2:22–25), as priest and as father,[52] and terrible consequences will follow. The tragedy will extend beyond the immediate family. Joining some dots in the First Testament story, one may infer that Eli was a descendant of Aaron, though possibly admitted to that line by adoption. "I definitely said that your household and your father's household would go about before me for all time. But now (Yahweh's affirmation) – a profanity to me. Because I honor people who honor

---

[52] Marvin A. Sweeney, "Eli: A High Priest Thrown under the Ox Cart," in Bodner and Johnson, *Characters and Characterization in the Book of Samuel*, 59–75.

me, but people who despise me will be slighted" (2:30). "A profanity to me" is a kind of expletive, and "the fact that he utters
the expletive is unparalleled in the Hebrew Bible"; it "shows the
depths of his disappointment and indignation."[53] Yahweh's words
indicate that "for all time" (*'ad-'ôlām*) may not mean "for all time."
Saul's story will implicitly take up this question and the question of whether Yahweh can have a change of mind about things
(13:13–14; 15:10–35), as will David's story when Yahweh commits
himself to David "for all time." A commitment on Yahweh's part
expects a reciprocal commitment. When Yahweh's beneficiaries
fail in their commitment, Yahweh is free to maintain his; it is an
aspect of the meaning of *hesed*, the word translated by expressions
such as "steadfast love" (2 Sam 7:15; 22:51). But Yahweh is also free
eventually to decide "That's it!" on the basis of the principle that
the relationship is reciprocal: "I honor people who honor me, but
people who despise me will be slighted." Eli's priestly line did not
acquire their position because they undertook a commitment, but
they had to maintain a commitment to be sure of staying in their
position.

So Yahweh is going to exercise his authority as judge on Eli's
household "for all time," and its waywardness will not be open
to expiation "for all time" (1 Sam 3:13–14). As the promise had
been for all time, now the threat is. Eli responds, "He is Yahweh:
that which is good in his eyes, he will do" or "he must do" (3:18).
Though it might be a simple recognition that the catastrophe must
happen, it is a slightly open statement, hinting that there might be
hope.[54] If the positive "for all time" (2:30) might not mean what
it says, maybe the negative one need not? Actually, the calamity

[53] Fokkelman, *Narrative Art and Poetry* 4:142.
[54] Cf. Auld, *I & II Samuel*, 60.

soon begins. Eli drops dead, as an old man who is "heavy" (kābēd); ironically, the word also means "honorable." His daughter-in-law declares that "the honor has gone from Israel" because of the covenant chest's capture and because of her father-in-law and her husband (4:21–22). She does not say "because of their death." Perhaps she knows the honor had gone long before.

VOCATION

Meanwhile, "the boy Samuel was gradually growing and was good both with Yahweh and also with people" (2:26). He grew up without his parents (who came to see him once a year) but "with Yahweh" (2:21). Then Yahweh "called" him (3:4). While he is then not quite the first person whom Yahweh "calls" (Yahweh is the subject of this verb in passages such as Exod 3:4; 19:3, 20; 31:2; 35:30; Lev 1:1), he is the only prophet in whose story "calling" has a key place; the verb comes twelve times in 1 Samuel 3. But initially it does not occur either to Samuel or to Eli to think that Yahweh might be calling to Samuel. One can perhaps hardly blame them, given that Yahweh's word had been rare, and vision had not been widespread (3:1). The implication is not that it had been widespread previously or had failed because of the waywardness of the age or of Eli and his sons. Rather, there has been little history of Yahweh speaking or giving visions or calling, such as would make it natural for Eli or Samuel to recognize what is going on.[55] The story implies as much when it comments that Yahweh's word had not yet revealed itself to Samuel (gālâ niphal; 3:7). This word "vision" comes here for the first time in the First Testament narrative, and there have been few references to "Yahweh's word" coming to anyone.

[55] McCarter, I Samuel, 97.

The amusing misunderstanding over who is calling in 1 Samuel 3 reflects how calling means summoning, which Eli and Samuel are used to Eli doing when Samuel is ministering before Eli. In Western thinking, "calling" or "vocation" implies being drawn into work that will express one's gifts, but in the First Testament, calling simply means summoning, a summons to do something that the boss wants done. The boss might be unwise to summon a person to a task for which they lacked the gifts, but the focus lies on the boss and the task, not on the servant and their gifts. In Samuel's case, we might guess that having the parents he did have would have prepared him well to be a servant of Yahweh, though the story does not quite make the point. It does invite the inference that his apprenticeship to Eli was important in this connection (2:11, 18–21; 3:1). Yet paradoxically, Samuel did not yet acknowledge Yahweh (3:7), which was the problem with Eli's sons (2:12). Samuel's sons will not be much better (8:3). Yahweh seems to make a habit of choosing odd people without obvious qualifications (Jacob, Moses, Samuel, Saul, David, Solomon…).

In due course Eli recognizes who must be calling to Samuel, and Yahweh takes his stand before Samuel (*yāṣab* hitpael; 3:10). It is the only occurrence of this phrase in the First Testament. Yahweh had already spoken in a voice so real that Samuel could take it to be Eli's. Something objective was happening. This voice is not inside Samuel's head. The reference to an appearance (*mar'â*, 3:15) reinforces the point. The term is less technical than the word that more specifically denotes a vision (*ḥāzôn* in 3:1). It suggests that Samuel did not have a vision of Yahweh, as Isaiah and Ezekiel did. Rather, Yahweh did actually appear to him. He will now be appearing in the future, letting himself be seen (*rā'â* niphal), revealing himself in Shiloh (*gālâ* niphal) (3:21).

The references to vision and word are indications that prophecy is now beginning, in response to people doing what is upright in their own eyes (Judg 21:25). But at least God's lamp has not gone out (which makes one think forward to 2 Sam 21:17; Ps 132:17) and the covenant chest is still at Shiloh, even if Eli is getting too old to be able to see (1 Sam 3:2–3) and has failed to get his sons to see. But he eventually realizes who is speaking to Samuel, and instructs him on how to respond and submit to Yahweh's word. Even here, "call" does not refer to a vocation or commission – there is no sending in the story. There is a message, but no instruction to deliver it, and it might be partly for Samuel himself. But Samuel assumes he has to deliver it, as perhaps the story takes for granted. Typically, the prophetic message relates to something unpleasant (compare Isa 6; Jer 1:4–19; Ezek 1–3). Samuel holds back from delivering it; but "the brave old man demands, with a firmness backed up by an oath, that Samuel not conceal 'anything of all that He told you'" (1 Sam 3:17).[56]

Samuel is now moving from being an assistant of Eli to being a servant of Yahweh, like Moses, Joshua, and in due course David. "Speak, Yahweh, because your servant is listening" (3:9). Insofar as the obvious meaning of Samuel's name is something like "Heard by El," Samuel "grows into his name."[57] Yahweh is with him (3:19) as he was with Joseph (Gen 39:2, 3, 21, 23), Joshua (Josh 6:27), and the judges (Judg 2:18), and will be with David (1 Sam 18:12, 14, 28).

---

[56] Uriel Simon, "Samuel's Call to Prophecy: Form Criticism with Close Reading," *Prooftexts* 1 (1981): 119–32 (128).

[57] Johanna W. H. van Wijk-Bos, *Reading Samuel: A Literary and Theological Commentary* (Macon, GA: Smith and Helwys, 2011), 46.

In 1 Samuel 3 he enters the scene a boy and an apprentice priest, and exits a prophet or a priest who is also a prophet,[58] and will also function as a "judge."[59]

Although the story says that people recognized him as a prophet (3:20), they would hardly have known what the word meant (it has been used previously of Abraham and Moses, somewhat loosely, and in Judg 6:8). Its implication here is that Yahweh lets himself be seen and reveals himself at Shiloh with Yahweh's word (as in 1 Sam 3:4–14), and that Yahweh's word thus comes to Israel as it did not previously (3:1) by means of Samuel's word (3:21–4:1). There was no slippage between Yahweh's word coming to him and his word coming to the people. As prophet and priest he was truthful or trustworthy or reliable (ne'ĕmān; 3:20). In place of Eli and his sons, Yahweh has declared the intention to "establish for myself a truthful priest such as acts with my mind and my spirit. I will build him a truthful household and it will walk about before my anointed for all time" (2:35). Samuel is a first fulfillment of the promise of such a priest, though his sons fail too. So "for all time" again does not work out, and the story will look for another fulfillment of the promise, which will by implication come in Zadoq. This failure is a concrete example of something broader. Replacing Shiloh by Jerusalem does not achieve much, nor does replacing Eli's line

---

[58] Robert Polzin, *Samuel and the Deuteronomist: A Literary Study of the Deuteronomic History. Part Two: 1 Samuel* (reprinted Bloomington: Indiana University Press, 1993), 49; Marvin A. Sweeney, "Samuel's Institutional Identity in the Deuteronomistic History," in Lester L. Grabbe and Martti Nissinen, eds., *Constructs of Prophecy in the Former and Latter Prophets and Other Texts*, Ancient Near East Monographs 4 (Atlanta, GA: SBL, 2011), 165–74.

[59] Mark Leuchter, *Samuel and the Shaping of Tradition*, Biblical Reconfigurations (Oxford: Oxford University Press, 2013), gives one chapter to each of these roles.

by Zadoq's, nor does introducing prophets, nor does appointing kings. When situations get desperate, God sometimes takes action, but it does not move things on. It is even true of Jesus's coming. But meanwhile, Yahweh's word comes to Samuel; Samuel's word comes to Israel; and Yahweh confirms all his words.

Actually, Yahweh says nothing about Samuel being a "prophet," though the narrator describes him thus: Yahweh "did not let any of his words fall to the earth, and all Israel from Dan to Be'er Sheba acknowledged that Samuel was trustworthy as a prophet of Yahweh" (3:19–20). He would apparently have been known as a "seer" (*rō'eh*; see 9:9). Etymology offers more clues to this word's meaning than is the case with "prophet" (*nābî'*), whose etymology is a matter of guesswork. Samuel sees things. He is also "a man of God" (9:6–10; 2:27) whom people can consult for a fee in order to "inquire of God" (9:9). The expression "man of God" in the First Testament does not have the connotation of piety that it has in English; it rather suggests someone through whom supernatural things happen.

The uniqueness of Yahweh's speaking to Samuel links with the significance of the action Yahweh is about to take, which will shock people's ears when they hear about it. Yahweh goes on to reiterate the message that the divine messenger has already delivered, about removing Eli and his household "on that day."[60] This expression covers more than that removing, though Yahweh does not here indicate what else "that day" will bring. For the moment, then, Yahweh's announcement raises suspense, until 1 Samuel 4 relates the main catastrophe of which the death of Eli and his sons is an incidental result.

---

[60] Marti J. Steussy notes that readings of the story normally stop before we get to that bit (*Samuel and His God*, Studies on Personalities of the Old Testament [Columbia: University of South Carolina Press, 2010], 1).

CHAPTER 3

Yahweh Who Designates a King
(1 Samuel 4:1b–12:25)

Samuel does not begin by telling readers its theme or its theological concerns, though with hindsight one can see them hinted
in its opening pages. They note that Samuel was the baby who
was "asked for" (*šā'ûl*; 1:28) and that Hannah sang of Yahweh's
"anointed" (2:10). The calamity that follows Yahweh's summons
of Samuel will lead into the anointing of one whom the people
ask for.

THE GOD OF BET SHEMESH

In MT's versification, the covenant chest's adventures begin when
"Samuel's word came to all Israel. And Israel went out to meet
the Philistines in battle" (4:1). By implication, Samuel's message
commissioned the battle, to bring about the fulfillment of the
threats in 2:27–34; 3:11–14.[1] But Samuel is missing from 4:1b–7:1,
NRSV links 4:1a with the preceding chapter, and more likely the
account of his recognition (3:19–4:1a) is anticipatory.[2] Through
what follows, then, Samuel is still a boy at Shiloh, Eli and his
sons are still in charge, and if anything, Samuel's absence from

---

[1] So Rashi and more explicitly Qimhi, in *miqrā'ôt gədôlôt*.
[2] Fokkelman, *Narrative Art and Poetry* 4:190.

the narrative frees him from any blame for what happens.[3] This story then has a dramatic beginning in 4:1b that does not give any background.[4]

There is also more than one view about the end of the story of the covenant chest, and some ambiguity about its meaning. Modern translations agree with MT against the medieval chapter division that the story ends with the people of Bet-shemesh getting the chest off their hands (that is, 7:1 is the end of the story). They are keen to pass it on because of a conviction expressed in their question, "Who can stand before [that is, stand in attendance on] Yahweh, this holy God?" (6:20). It is a key theological question raised by the story, which in effect 7:2–17 will answer.

The Israelites and the Philistines were both seeking to consolidate and extend a hold on land, the Israelites aiming to expand westward and the Philistines northward. They meet in the borderlands in between. Joshua 13 had noted that Israel had not yet got control of the Philistine areas, and Judges has reported ongoing clashes between the Israelites and the Philistines, who dominate the Jezreel plain. One could see the engagement's theological rationale as lying in the Israelites' destiny to control the whole of Canaan, which (sort of) answers the question why Yahweh is on Israel's side and not the Philistines' in this battle,[5] but the story does not make that point. The narrative takes war for granted, and specifically takes for granted Israel's engagement in war.

Whoever started it, Israel's reversal in a first engagement makes the Israelite elders ask a good question, "Why has Yahweh

[3] Ralph W. Klein, *1 Samuel*, WBC 10 (2nd ed., Nashville, TN: Nelson, 2008), 35.
[4] LXX has an extra sentence explaining that the Philistines started the conflict (cf. NRSV).
[5] Peter D. Miscall, *1 Samuel: A Literary Reading* (Bloomington: Indiana University Press, 1986), 38–39.

knocked us down today in front of the Philistines?" (1 Sam 4:3a).
Actually, the narrative did not say that Yahweh had done this, but
if it is the right question, earlier narratives have suggested one or
two possible answers (see, e.g., Josh 7; Judg 3:4; 10:6–7). It turns
out, however, to be a rhetorical question.[6] There is no discussion,
"no consultation of anyone – prominently Samuel. Rather, at once
the solution."[7] "They have been left in the lurch."[8] Their solution
is to fetch "the chest of the covenant of Yahweh" from Shiloh "so
that he may come among us and deliver us from our enemies' fist"
(1 Sam 4:3b). The covenant chest had rings and poles to make it
portable, and it had been carried around in a similar connection
before (see Josh 6). Bringing it would mean bringing the rocks
engraved with the basic terms of the covenant, which were inside
it, along with the griffin-like creatures (the "cherubim") on top of
it, and the assumed presence of Yahweh sitting enthroned over it.
The God enthroned is Yahweh Armies, which would be significant
in the circumstances. The elders are pardonably hazy about the
relationship between Yahweh's presence in the tent and his presence in the battle, but anyway he has evidently not been exercising
his sovereignty as Yahweh Armies on Israel's behalf and he needs
to be reminded of the covenant, of his pledge to them.[9]

The chest's arrival issues in an earth-shaking shout among the
Israelites. When intelligence reaches the Philistines regarding the
explanation, it issues in fear among the Philistines of the "powerful gods" who are now present in the Israelite camp. They thus

---

[6] Cf. David G. Firth, *1 & 2 Samuel*, Apollos Old Testament Commentary 8 (Nottingham: Apollos, 2009), 85.
[7] Green, *How Are the Mighty Fallen*, 138.
[8] Fokkelman, *Narrative Art and Poetry* 4:201.
[9] Lyle Eslinger, *Kingship of God in Crisis: A Close Reading of 1 Samuel 1–12*, Bible and Literature Series 10 (Sheffield: JSOT Press, 1985), 166.

have half of an understanding of Israelite theology, and they articulate the Israelites' own implicit assumption, that the chest's presence means the presence of the God who delivered Israel from
the Egyptians by hitting them with his hand, and specifically by
bringing down epidemics upon them (4:8; cf. Exod 3:9, 19–20;
6:1; 7:4, 5). Unfortunately, their insight galvanizes them for a fight
and they defeat the Israelites, capture the chest, and kill Eli's sons,
though they fail to see the implications of knowing that Yahweh's
hand operates by bringing epidemics. Yahweh's hand and the
Philistines' fist and hand are key motifs in the story (1 Sam 4:3,
8; 5:6, 7, 9, 11; 6:3, 5, 9) and its sequel (7:3, 8, 13, 14). The fist (*kap*)
suggests a hand that grasps in a way that cannot be evaded, though
also a hand that hits – which is also the implication of the more
general word for hand (*yad*). The Philistines' gods losing both fists
and hands (5:4) adds to the pointed nature of the story. While the
Philistines' awareness of Yahweh as the God who brought the
Israelites out of Egypt makes them like Rahab, they do not draw
the inferences that she did. The Israelites resemble the Israelites in
the Rahab story, but not enough.

When Eli hears about the defeat, his sons' deaths, and specifically the chest's capture, the aged priest and judge drops dead. By
implication, 2:27–34 and 3:10–14 find fulfillment. The news (especially the news about the chest) sends Eli's pregnant daughter-in-
law into labor, and she also dies, but not before she names her
child Ikabod. The name would literally mean "Where is honor"
or "Alas, honor" or "Dis-honor," but she explains it as meaning "honor has gone into exile from Israel." The chest has gone
to Philistia; the honor has gone there. The simple term "honor"
(*kābôd*) hardly refers to Yahweh: It is Israel's honor that gone into
exile and been replaced by shame (cf. the collocation in Ps 4:2[3];
Isa 61:6–7).

In due course, the Philistine priests and diviners advise their people to give honor to Yahweh, who might then lighten his hand on them, their gods, and their country (1 Sam 6:5). It is the only other reference to honor in Samuel; the only reference in Joshua and Judges occurs when Joshua urges Achan to give honor to Yahweh before he dies (Josh 7:19), though the Exodus story relates how Yahweh had decided to gain honor from the Egyptians (*kābēd* niphal, Exod 14:4, 7, 18). So here the Philistines realize that they had better give it. They no more think of Yahweh as simply located in the chest than the Israelites do. But they have discovered that the chest is too hot to handle. "Israel may be defeated in spite of its possession of God's ark and the ark itself may be seized, but all this is not to imply that God has lost any of his power over other people's gods."[10] Not only does Yahweh raise his hand against the Philistines' images; the people themselves are afflicted by epidemics. Although the chest's presence does not exactly mean Yahweh's presence, it does draw forth Yahweh's action. In another ironic link, the Israelites' cry (*šawʿâ*) for deliverance (*yašûʿâ*) had gone up to God in Egypt (Exod 2:23, the only preceding occurrence of this word for "cry"), and the Philistines' "cry" now goes up to the heavens (1 Sam 5:12).

The Philistines realize they must send the chest off to its "place" (*māqôm*; 6:2), apparently its country not its sanctuary (which they have destroyed?).[11] Their diviners and priests advise sending it with a reparation offering to make up for the offense they have committed against Yahweh. The chest and offering are set on a new cart hauled by milch cows. Though separated from their calves,

---

[10] Polzin, *Samuel and the Deuteronomist*, 64.
[11] Israel Finkelstein, ed., "Excavations at Shiloh 1981–1984: Preliminary Report," *Tel Aviv* 12 (1985): 123–80 (173).

they make straight for Bet-shemesh, which proves that they know where the chest's home is, in Israel. The people there welcome it and make offerings to Yahweh. But then some of them look at the chest (or look into it) and Yahweh strikes down a large number, which leads the town to ask that question, "Who can stand before Yahweh?" Something like electricity attaches to holy ones. While one might be nervous about being in the presence of any holy one, a particular nervousness could attach to standing before Yahweh as *the* holy one, and particular vulnerability attaches to people who "stand before" the holy one in the sense of serving him. The wording suggests that the disaster at Bet-shemesh happened in the context of some act of service that somehow turned out to be an act of contempt and led to a catastrophe.

The chest means death and destruction. If the Israelites properly laughed through the story of the Philistines and the trouble they got into with the covenant chest, "laughter may have died on their lips on hearing the end of the story."[12] The chest really does convey the presence of Yahweh, the powerful God. You cannot take him for granted, but neither can you mess with him, whether you are Philistine or Israelite. "The ark in and out of battle entails defeat and disaster for both communities."[13] Both of them get the chest (4:3, 11, 17, 21, 22; 5:1), both shout (4:5, 14; 5:9, 11), Yahweh afflicts both, Yahweh strikes both down.

The story does not really make sense, which is why that question "Who can stand?" did make sense.[14] Yahweh does not explain what has happened. No one says the Israelites should repent; that possibility arises only twenty years later (7:2–6). The narrator does

---

[12] Van Wijk-Bos, *Reading Samuel*, 52.
[13] Polzin, *Samuel and the Deuteronomist*, 55.
[14] Antony F. Campbell, *1 Samuel*, FOTL 7 (Grand Rapids, MI: Eerdmans, 2003), 81.

not explain what has happened. Interpreters speak of omniscient narrators; in the Scriptures, narrators may have some supernatural knowledge, but if they possess omniscience, they keep it to themselves. There is no theodicy in this story. "He is Yahweh – he does what is good in his eyes" (3:18).[15]

Once again, however, having asked a question, the Israelites do not wait for an answer, but take action,[16] sending the chest off to Qiryat-ye'arim. It is not too far, and nearer than Shiloh, which now loses its significance as Israel's central sanctuary even if it has not been destroyed. Further, Qiryat-ye'arim seems not to count as a fully Israelite town; it belonged to the Gibeonites (Josh 9:17). After the Gibeonites tricked Joshua into not eliminating them, he let them become manual laborers, looking after practical and menial aspects of worship, which fits the role they receive here. They set someone apart to look after the chest, making him holy (1 Sam 7:1).

BEING THE PEOPLE OF GOD

The return of the chest is not an indication that relationships between the Israelites and the Philistines are resolved. The Israelites still need rescuing or delivering from the Philistines (7:3, 8). They are now to have an "ostensibly" important meeting with the Philistines, but a more important meeting with Yahweh.[17] Samuel has grown up, and Yahweh has been speaking through him and fulfilling his words. He has come to be recognized to be

---

[15] Eslinger, *Kingship of God in Crisis*, 199.

[16] Miscall, *1 Samuel*, 34–35.

[17] Walter Brueggemann, *First and Second Samuel*, Interpretation: A Bible Commentary for Teaching and Preaching (Louisville, KY: John Knox, 1990), 50.

trustworthy as a prophet (3:19–4:1a), and his moment has arrived. He declares that Israel must turn to Yahweh with their entire mind (7:3). Turning (*šûb*) is something one does with one's body, but it needs to involve the mind (*lēbāb*). It means not just mind or inner person as opposed to something outward, nor an outward turning without a change in inner attitude, nor a half-hearted such change, but a turning of the whole mind. Israel needs to jettison alien gods, the Ba'als and the Ashtarts, fix their mind on Yahweh, and serve Yahweh alone. Samuel's challenge resembles similar challenges in Joshua (24:14–15, 20, 23) and Judges (2:11–13; 10:6–16). It suggests a recurrent issue for the people of God, an inclination to put faith in the culture's resources instead of the God who had proved himself in the past. And it suggests a need to clean things up in this connection from time to time. Is there a link with Israel's letting the chest sit in a Gibeonite town for twenty years? There are times when one has to wait, and times to take action. Such a moment has arrived.

Perhaps it is a prophet's job to recognize such a time and then to discern the action that needs taking. There is a negative action, the jettisoning, and then a gathering, at Mizpah (1 Sam 7:5). It is one of the centers of Samuel's activity (7:16) and it recalls another historic occasion (Judg 20). Here Samuel pleads for them. It is his responsibility and vocation both as priest and prophet, and they urge him not to be deaf to them or to fail to cry out to Yahweh for them (1 Sam 7:8, 9). They draw water and pour it before Yahweh, and they fast. It is the only First Testament reference to a water libation, though the practice is known from elsewhere and appears in the Mishnah (*Sukkah* 4:9); it might symbolize pouring out yourself (Tg; cf. Lam 2:19),[18] or it might go along with fasting

---

[18] Peterson, *First and Second Samuel*, 51.

and denote that people were not even drinking water. People would often make a burnt offering when they were pleading with Yahweh for something, as we might make a gift to someone when we ask a favor. While it can be a sign of a sad understanding of the relationship, it can be a sign that we are not asking for a favor in a way that costs us nothing (2 Sam 24:24). Samuel makes a particularly sacrificial burnt offering for them (1 Sam 7:9): The whole event forms a marked contrast with 2:12–17. They acknowledge, "We have offended against Yahweh" (7:6).

Yahweh answers and thunders (7:9–10); the thunder constitutes the answer. The two aspects to an answer to prayer become one.[19] Only here in Samuel does Yahweh "answer" a prayer, and only here in First Testament narrative does Yahweh thunder. Perhaps there was literal thunder that encouraged Israel and panicked the Philistines or perhaps the language has its regular metaphorical significance. Either way, Yahweh somehow throws the Philistines into confusion (hāmam) and they collapse (nāgap niphal), the verb that applied unhappily to Israel in 4:2, 10. Typically, the event involves both Yahweh's action (he is the subject of two verbs), and the Philistines' action or reaction, and Israel's action or reaction (7:10–11). But all Israel has to do is give chase. Not so typically, they do not have to fight. This victory resembles the conquest of Jericho more than most victories in Joshua, Judges, or Samuel. It thus provides an alternative model of the interaction of Yahweh's activity and Israel's activity.

So Yahweh "helped" the Israelites "thus far" (7:12). Both expressions may be misleading. "Helped" ('āzar) often suggests more than assisting and supporting people, as they play their part. Rather, somebody powerful (such as God) takes action on behalf

---

[19] See the section earlier on "Prayer and Promise."

of someone who cannot do anything. The verb comes in company with words for "delivering" (e.g., Pss 37:40; 79:9; 109:26). And "thus far" does not imply "so far but who knows what will happen now," but "to this very point" (CEB). We are coming to a climax in the story (1 Sam 7:13–17). Israel has returned to Yahweh, Yahweh has put paid to the Philistines, Israel has recovered its land, and there is peace between the Israelites and the pre-Israelite peoples of Canaan, the Amorites. Samuel the priest and prophet is exercising authority (*šāpaṭ*) around Israel, sorting things out where necessary at Bethel, Gilgal, and Mizpah, acting as "judge" in succession to Eli. At last there is someone to succeed Moses and Joshua.[20] He has built an altar in his home town at Ramah, which perhaps replaces Shiloh as a key sanctuary. Everything looks good.[21] But it will turn out that there is an ambiguity in that expression "thus far."

The event illustrates a key sequence in the life of the people of God, maybe two. They acknowledge their waywardness, they turn away from other servitudes and trusts, and they turn to God in worship that costs them something. As a weak people they cry out, and God answers in word and deed. The people do what needs doing to enter into the benefits of that sequence. Of course, often people do not turn or cry out, and God does not always answer in word and deed. Part of the theological genius of narrative is to tell of something that has happened and/or could happen without implying that it always happens. It issues an invitation, but it makes no promise.

Samuel himself is capable of issuing exhortations and not quite making promises. He will subsequently review the story of Israel

---

[20] Campbell, *1 Samuel*, 86.
[21] Rosenberg, "I and 2 Samuel," 125–26.

from the exodus (12:10). It is a story of Yahweh's acts of faithfulness (his ṣᵊdāqôt, 12:7: cf. Judg 5:11; Ps 103:6; Isa 45:24; Dan 9:16;
Mic 6:5), a salvation history. It is also a story of Israel's putting
out of mind, wrongdoing, abandoning, and serving other deities,
a history of waywardness. "If you live in awe of Yahweh, serve
him, listen to his voice, do not rebel against Yahweh's voice, and
are after Yahweh your God…" (1 Sam 12:14). Then "it will be well,"
the NRSV goes on. But Samuel does not say so. The if-clause runs
out in an ellipsis.[22] In contrast, the negative if-clause that follows,
"if you do not listen," does explicitly go on, "Yahweh's hand will
be against you" (12:15). As many psalms presuppose, sometimes
Israel will be faithful and blessing will not follow; there is slippage
between act and experience. While Samuel speaks in the terms
of Deuteronomy's expectations, he also implicitly recognizes
that Deuteronomy's promises about obedience and blessing will
not always work out. Fortunately, the rules about disobedience
and trouble do not always work out either. It is just as well here,
because "the issue at stake is the destruction of Israel rather than
[merely] the failure of the monarchy."[23]

Once again Samuel gives a sign to show he speaks the truth.
This time it is a scary sign, as a result of which the people are in
awe of Yahweh and of Samuel (yārē'; 12:18). Or are they afraid of
Yahweh and of Samuel? They now describe Yahweh as "your God"
not "our God."[24] Samuel does tell them not to be afraid (12:20).
They are the gentlest words of his tough ministry. "Yahweh will
not give up on his people, on account of his great name, because

---

[22] But the expression is odd, and KJV follows Tg, Vg in making the last clause,
"are after…" (which is unique as an alternative to "go after" Yahweh), the
apodosis.

[23] Chapman, 1 Samuel as Christian Scripture, 61.

[24] Eslinger, Kingship of God in Crisis, 415.

Yahweh determined to make you a people for himself" (12:22). He has to be faithful to himself and stick by decisions he has taken and commitments he has made. It is his people's great security. Yet they should not take too much for granted. If they live in a grossly dire fashion, they will be swept away like Sodom and Gomorrah (*sāpâ* niphal, 12:25; cf. Gen 18:23–24; 19:15, 17). Does this threat contradict the reassurance and set alternative prospects ahead of them, so that they choose? The ambiguity about their position parallels and links with the ambiguity over whether their own faithfulness issues in blessing. And at the end of 1 Samuel 12, Samuel returns to his grim warning, and "swept away" is his last word.[25]

Prophets and priests live life in an identification with two sides in a relationship,[26] speaking for Yahweh to their people and to their people for Yahweh. In Samuel's role, praying and teaching go together (12:23); neither is complete without the other.[27] It thus fortunately continues to be his job to intercede for his people. If he stops, he would be doing wrong against Yahweh (*ḥāṭāʾ*; 12:19–23). Yahweh is committed to staying faithful to Israel notwithstanding its faithlessness, and Samuel's pleading is the practice that holds Yahweh to his intention rather than (for example) allowing him to give in to a justified inclination to abandon Israel. It would be foolish of them to tempt Yahweh in that direction. He is, after all, the one who undertook all those acts of faithfulness and rescue (12:6–11), whereas the gods to whom they might alternatively turn

---

[25] Fokkelman, *Narrative Art and Poetry* 4:532.

[26] Viktorin Strigel, *Libri Samuelis, Regum et Paralipomenon* (Leipzig: Vögelin, 1569), 41; cf. Cooper and Lohrmann, *1–2 Samuel, 1–2 Kings, 1–2 Chronicles*, 51.

[27] Michael Widmer, *Standing in the Breach: An Old Testament Theology and Spirituality of Intercessory Prayer* (Winona Lake, IN: Eisenbrauns, 2015), 202–5.

are empty (*tôhû*). They cannot do anything useful and they cannot rescue (12:21). The same applies to their kings.[28]

Much of the "sermon" in 1 Samuel 12,[29] read during the divided monarchy and after 587, would remind people of Yahweh's acts of faithfulness and their rebellions, urging them to start following Yahweh's way, and promising them that he would not let go of them. Samuel does not describe the relationship between Yahweh and Israel as covenantal except in referring to the covenant chest, and the word *covenant* can have many meanings. If we mean by a covenant a solemnly undertaken committed reciprocal relationship, then the relationship between Yahweh and Israel is covenantal and Israel needs to be committed to it, as Yahweh is. But covenants can be terminated by one party or the other. The relationship between Yahweh and Israel is better than covenantal. It is more like a family relationship. Yahweh will not make use of any basis for terminating it. It is more or less impossible to stop being the parent of your children.

WHY AND WHY NOT HAVE A KING

The account of why and how Saul becomes king and then loses his warrant as king is substantial, complex, mysterious, and jerky. It is substantial because his reign is a turning point in Israel's story, and it can illustrate key issues. The jerkiness (e.g., the move from 8:1–22 to 9:1–10:16) parallels the way one episode in a television series may make a jump from where the previous episode ended before possibly bringing things together. The complexity

[28] Lyle Eslinger, *Into the Hands of the Living God*, JSOTSup 84 (Sheffield: Sheffield Academic Press, 1989), 117.

[29] H. W. Hertzberg, *I & II Samuel: A Commentary*, OTL (London: SCM, 1964), 97, following Martin Noth.

generates a portrait of Saul as a complicated and enigmatic person who is not amenable to confident unequivocal description or judgment. He thus resembles other biblical characters such as Jacob, Rebekah, David, and Mary. The mystery extends to God's relationship with Saul, as is the case with God's relationship with Moses and Job; his attitude to kingship in general is "enigmatic."[30] The jerkiness and the different angles on central government also reflect the narrative's combining several versions of why and how Israel came to have kings, like a movie script that merges several screenwriters' work. The several versions, telling the story from different angles, cannot be put end to end, but together they comprise a richly diverse account. It illustrates another aspect of the genius of narrative: It can portray people and issues in the appropriately complex way. During the divided monarchy and after 587, it might aid the Judahite community in thinking about monarchy and about the future, though it would not tell them the answer about what to think. The further genius of narrative is that it forbids its readers taking too much for granted, thinking it has come to an end when it had not.

"Samuel is not a political book" but it is "a book about politics" that suggests "a revolutionary transformation in biblical political theology" in denying that "the king is God," asserting instead that "God is the king," and seeking to wrestle with what human kingship can therefore mean.[31] "The centrality of human power in relation to the divine lies on the surface in Samuel."[32] Thus, "how human kingship could exist within an authority structure that

---

[30] Gilmour, *Representing the Past*, 187, 194, 198.

[31] Moshe Halbertal and Stephen Holmes, *The Beginning of Politics: Power in the Biblical Book of Samuel* (Princeton: Princeton University Press, 2017), 2, 4, 5.

[32] J. G. McConville, *God and Earthly Power: An Old Testament Political Theology Genesis–Kings*, LHBOTS 454 (London: T&T Clark, 2006), 133.

allowed Yahweh to remain the 'Great King' is one of the key questions addressed by the books of Samuel."[33] Yet only once in Samuel
is Yahweh termed "king" (1 Sam 12:12), against 299 references to
human beings as kings. It looks as if Yahweh prefers to be seen
as "deliverer" rather than as "king" (môšîaʿ rather than melek);[34]
these two words come together in one of Samuel's rebukes of the
people's desire for a king (10:19; see also 14:39; 2 Sam 22:3).

The first king emerges:

1. Because the hereditary principle for government did not
    work (8:1–5). Samuel was no more fortunate or effective as
    a parent than Eli had been, and he had not confronted his
    sons, as Eli at least had.[35] Samuel thus confirms a point that
    emerges from Eli's story. An irony then emerges, since Israel
    soon falls into hereditary assumptions about kings and
    repeats the same experience over the hereditary principle.
    Another irony is that the other disappointed father in
    Israel's story was Gideon, the man who refused to be ruler
    over Israel (Judg 8–9).

2. Because the previous form of government did not work, in
    that the people with authority misused their authority to
    benefit themselves (1 Sam 8:2). The beginning of this narra-
    tive establishes that the exercise of authority (šāpaṭ, mišpāṭ)
    is a key theme.[36] It is misleading that mišpāṭ is conven-
    tionally translated "justice," because it refers concretely to
    the exercise of authority, in giving judgment and in other

---

[33] V. Philipps Long, I & II Samuel (Grand Rapids, MI: Zondervan, 2009),
    Introduction.

[34] Karl Barth, Church Dogmatics III/1 (reprinted London: T&T Clark, 2010), 438.

[35] Van Wijk-Bos, Reading Samuel, 58.

[36] Jerry Hwang, "Yahweh's Poetic Mishpat in Israel's Kingship," Westminster
    Theological Journal 73 (2011): 341–61.

contexts. But it does imply the *proper* exercise of authority. An implication of the elders' appeal is the traditional Middle Eastern assumption that it is a king's business to see to the exercise of authority in a way that is fair and protective.[37] The further irony emerges that the exercise of authority by Israel's kings will hardly be better than that by Samuel's sons, like all forms of authority known to humanity.

3. Because the elders, whose previous appearance had been to ask why Yahweh had defeated the Israelites and then to jump to a dubious solution (4:3), again see a problem and jump to a dubious solution (8:4–5). Their reasoning does recall the observation at the end of Judges about people deciding for themselves what was upright when there was no king, which implied that a king would solve the problem. But why should a king make a difference if a figure like Samuel did not?

4. Because the elders want Israel to be like other nations (8:5). It might seem that moving towards strong central government is indeed a natural or inevitable sociological development as the nation grows and develops. The story in 1 Samuel 8–12 is then an account of a nation going through a necessary "rite of passage."[38] But "like other nations" is "a bid … for ordinariness" as a means to survival.[39] Israel was designed to be and to model something different. So the elders who ask for a king adduce bad reasons as well as defensible ones (that the Samuel sons are not suitable as successors to their

---

[37] Campbell, *1 Samuel*, 98–100.
[38] Marcel V. Măcelaru, "Israel in Transition: Liminality and Status Change In 1 Samuel 8–15," in Corneliu Constantineanu and Marcel V. Măcelaru, eds. *Bible, Culture, Society* (Osijek: Evanđeoski teološki fakultet, 2009), 39–64.
[39] Rosenberg, "I and 2 Samuel," 126.

father), and they seem persuaded not a bit by what Samuel warns.[40]

5. Because the people are thereby rebuffing Samuel as the person put in authority by Yahweh (though they could claim that Deut 17:14–20 allows the appointment of a king – by Yahweh) and/or rebuffing Yahweh himself, in keeping with their consistent practice (8:6–8). The king's appearance "opens a new way to apostasy from the first commandment."[41]

6. Because Yahweh is prepared to do as they say (8:7), though he first wants Samuel to get them to think about the implications of their proposal. God "gives them up" to their own desires (cf. Rom 1:24, 26, 28).[42]

7. Even though they will find having a king is expensive (8:9–17). Central government costs money, even if it tries to be economic, though in practice governments do not try hard to be economic in the way they themselves live off the back of their people. "From Samuel's perspective, what characterizes a king above all is that he will *take*."[43] He can later claim to have been cheaper, even if his sons were not (12:1–5; "take" recurs there, too).[44] But a government has to be fed, and the people are going to have to foot the bill. To be less anachronistic, it is all going to cost labor, the price being mostly paid by people other than the elders themselves.[45]

[40] Barbara Green, *David's Capacity for Compassion: A Literary-Hermeneutical Study of 1-2 Samuel*, LHBOTS 641 (London: T&T Clark, 2017), 53.
[41] Hertzberg, *I & II Samuel*, 73.
[42] Barth, *Dogmatics* III/1, 439.
[43] Van Wijk-Bos, *A People and a Land 2*, on the passage.
[44] Birch, "The First and Second Books of Samuel," on the passage.
[45] See Gale A. Yee, "'He Will Take the Best of Your Fields': Royal Feasts and Rural Extraction," *JBL* 136 (2017): 821–38.

There is yet more irony in the fact that this warning is labeled as a description of the way the king will exercise authority, of his *mišpāṭ*. One would have hoped that a description of the king's *mišpāṭ* would have been more positively prescriptive for the people's sake, like (one hopes) the account of it in 10:25 (cf. 2 Sam 8:15). Here the king's *mišpāṭ* is simply what he will legitimately be entitled to do in making kingship work (it does mean more than "custom" or "manner").[46] But at least the "rule" may draw attention to limits that a king must respect.[47]

8. Even though the king will be one who thus puts them into servitude and makes them cry out, instead of being a liberator when they cry out (1 Sam 8:18).[48] And when they do cry out thus, Yahweh will not respond. They have chosen their alternative bed and they will have to lie in it. To put it more positively, they will learn a painful lesson if they insist on their request. To put it even more positively, though the monarchy will fail, it is nevertheless "a sign act" that "will provide a continuing testimony to God's righteousness, to the people's faithlessness, and to the difference between a human kingdom and the kingdom of God."[49]

9. Because they nevertheless insist on having a king, feeling the need of someone to fight their battles (8:19–20). In itemizing the cost, Samuel made more explicit that having a king like other nations implies the general

---

[46] Cf. McConville, *God and Earthly Power*, 138–39.
[47] See Jonathan Kaplan, "1 Samuel 8:11–18 as 'A Mirror for Princes,'" *JBL* 131 (2012): 625–42.
[48] Auld, *I & II Samuel*, 93.
[49] Chapman, *1 Samuel as Christian Scripture*, 59.

assumption that the main task of a government is its people's protection. The Philistine imbroglio has shown this necessary in the past, and the surprising fact that there is apparently now a Philistine base in the vicinity (10:5) also suggests the need. In a moment Yahweh will refer to the people's need for deliverance from the Philistines and to the cry they have uttered (ṣəʿāqâ; 9:16), like the one they uttered in Egypt (Exod 3:7, 9). Yes, they want a king to lead them in battle, a *real* king, not an occasional human judge and an invisible divine king. This aspect of their request looks like an afterthought and might be intended that way.[50] But as Samuel said, a military requires expenditure.

10. Because Yahweh agrees (1 Sam 8:21–22). What else was he to do? Turn his back on them as they had turned their backs on him? Insist on appointing another non-kingly leader? In the Scriptures and in the subsequent life of the people of God, he is consistently trimming what he wants to what is practicable, not least in the forms of leadership he allows to develop. "The mysterious forbearance of God and the continuing perfidy of God's people walk side by side."[51] "He gave them a king, as it is written, according to their heart, but not according to His heart."[52] The monarchy is "an unwelcome but inevitable reality."[53]

[50] Diana Vikander Edelman, *King Saul in the Historiography of Judah*, JSOTSup 121 (Sheffield: Sheffield Academic Press, 1991), 41.

[51] Polzin, *Samuel and the Deuteronomist*, 81.

[52] Augustine, "Letter 130," in *Letters* (Washington, DC: Catholic University of America, reprinted 2008) 2:376–401 (396); cf. Franke, *Joshua, Judges, Ruth, 1–2 Samuel*, 224.

[53] P. Kyle McCarter, *II Samuel: A New Translation with Introduction, Notes and Commentary* (AB 9; Garden City, NY: Doubleday, 1984), 8.

HOW AND HOW NOT TO HAVE A KING

"We move from why it was done to how it was done."[54] The argument between the people (or the elders representing them), Samuel, and Yahweh ends with Samuel sending everyone back to their hometown. A decision has been reached. How will it be implemented? Will the elders consult? Will there be nominations and an election? Will Samuel spend time consulting with Yahweh? Who would Yahweh want as king (cf. Deut 17:15)? The answer is that Yahweh will designate Saul.

1. He is someone with an impressive family background, and he is himself impressive in appearance (1 Sam 9:1–2). But it will transpire that the narrative is playing with the auditors in implying that these are important considerations. And maybe it is significant that he comes from little Benjamin (9:21; cf. Ps 68:27[28]), with its shameful background (Judg 19–21).

2. "Saul makes his first appearance in the Bible as an agreeable young man, motivated only by a sense of family duty, unassuming, deferential, and, as far as we can see, without high ambition."[55] He is also not as knowledgeable or as bright as his boy (1 Sam 9:3–10), which warns us more overtly that things may not turn out well.

3. Saul and the boy arrive at a certain town while looking for some lost donkeys. Maybe it is Ramah, as Samuel has a house here (9:18). By no coincidence Samuel is going to be there, leading worship at the shrine, the first (almost the only) individual *bāmâ* ("high place") in the First Testament

---

54 Auld, *I & II Samuel*, 96.
55 McCarter, *I Samuel*, 184.

story (9:11–15). Yahweh has told him that someone is coming whom he is to anoint. Yahweh prefers to speak of the
prospective leader as a commandant (*nāgîd*), whose task is
to restrain or control or marshal Israel (*ʿāṣar*; 9:16–17). Both
noun and verb are elusive words, but a main point about
them is that they do not mean "king" or "reign." A commandant suggests someone chosen, designated, exalted, and
anointed by Yahweh,[56] someone "announced" by Yahweh
(the verb *nāgad* comes eight times in 9:1–10:16), someone
under Yahweh's direction, more like a prophet than a king.
It confronts any idea of a leader who engages in decisive initiatives on the basis of his own vision of what a situation
needs. Thus, Yahweh here four times calls Israel "my people" (9:16–17);[57] he uses the expression only once more in 1
Samuel (2:29). Despite Deuteronomy 17:15, the idea of the
leader being someone God "chooses" stands in some tension with the usual talk of the people as the entity that is
chosen by God, a more common theme in Deuteronomy.
"Monarchy potentially endangered this belief in the election
of the people as whole."[58]

4. He is the one to whom Israel's entire desire or delight
(*ḥemdâ*) relates or belongs or attaches (1 Sam 9:20). Samuel's
noun could imply something proper (Pss 19:10[11]; 106:24)
or something wrongful (Deut 5:21[18]; Josh 7:21).

5. Saul's response, "What, me?" (1 Sam 9:21), matches a common pattern when Yahweh summons people, but that parallel does not make the response less significant. It suggests
he has not been aspiring to such a designation, whatever

[56] Cf. G. F. Hasel, *TDOT* 9:199.
[57] Cf. Eslinger, *Kingship of God in Crisis*, 307.
[58] Murphy, *1 Samuel*, 63.

Samuel means when he says he knows what Saul has in his mind, about which he promises to talk to him (9:18–19). Saul does not take Gideon's stance of simply refusing to "rule" over the people (*māšal*; Judg 8:22–23), on the basis of Yahweh's being the one who rules; but then, it was the Israelites not a prophet who approached Gideon.

6. Saul thus becomes the first person to be anointed as a ruler (as opposed to being anointed as a priest). In effect, Samuel crowns him and declares that Yahweh has anointed him (1 Sam 10:1).

7. He gives Saul signs that what he says is true (10:2–13), as Yahweh did for Moses and for Gideon. It can be another feature of a summons by Yahweh. The signs' fulfillment will also be an indication that Samuel is the prophet whom Saul can and must trust and follow (cf. Deut 18:21–22). The climactic sign is that he will find himself joining a group of prophets in "acting like a prophet" (*nābā'* hitpael) as Yahweh's spirit or wind or breath comes dynamically upon him (1 Sam 10:6). Translations such as "in a prophetic frenzy" (NRSV) or "speaking in ecstasy" (NJPS) do not clarify the verb's meaning. In the eighteenth-century First Great Awakening, groaning, screaming, and collapsing could be signs of God's having an impact on a person, and such phenomena have recurred in more recent Pentecostal and charismatic movements. Like prophesying or speaking in tongues, the experience may imply a heightened consciousness, but it need not do so. It does imply Saul acting in a way he normally did not. He will thus "turn into another man" (10:6). To put it a different way, God gives him another mind or attitude (10:9), an anticipatory summary of what happens when he meets the prophets. By nature Saul is just a regular guy, without gifts

of leadership or aspirations to leadership, like people such as Moses, Joshua, and Gideon. If the fulfillment of Yahweh's purpose depends on Yahweh, the leader of Israel does not need leadership gifts. The coming of Yahweh's spirit will look after such matters. Yahweh gives him another mind, "a spirit of royal might,"[59] instead of one that just knows about cattle,[60] and he is now a man who can sing praise (cf. Tg).

8. He is then to do what his hand finds to do, given that God is with him (10:7). Again puzzlingly, however, Samuel adds that he is to go down to Gilgal by the Jordan and wait for a week for Samuel to come to offer sacrifices and make known to him what he is to do (10:8). The sequence of events in 1 Samuel 11–13 will partly clarify things.

9. Meanwhile, once again the narrative jumps (10:17–27). Samuel summons the people to Mizpah again, reasserts a rebuke for their rebuffing Yahweh in saying they want a king, but gets them to assemble by families so they can identify by lot the person of Yahweh's choice. The process might seem worrying, as the last person identified this way was Achan (Josh 7), but it will apparently be okay for the appointment of Matthias (Acts 1:26). The method underscores the assumption that determining who should be king is not a matter of discerning who has the leadership qualities, or even the personal qualities, but of discerning who is Yahweh's choice. The private and secret anointing (1 Sam 10:1) and the public identification confirm each other.[61]

---

[59] Rashi, in *miqrā'ôt gədôlôt*.

[60] Andrew Willet, *An Harmonie upon the First Booke of Samuel...* (Cambridge: Greene, 1607), 62.

[61] Cf. Jeffrey L. Cooley, "The Story of Saul's Election (1 Samuel 9–10) in the Light of Mantic Practice in Ancient Iraq," *JBL* 130 (2011): 247–61.

10. Saul is hiding with the stuff belonging to the gathering, but it does not stop Samuel designating him. Like declining to tell his uncle about his anointing (10:15–17), hiding is a sign of being someone who does not push himself forward and/ or a sign of "Saul's premonition that ruling is a burden from which he must hide."[62]

11. The people acclaim him. Samuel gives the people another description of how the king will exercise authority, his *mišpāṭ* (10:25), different from the earlier one (8:11–18): NRSV here renders the phrase "the rights and duties of the kingship." Perhaps it is the kind of thing that appears in Deuteronomy 17:14–20. Samuel writes it down and sets it before Yahweh, and everyone goes home. There are some people who are not impressed by Saul, but he keeps quiet (1 Sam 10:25–27), which might be a sign of wisdom (Prov 11:12).

HOW TO BE A KING

The Philistines were not Israel's only problem at this time (1 Sam 11:1–5). According to Judges 11, the Ammonites claimed the Israelite territory east of the Jordan, are now trying to drive the Israelites out of Jabesh-gilead there, and are intent on disabling people who remain.[63] News reaches Saul, who is out plowing. It will seem surprising if he has already been acclaimed as king, but if a main point about a king is to lead the people in battle, the need for him to function as king arises only now. Or maybe 1 Samuel 11 provides a third account of a proper process whereby Yahweh might indicate that a person should become king rather than being

---

[62] Murphy, *1 Samuel*, 88.
[63] 4QSam^a gives a fuller version of the background: see NRSV.

merely someone with authority like Gideon, Eli, or Samuel. It is
then parallel to the accounts in 1 Samuel 10 rather than chronologically sequential: There is private anointing, public identification,
and active demonstration that Yahweh is at work through him.
All three are important indicators of Yahweh choosing Saul and
thus of the argument for recognizing him as king. Anyway, the
Ammonite action tests whether Saul can fulfill the role of king.[64]
Once again Yahweh's breath or wind or spirit overwhelms Saul,
and his anger blazes (11:6). Yes, he is a different person, and "Saul's
finest hour" follows.[65]

Some recent events in the United States and in Britain may
help us understand the way Samuel speaks about a spirit of anger,
and the latter may help us understand these events. A spirit of
anger and/or affront and/or fear and/or compassion and/or
worry has overwhelmed many people in connection with rac-
ism, imperialism, and global warming, and led to public demon-
strations over these matters and to people taking violent action
against property and/or people. This spirit was not something
that was previously active in them, though it may have been
latent. It aroused them from outside and turned them into different people (demonstrators often comment "I am not the kind
of person who usually does this sort of thing, but…"). To speak
of this spirit overwhelming them is not to indicate approval of
it; Samuel will later speak of a bad spirit overwhelming Saul, and
some of the ways in which a spirit has overwhelmed people in
Britain and in the United States have been bad. But in this case
with Saul, the anger is God's, as is the case (for instance) with
God's spirit of wisdom (Exod 28:3).

---

[64] Edelman, *King Saul*, 59.
[65] Miscall, *1 Samuel*, 66.

If this spirit overwhelms someone, it comes from outside, and with force. The Hebrew expression (*ṣālaḥ* followed by the preposition *ʿal*) is used almost exclusively in references to a spirit coming onto a person (Judg 14:6, 19; 15:14; 1 Sam 10:6, 10; 11:6; the preposition is *ʾel* in 16:13; 18:10, suggesting into rather than onto). The spirit lays hold on them. Whereas LXX and Vg translate "jump on," forcefulness rather than suddenness is the connotation. NRSV's "possess" might be misleading, while Tg's "dwell" undertranslates. The spirit's overwhelming people does not mean overriding their will or making them act in an involuntary way, but it does mean that a force from outside pushes them into behaving in a way they otherwise would not.

Energized by the anger generated by God's breath or wind or spirit, Saul does what his hand finds to do, God being with him (10:7). He summons an Israelite fighting force (threatening them Mafioso-style with death if they hold back),[66] and leads them in striking down the Ammonites. The story does not refer to Yahweh acting, but Saul subsequently declares that Yahweh has effected deliverance for them. The three references to deliverance in the chapter make clear that it is not Saul who is meant to be celebrated as a result of what happens.[67] But what happens is reason for being merciful to the people who had doubts about him (11:7–13), and reason to "renew" the kingship; so they "made Saul king" there.

In due course, the people of Jabesh will star in the final act in the drama of Saul's life (31:11–13). For them, "Saul would always be the one who rescued them from extreme danger, their redeemer-king." And the first great act of Saul as king will have a substantial link to the promise of a king "who would embody

---

[66] Robert Alter, *The David Story: A Translation with Commentary of 1 and 2 Samuel* (New York: Norton, 1999), 62.

[67] So Hertzberg, *I & II Samuel*, 93.

justice and righteousness, who would defend the cause of the poor and the needy, who would uphold the rights of the stranger, the orphan, and the widow. Great expectations were thus shaped against the concrete background of failed monarchs, or unjust and greedy ones."[68]

---

[68] Van Wijk-Bos, *Reading Samuel*, 153–54.

CHAPTER 4

Yahweh Who Rebuffs a King
(1 Samuel 13:1–20:42[21:1])

Samuel does not aim to write a biography of Saul or a chronicle of his reign (any more than of David).[1] Its focus is now his failure to live up to his vocation. Narratively, Saul features in Samuel primarily as a "negative contrast to David."[2] Nor does the account of his failure and downfall work in chronological sequence. Several individual chapters each cover the entire story, so that they resemble a set of paintings portraying the same scene from different angles. Chronologically, 1 Samuel 15:1–35 does not simply follow on 13:2–14:52; nor does 16:1–23 simply follow on 15:1–35; and so on.

While leadership qualities do not determine who Yahweh designates as leaders, the leaders' response to Yahweh's choice – how they respond morally and how they respond in relation to Yahweh – makes a difference to them and to their people. Saul is now a king, like other kings; but he is "thrown back wholly upon the Spirit of Yahweh, and therefore he stands or falls by the fact that he does His will, that as a king and lord among men he is His

---

[1] Cf. Firth, *1 & 2 Samuel*, 180.
[2] Steven L. McKenzie, "Saul in the Deuteronomistic History," in Carl S. Ehrlich with Marsha C. White, eds. *Saul in Story and Tradition*, Forschungen zum Alten Testament 47 (Tübingen: Mohr, 2006), 59–70 (59).

servant." Everything depends on his management of his position as both lord and servant.[3]

THE FOG OF WAR[4]

From the beginning, the Samuel narrative has from time to time left things unclear. Why did Yahweh close Hannah's womb? Did Eli mean "the God of Israel will give you what you asked" or "may the God of Israel give you what you asked"? When Elqanah said, "may Yahweh establish his word," what word did he refer to? Is Ramathaim the same as Ramah? Sometimes the answers to these questions might have been evident to the narrative's first auditors, sometimes the gaps are there by the nature of a story because it is impossible to include everything, sometimes we can work out the answers, sometimes the author may have just wanted us to think about them. The way 1 Samuel 13–20 opens signals something similar about how it will proceed:[5] "Saul was a man of [blank] years when he became king and he reigned [blank?] two years over Israel" (13:1). The account of the battle at Mikmash and of the first threat of Saul's losing the throne (13:2–14:52) manifests the densest compendium of such unclarities in Samuel.

Some battle accounts in the First Testament tell a coherent story of leaders making deliberate and careful inquiry of Yahweh and/or of Yahweh giving clear and explicit instructions and/or of leaders then taking effective and decisive action with a positive and conclusive outcome. This battle account is not an example. The battle

---

[3] Karl Barth, *Church Dogmatics* III/1 (reprinted London: T&T Clark, 2010), 442, 443.

[4] The phrase is traditionally attributed to the Prussian general Carl von Clausewitz, though there is no record of his using the actual expression.

[5] Cf. Jobling, *1 Samuel*, 79–80.

begins as a human initiative (13:2–7). There is no overwhelming by God's spirit or blazing of anger, though neither is there any critique of the initiative. Perhaps Saul is doing what his hand finds to do, in accordance with Samuel's encouragement (10:7). But who is this Jonathan who strikes down a Philistine garrison – or does he strike down a Philistine garrison commander (*nāṣîb*, 13:3)? We have not heard of this Jonathan before. Or is it Saul who does the striking down (13:4)? Was the army "called out" by him or did it simply muster, as LXX and Vg imply (the verb is *ṣāʿaq* niphal)? What is the relationship between Jonathan's forces and Saul's forces in the engagements that follow? Are Gibeah of Benjamin, Geba of Benjamin, and Geba the location of the Philistine base different places (13:2–3, 16), and are any of them the same place as Gibeah of God where the Philistine base/garrison also is (10:5) and/or as Gibeah of Saul (11:4)?

And where is Samuel? Alongside that earlier encouragement, he had spoken of the making of offerings (which would be the natural accompaniment of seeking Yahweh's blessing), and he had added that he of course would come to make the offering. Why does he not show up within the timeframe he himself set, when the army is beginning to run for cover? When Saul "forces himself" and makes the offering, is he at fault? Is Samuel at fault in his absence or his judgment? "Samuel may think that Saul has failed the test, but the narrator betrays no trace of any attitude of judgment or cheap superiority over the doomed king."[6] Why does Yahweh not speak? Is he being tough? Should Saul have acted instead of sacrificing? When Samuel arrives and tells Saul he has been a fool for ignoring Yahweh's command, what command does he refer

---

[6] J. P. Fokkelman, *Narrative Art and Poetry in the Books of Samuel, Volume II: The Crossing Fates (I Sam. 13–31 & II Sam. 1)* (Assen: van Gorcum, 1986), 38.

to (Yahweh, as opposed to Samuel, issued no command about Gilgal)? Are the words of condemnation Samuel's or Yahweh's?

For ignoring that command, Saul's reign "will not stand" (*qûm*, 13:14). Is it his own reign, which will actually last quite a while but come to an end with his death by his own hand, or is it his dynasty? In the former case, this note is one of the indications that the story anticipates the long process that does end in his death. In the latter case, there is an irony, because this story shows his son as having the character and gifts that a king might need, even while also suggesting an uneasy relationship or non-communication between father and son that will worsen as the chapters unfold. Does the declaration that Saul's reign will not stand lie behind Jonathan's not succeeding his father even though he is eminently qualified? Is the narrative simply informing the auditors of where the story is bound to go? Or does the threat to Saul presuppose an "unless"? Does it imply "may not stand"? The ambiguity of Samuel's declaration parallels the ambiguity of his instruction in 10:8.[7]

"Yahweh has sought for himself an individual after his own heart" (13:14). Will he be someone whose heart or mind matches Yahweh's, "an individual doing his will" (Tg)? "Yahweh has ordered him to be commandant over Israel" (13:14). Saul had been that person. Who might it now be? It will be David, but at the moment it might be Jonathan, "who is everything good that Saul is not."[8] But is that what Yahweh means? Other occurrences of phrases such as "an individual after his own heart" suggest that it simply means someone on whom Yahweh's heart or mind has set itself (cf. 14:7), someone of Yahweh's own choice. David will indeed be that person, but it will turn out that an irony would

[7] Edelman, *King Saul*, 79–80.

[8] Paul Borgman, *David, Saul, and God: Rediscovering an Ancient Story* (New York: Oxford University Press, 2008), 17.

attach to a description of David as ultimately someone whose
heart or mind matches Yahweh's.

One could have expected the exchange between Samuel and
Saul to lead to a defeat in which Saul perishes. Instead, it leads
to a victory achieved by a brave ruse of Jonathan's, aided by his
boy. Perhaps Yahweh will act on our behalf (14:6), Jonathan spec-
ulates, and thinks up a sign that will tell them whether Yahweh is
doing so. Is Jonathan ambitious to outdo his father, like Absalom?
Anyway, Yahweh cooperates, the earth shakes, there is a supernatural panic among the Philistines, and a commotion (14:15–16).
Saul has the Shiloh priest, Eli's great-grandson, with him. Why
was he not at Gilgal, and is Saul to consult the representative of
Eli's condemned and deposed line? According to MT, he has the
covenant chest with him: Is it not at Qiryat-ye'arim? In LXX he
has only a chasuble, which seems more plausible, but why would
MT have "chest" instead? The chasuble presumably contains the
"Illumination and Completeness" (Urim and Thummim) through
which Saul hopes to consult Yahweh, but what is he asking, and
in 14:41 why does MT lack most of the later presumed reference to
Urim and Thummim? And when he decides (before the process
can be completed) that they had better go into battle anyway and
give chase, is it not surprising that "Yahweh delivered Israel"
(14:23), especially when only here in 1 Samuel 13–14 is Yahweh the
subject of a verb?

Was Jonathan then right that Saul was unwise in requiring
his army to fast until the fighting was over (14:29–30), or was
fasting a proper act of discipline (cf. 7:6)?[9] When his troops
hungrily barbecued at the end of the initial victory, were they

---

[9] So Bede, *In primam partem Samuhelis libri iv* 2:14, as quoted by Franke, *Joshua,
Judges, Ruth, 1–2 Samuel*, 250–51.

failing to observe the proprieties about draining the blood from an animal before barbecuing it, or does eating *over* the blood imply divination? Is the altar that Saul then builds the same thing as the rock just referred to, or something more proper (14:31–35)? When it transpires that Jonathan had unwittingly broken the fast, was Saul amenable to the death of his son, who has been showing himself more a person of initiative and trust in Yahweh than Saul is, and who might be the person Yahweh has in mind to replace him? When the troops redeem him, how did they do so?

It is impossible to be clear on much of the story. Sometimes leaders may take action that they identify, within the parameters God lays down (but sometimes the plan turns out to be wrong); sometimes leaders get concrete instructions. Sometimes leaders may specify a sign through which God may confirm something as a good idea (but sometimes God may not cooperate). Sometimes leaders may take an initiative and God may work through it (but sometimes God may not). Most troublesomely, sometimes leaders may take an action in good faith but it turns out that God disapproves, and disaster follows. As Qohelet might have put it, one can never be sure of acting in a way that seems good in God's eyes and that he therefore blesses, rather than of doing the opposite. With this text, "it is easier to speak of impact than of meaning or intention.... The text embraces remarkable of levels of ambivalence."[10] It does reflect how decisions within the people of God reflect issues of power and personality.[11] And as Qohelet might also have put it, when things in a story are clear, we can rejoice. When things are unclear, we just have to deal with it.

---

[10] Campbell, *1 Samuel*, 150.
[11] Birch, "The First and Second Books of Samuel," in his "Reflections" on 13:1–23.

One ultimately wrestles with how to gain insight from a narrator who seems to claim authoritatively that it is humanity's fate, even nature, to remain ignorant in the face of God's omniscience, yet ever compelled to strive for knowledge and understanding…. The Deuteronomic narrative style, for all its authoritative manner, still involves a profound contemporaneity and sublime relativity that revels in the mystery and ambiguity of life. No matter that the reader gives the narrator of chapters 13–15 and the God within them their basic due of communicative omniscience and reliability; the story that begins with Jonathan's initiative and ends with Saul's rejection never fails to highlight life's rich complexities…. [It aims] to provoke humanity toward an everpresent quest for the truth, even as we are disposed to recognize our relative ignorance.[12]

DEVOTING

The possibility that 13:13–14 was an anticipatory judgment fits the way 14:1 does not seem to presuppose it. Saul's mistake in 13:2–12 was a misjudgment that typifies his rule and was the kind of act that led to his downfall. The account of his downfall compares with the account of his rise, where the sequence of the stories is partly parallel. It fits that the story about Jonathan and the fast closes with a summary account of Saul's achievements and family (14:47–52). We have read the whole story of his reign here. But now (in the narrative) Samuel gives Saul another command. In effect, the narrator later confirms it did come from Yahweh (15:2–3, 10–11). Amusingly, whereas 13:1–14:52 is full of ambiguities that give premodern, modern, and postmodern interpreters scope to read them their own way and thus to affirm the story, 15:1–35 manifests some clarities that disturb premodern, modern,

---

[12] Robert Polzin, *Samuel and the Deuteronomist*, 150, 151.

and postmodern interpreters, though it also has its own ambiguities over the actions, words, and motives of Saul, Samuel, and Yahweh.[13]

Yahweh is set on "attending to" Amalek. The verb (*pāqad*) is neutral in meaning; it earlier referred to Yahweh's "attending to" Hannah, with the result that she had several pregnancies (2:21). Here it implies negative attention. It relates to what Amalek did to Israel on its way out of Egypt. That attack was unprovoked, but the first account of it (Exod 17:8–15) does not portray it as very terrible, though afterwards Yahweh undertook to obliterate Amalek's memory (the story might therefore seem self-defeating, as it perpetuates that memory). But a later reference says that Amalek "met with you on the way and attacked you from behind, all who were shattered behind you, and you were faint and weary, and it was not in awe of God" (Deut 25:18). The Amalekites were "wrongdoers" (*ḥaṭṭā'îm*). But like Exodus, 1 Samuel 15 does not refer to the ethical point that Deuteronomy makes, though Samuel later says to the Amalekite king:

> As your sword bereaved women,
>> so your mother will be bereaved from among women.
> (1 Sam 15:33)

Yahweh therefore now commissions Saul to attack Amalek and "devote" men, women, children, and animals. LXX, Vg, and Tg translate the verb (*ḥāram* hiphil) "destroy," but LXX in its expansive rendering in 15:3 adds "anathematize," which gets nearer the verb's distinctive meaning. In its first occurrences in the Torah, the verb and the related noun (*ḥērem*, Lev 27:21–28) simply mean

---

[13] See, for example, David M. Gunn, *The Fate of King Saul: An Interpretation of a Biblical Story*, JSOTSup 14 (reprinted Sheffield: JSOT Press, 1989), 129, on "the dark side of God."

giving something to Yahweh in irrevocable fashion. Killing is neither essential to "devoting" nor does it get to the idea's essence, though most First Testament references do refer to killing. The same is true of references elsewhere. The inscription commissioned by Mesha, the king of Moab, to commemorate a victory over Israel a couple of centuries later refers to devoting people to his god in this way.[14] One significance of such killing is that the killers gain nothing from their action.

The story gives no indication that Israel is seeking redress for the attack two or three centuries previously, in which Israel in any case won a victory. Nor does it indicate that the Amalekites, who live far away in the Negeb, are a problem to Israel at the moment. Saul is to undertake the action because Samuel says that Yahweh says so: "I am the one Yahweh sent to anoint you as king over his people, over Israel: so now listen to the sound of Yahweh's words" (1 Sam 15:1). Saul does as he is told, though sparing the Kenites who live among the Amalekites but had shown commitment (*ḥesed*) to the Israelites when they left Egypt (Judg 1:16 is the nearest we have to a clarification of that reference). He also spares the Amalekite king and the best of the domestic animals and other things of value.

"Devoting" in the sense of killing as a divine punishment raises a number of questions. Can it ever be right for God to kill? The Scriptures assume throughout that it can be right. Could it be right to kill this generation of Amalekites for something that their ancestors did, and to include their children and their animals? The Scriptures assume that one generation is tied up for good or ill with previous generations, and that children are tied up for good

---

[14] See, for example, Christopher B. Hays, *Hidden Riches: A Sourcebook for the Comparative Study of the Hebrew Bible and Ancient Near East* (Louisville, KY: Westminster John Knox, 2014), 193–99.

or ill with the destiny of their parents. So are a family's animals. Can it be right for Yahweh to use Israel as his agents in punishing other human beings? The Scriptures assume that it can be. Is this belief not dangerously open to misappropriation by other peoples? Yes, but then most things in the Scriptures are, and the danger is maybe no greater than converse convictions such as the idea that God does not punish people for their wrongdoing or that our children and our animals do not suffer through our wrongdoing. Like moving from "is" to "ought," it is tricky to move from "God told them to do it" or "God once did a certain thing" to "God is telling you to do it" or "God regularly does this thing," as maybe Israel knew well. As is the case with the analogous story of Abraham's offering of Isaac (Gen 22), Israel did not assume that Yahweh regularly issued this kind of command, nor that he generally related in this way to other peoples in its world.[15] Indeed, the First Testament refers to "devoting" almost exclusively in connection with Israel's arrival in Canaan.[16]

There is a difference between assumptions in this story and teaching that Jesus will give, though the difference needs stating carefully. It is not that Jesus introduces the idea of loving and forgiving enemies,[17] which is a principle implied elsewhere in the First Testament and in Samuel itself. Indeed, we have noted that in Saul's day Amalek was not Israel's enemy. And Jews feel as uneasy about the instruction to destroy Amalek as Christians do.[18]

---

[15] Cf. Murphy's comments on the approach of "the Western medieval Christian tradition" to this story (1 Samuel, 133–34).

[16] C. L. Crouch, War and Ethics in the Ancient Near East: Military Violence in Light of Cosmology and History, BZAW 407 (Berlin: de Gruyter, 2009), 177.

[17] See, for example, Tony W. Cartledge, 1 & 2 Samuel, Smyth & Helwys Bible Commentary (Macon, GA: Smyth & Helwys, 2001), 194, 197, 198.

[18] See, for example, Avi Sagi, "The Punishment of Amalek in Jewish Tradition: Coping with the Moral Problem," Harvard Theological Review 87 (1994): 323–46.

Conversely, Jesus does affirm that judgment will come on nations that neglect his family (notably, Matt 25:31–46). The difference is that he describes God as bringing this judgment at the end of the age rather than picturing God being involved thus in this age, and the judgment involves eternal punishment. It is not obvious that these differences imply a theological or ethical advance on Samuel as opposed to expressing different insights. Jesus also describes, without disapproval, an oppressive servant being hacked to piece like Agag (Matt 24:51). Of course, these are "only parables." But then 1 Samuel 15 is "only a story." Whatever degree of historicity it may have, its account of Saul devoting the entire Amalekite people is not simply factual. The Amalekites are alive and well later in 1 Samuel (27:8; 30:1, 13) and Agag is reincarnate as Haman "the Agagite" in Esther, where his opposite number is Mordecai, the descendant of Kish.[19] Amalek "is now an emblem of evil rather than an historical entity," like Nineveh in Jonah.[20] It stands for an embodiment of disorder that attempted to reassert itself after Yahweh put disorder down at the Red Sea.[21] The action that Yahweh commissions had what might be called an eschatological significance that took it closer to those parables. It embodied a commitment to eliminate evil.

Saul gets into trouble for compromising on what Yahweh commanded in this connection, though he has more than one excuse ("I saved the best animals to sacrifice to Yahweh, and also I gave into pressure from the people"). But the symbolic significance of

---

[19] Philip R. Davies, "Saul, Hebrew and Villain," in Diana V. Edelman and Ehud Ben Zvi, eds., *Remembering Biblical Figures in the Late Persian and Early Hellenistic Periods: Social Memory and Imagination* (Oxford: Oxford University Press, 2013), 131–40 (137–38).

[20] Fokkelman, *Narrative Art and Poetry* 2:87.

[21] Cf. Philip D. Stern, *The Biblical Ḥerem: A Window in Israel's Religious Experience*, Brown Judaic Studies 211 (Atlanta, GA: Scholars, 1989), 165–78.

this compromise makes Yahweh relent over making Saul king. As it was explicit that the attack on Amalek was Yahweh's idea not Saul's, it is explicit that Saul's rebuff is Yahweh's idea not Samuel's. Samuel himself is angry (ḥārâ; some translations have him "upset," but "angry" is the verb's regular meaning). Is he angry with Saul or with Yahweh? He cries out to Yahweh all night: Is he pleading with Yahweh to change his mind? If so, it is "a failed intercession"; he cannot achieve what Moses achieved (Exod 32:11–14).[22] He goes to see Saul, accuses him of profiting from the venture, adds a rhetorical question, then adds a pair of lines that move from comparative to absolute:[23]

> Is there delight for Yahweh in burnt offerings and sacrifices
>   like listening to Yahweh's voice?
> There: listening is better than a sacrifice,
>   to heed is better than rams' fat.
> Because rebellion: the wrongdoing of divination,
>   presumption: the trouble of effigies.
> Because you rebuffed Yahweh's word,
>   he is rebuffing you from being king. (1 Sam 15:22–23)

These classic lines compare with prophetic indictments such as Hosea 6:6 and Amos 5:21–24. Yet the comparison would be bizarre if they related to a straightforward historical action involving Saul's showing mercy in his act of slaughter. Hosea and Amos are contrasting burnt offerings and sacrifices with commitment and faithfulness (ḥesed and ṣədāqâ), not with unsparing slaughter. But if Amalek stands for forces of disorder and opposition to Yahweh, the indictment makes more sense, and it also compares with the

---

[22] Jean-Pierre Sonnet, "God's Repentance and 'False Starts' in Biblical History (Genesis 6–9; Exodus 32–34; 1 Samuel 15 and 2 Samuel 7)," in André Lemaire, ed., *Congress Volume Ljubljana 2007*, VTSup 133 (Leiden: Brill, 2009), 469–94 (487).

[23] Miscall, *1 Samuel*, 108.

equivalent indictment in Jeremiah 7:16–26. Compromising over Amalek is indeed like compromising over divination by means of effigies (tərāpîm), which I take to be representations of family members who have passed, who can be honored and remembered by means of them and can also be consulted for information (especially about the future) that they now possess through being beyond the confines of this world. Divination by consulting Yahweh (the "Urim and Thummim," in fact) would be okay for Israel. Divination by means of effigies might be understandable on the part of other peoples, but Israel's use of such means would be an act of rebellion and a rebuff of Yahweh's word. Compromising over repudiating the opposition to Yahweh symbolized by Amalek belongs in the same category. "Here, then, was Saul's sin. He wished to be more merciful than God."[24]

RELENTING

When Samuel declared that Saul's reign would not stand, might the pronouncement presuppose an "unless," like Jonah's equivalent pronouncement to Nineveh? Saul certainly hopes that Yahweh leaves open the possibility of repentance and of finding forgiveness: "please carry my wrongdoing" (1 Sam 15:25). The verb "carry" (nāśā'), the regular term for forgiveness, suggests declining to require a person to carry the consequences of their wrongdoing and agreeing to carry them oneself. "Go back with me so I may bow down to Yahweh," Saul adds. But Samuel refuses. "You have rebuffed Yahweh's word, and Yahweh has rebuffed you from being king." He is giving the kingship to Saul's "neighbor … a

[24] John Calvin, Sermons on 2 Samuel (Edinburgh: Banner of Truth, 1992) 1:112; as quoted in Cooper and Lohrmann, 1–2 Samuel, 1–2 Kings, 1–2 Chronicles, 62.

better man" than him, a good man as he is not. And "the Glory
of Israel will not act falsely and will not relent, because he is not
a human being, to relent."[25] This rebuff does not dissuade Saul.
He again acknowledges his wrongdoing and does bow down to
Yahweh (15:24–29). But there is no indication of a response. And
Samuel grieves over Saul (15:35). It is not only as if Saul's reign is
over; it is as if Saul is already dead.[26] They never see each other
again.

First Samuel 13 and 15 parallel other stories where calamity
follows a mistake or wrongdoing that does not seem gigantic:
Compare 2 Samuel 6; also Genesis 3; Exodus 32; Joshua 7; Acts
5. They offer some comfort in reflecting the way life works. But
none of these examples happens at an ordinary moment. All
have special significance because of the context to which they
belong. Here, the context is Israel's "No" to Yahweh as king (1
Sam 12:12).

> This No must be broken with the revelation of the divine Yes
> of the kingdom instituted by God.... And in order to represent
> this Israelite No and at the same time the fact that it is broken
> by the divine Yes, Saul must first become king. No gross, no
> blatant personal sin of Saul is needed to exhibit this negative
> aspect of the grace of the kingdom willed and created by God.
> All that needs to be seen is that he is just the person and ideal
> which the nation has foolishly imagined, and can only imagine,
> as its king. And it is this which is made evident in the double
> sinning which is microscopic to human eyes, but gigantic and
> absolutely decisive in God's eyes.... It is because Saul represents
> Israel in its resistance to Yahweh being its king that he has to
> be rejected.[27]

---

[25] For MT yəšaqqēr, act falsely, 4QSamᵃ has yšyb, LXX "turn back" (cf. NRSV).
[26] Fokkelman, *Narrative Art and Poetry* 2:110.
[27] Karl Barth, *Church Dogmatics* II/2 (reprinted London: T&T Clark, 2010),
178, 179.

The underlying cause of Saul's rejection lies not in his action in 1 Samuel 13 but in the attitude of Yahweh towards him or in something he represents: "I gave you a king in my anger, and I took him in my wrath" (Hos 13:11).[28] While monarchy was a development that Yahweh had not wanted, and he had appointed a man who would not fulfill the job description, the narrative does not quite suggest that he had deliberately appointed someone who would fail. "Fate and flaw" are part of Saul's story, though especially fate. Saul does become "kingship's scapegoat."[29]

Whereas some Christian readers have been offended at the idea of God commanding Saul to devote the Amalekites, other Christian readers have been offended at the idea of God relenting or regretting or repenting or having a change of mind (*nāḥam* niphal) after making Saul king. It has been an axiom of Christian thinking that God does not change his mind. It would imply inconsistency or a recognition that one had made a mistake. When Samuel speaks thus, then, he must be using anthropopathic language.[30] The expression indeed does involve anthropopathic language, but the same applies to talk of God having compassion. Nearly all language about God involves describing him in human terms. It is the only way we have to think and speak of God. Fortunately, our being made in God's image means we can use human analogies so as to think and speak of God truthfully.

The question is what this example of anthropopathic language tells us about God. And relenting can indeed be an aspect of the

---

[28] Gunn, *The Fate of King Saul*, 40, 113.
[29] Gunn, *The Fate of King Saul*, 30, 125.
[30] Tsumura, *The First Book of Samuel*, commenting on 15:11. Steven J. Duby has a careful study of anthropopathic or metaphorical approaches in "'For I Am God, Not a Man': Divine Repentance and the Creator-Creature Distinction," *Journal of Theological Interpretation* 12 (2018): 149–69.

dynamic relationship between God and humanity.[31] God is not locked into the alleged inflexibility of a Median or Persian king (Dan 6:8[9]). But God relents for reasons and not randomly, in the way that a human being might (1 Sam 15:29; cf. Num 23:19). Jeremiah 18:1–11 speaks of there being a principled basis for God's relenting, both from promises and from threats. Human turning from wrongdoing can cause Yahweh to cancel a declaration of intent, as the Jonah story shows.

Does Saul's acknowledgment of wrongdoing not count as such a turning? It contains no expression of regret, though that feature does not have the importance in the Scriptures that it has in Christian spirituality. But neither does Saul's acknowledgment explicitly refer to turning, which is the essence of repentance in the Scriptures. And it is accompanied by the making of excuses, which always undermines an apology. Further, Saul oddly asks for Samuel's forgiveness, not Yahweh's. So Saul's equivocation or shiftiness could give Yahweh or Samuel a basis for declaring that Saul's confession does not count as turning.

After being confronted over wrongdoing that looks much more reprehensible than Saul's, David will use the same expression as Saul, "I did wrong" (ḥāṭā'tî, 15:24; cf. 2 Sam 12:13), and his prophet's response will be enigmatic, but less negative than Samuel's to Saul. Samuel reiterates that Saul has rebuffed Yahweh's word, and that consequently Yahweh has rebuffed him as king. Apparently, Saul's confession does not undo his repudiation of Yahweh's word, nor does it cause Yahweh to

---

[31] Benjamin J. M. Johnson, "Characterizing Chiastic Contradiction: Literary Structure, Divine Repentance, and Dialogical Biblical Theology in 1 Samuel 15:10–35," in Marvin A. Sweeney, ed., *Theology of the Hebrew Bible, Volume 1: Methodological Studies* (Atlanta, GA: SBL, 2019), 185–211 (206).

reverse his repudiation of Saul as king. But Samuel then seems to add an explanation: Yahweh does not act falsely and does not relent. Both are odd statements, the first because its relevance is not immediately obvious, the second because Yahweh has told Samuel that he *has* relented, of making Saul king (15:11); the narrator will soon repeat the point (15:35).

Sometimes contradictory statements in the Scriptures have to be allowed to stand and be in dialog and tension; it is a characteristic of Qohelet. "Yahweh does not relent; Yahweh has relented" could simply mean that there is no predictable, calculable link between human turning and divine turning.[32] Whether or not God turns or relents is an aspect of God's freedom, an aspect of "I will be what I will be" (Exod 3:14).[33] We may trust that there are reasons for his acting in one way on one occasion and in the other way on another occasion, but we may not know what the reasons are.

Here, however, Samuel offers that explanation: God "will not act falsely and will not relent, because he is not a human being, to relent" (1 Sam 15:29). One implication might indeed be that Yahweh does not relent without reason, as a human being may. Christian unease over the notion of God relenting has this concern. And Yahweh's capacity for relenting does not mean he is fickle.

And here, the comment about not relenting follows up the comment about not acting falsely, and the double statement follows the declaration that "Yahweh has torn Israel's kingship from you today and given it to your neighbor" (15:28). As Samuel has put it earlier, "Yahweh has sought for himself an individual in

---

[32] Polzin, *Samuel and the Deuteronomist*, 140–45.
[33] Van Wijk-Bos, *Reading Samuel*, 87.

accordance with his mind [or an individual after his own heart]. Yahweh has ordered him to be commandant over Israel" (13:14). Chronologically, the commission has not yet happened, but within the frame of this narrative it has happened, and Yahweh is not going back on it. To do so would mean breaking a commitment, which Yahweh would not do.[34] The logic in 1 Samuel 15 parallels Balaam's more explicit statement in the other passage about Yahweh not relenting (though it uses the hitpael rather than the niphal):

> God is not a person so he lies,
>   a human being so he relents.
> Would he have said and will he not act,
>   spoken and will he not implement it? (Num 23:19)

Sometimes God makes a definitive decision on which he will not go back, as another of Jesus's parables illustrates (Luke 16:19–31). In this story it is too late for Saul to repent because Yahweh has made a commitment to David. "Samuel's former warning in 13.13–14 becomes a divinely decreed reality."[35] Yahweh has decided to appoint someone else as commandant over Israel, someone who is good compared with Saul (1 Sam 15:28). Good compared with Saul? A deserter, a usurper, a calculator, a womanizer, a traitor, an outlaw, a mercenary, a murderer? If the bad thing about Saul was his laxness in relation to the Amalekites (15:19), is David better because he is more ruthless? After 16:12, the only other "good" person in 1 Samuel is Abigail in 25:3, who is good in understanding. Perhaps "good" simply means "good in Yahweh's eyes," someone his mind has set upon (13:14).

---

[34] Terence E. Fretheim, "Divine Foreknowledge, Divine Constancy, and the Rejection of Saul's Kingship," *CBQ* 47 (1985): 595–602 (597–98).

[35] Edelman, *King Saul*, 104.

ONE KING ANOINTED, ONE KING ASSAILED

Sent without explanation but with danger to anoint a son of Jesse in Bethlehem, Samuel sees Eliab (16:6), who is perhaps assumed here to be Jesse's eldest (cf. 1 Chr 2:13). He has the appearance and height that had been important when Yahweh chose Saul.[36] But Yahweh does not look at things as human beings do (cf. Isa 55:8).[37] Yahweh has looked at Eliab's mind or thinking or inner attitude. The significance of this comment may emerge when Eliab gets angry and disdainful to David later (1 Sam 17:28).[38] The person Yahweh has chosen will not be qualified by seniority, appearance, or height, but by thinking and attitudes. The "not this but that" should not be misunderstood. It evidently means "not so much this as that" or "less this than that," because the one Yahweh has his eye on actually is a tanned, brown-eyed handsome young man (16:12). Yet apparently Yahweh can see something in David's attitude that he could not see in Eliab. On the other hand, when Eliab says those tough things about David's impudence and the ambitiousness of his thinking and attitude (17:28), he is not far wrong.[39] "From the moment David first speaks (17:26), he seems to manifest a distinctive spark of ambition."[40] "Even before 2 Samuel 11, ominous signs appear throughout the story and foreshadow David's moral demise."[41]

Samuel anoints David, and Yahweh's wind or breath or spirit overwhelms him, as it did Saul (1 Sam 16:7, 12–13). The anointing

---

[36] Qimhi, in *miqrā'ôt gədôlôt* on the verse.

[37] Miscall, *1 Samuel*, 117.

[38] Rashi, in *miqrā'ôt gədôlôt* on the verse.

[39] Lyle Eslinger, "'A Change of Heart': 1 Samuel 16," in Lyle Eslinger and Glen Taylor, eds., *Ascribe to the Lord: Biblical and Other Studies in Memory of Peter C. Craigie*, JSOTSup 67 (Sheffield: Sheffield Academic Press, 1988), 341–61.

[40] Rosenberg, "I and 2 Samuel," 128.

[41] Robert B. Chisholm, "Cracks in the Foundation: Ominous Signs in the David Narrative," *Bibliotheca Sacra* 172 (2015): 154–76 (156).

is a family event not a public one, and while Samuel knows what
it means and the audience of the story knows, who can tell what
the family would have thought at the time? Samuel had anointed
Saul without anyone else knowing what it signified, and God's
spirit had come on him and he had prophesied. Is David to be a
prophet? Or a priest (priests are anointed)?

As happened after Samuel anointed Saul and God's spirit came on
him, life then goes on as normal for a while. But alongside God's spirit's overwhelming David is its leaving Saul (16:14). The implication is
not the one that could apply in Christian language usage, where the
Holy Spirit's departure would imply losing one's relationship with
God. Saul is not being cast off as a person or cut off from Israel. The
narrative is talking about the arrival and departure of Yahweh's spirit
in connection with appointment as king and resourcing for that role.
Saul is being fired from being king, or being given notice of his firing,
and the withdrawing of Yahweh's spirit is tied up with Yahweh's giving up on him as king. On the other hand, the coming of Yahweh's
spirit on David and Yahweh's being with him do not issue from any
deserving on his part. He is simply the person God chose. Maybe
Yahweh had reasons, but the narrator does not tell us what they
might have been, beyond the comment about attitude.

Whereas Yahweh has left Saul, David has great success in battle and great popularity. His appointment as commander-in-chief
"was good in the eyes of the entire people and also in the eyes of
Saul's servants" (18:5). "He was successful ... successful ... successful ... successful" (18:5, 14, 15, 30). People "loved him ... loved
him ... loved David ... loved David ... love you ... loved him"
(18:1, 3, 16, 20, 22, 28).[42] "Love seems to come to him as gift and

---

[42] Cf. Walter Brueggemann, "Narrative Coherence and Theological Intentionality
in 1 Samuel 18," *CBQ* 55 (1993): 225–43 (239–40).

destiny."[43] "Yahweh was with him … with him … with him" (18:12, 14, 28). While there will be no other references to God's spirit being involved with David (the exception in 2 Sam 23:2 proves the rule), the phrase about God being with him recurs (cf. 16:18; 17:37; 2 Sam 5:10). It is another way of making the same point. Saying that Yahweh's spirit came on David makes a link with the Saul story, but Yahweh's being with David is more intrinsic to and characteristic of his story. It means he defeats Goliath and has other victories and achievements, which are soon worrying Saul. In Christian usage, God being with you suggests having a sense of God's presence. In the Scriptures, it suggests an objective fact with visible implications (cf. 1 Sam 10:7; 20:13; 2 Sam 7:3, 9; cf. Matt 28:20; Luke 1:28).

For Saul, in addition, "a bad spirit from Yahweh assailed him" (1 Sam 16:14). The translation "evil spirit" is misleading. While the adjective (*ra'*) can mean something morally or religiously bad (1 Sam 15:19), it can also denote something painful and tragic (10:19), which is the implication when God is doing the sending (e.g., Isa 45:7). References to a bad spirit cluster uniquely in 1 Samuel (16:14, 15, 16, 23; 18:10; 19:9). "Evil/bad spirit" is hardly a way of describing mental disturbance; the Scriptures have other terms for what Western thinking might call depression or mania. And the "bad spirit" between Abimelek and the Shechemites (Judg 9:23) seems different from this bad spirit, as do the deceptive spirit in 1 Kings 22 and the jealous spirit in Numbers 5.

Paradoxically, there may be more comparison with the wise spirit of Exodus 28:3 and Deuteronomy 34:9, in that both relate

---

[43] Birch, "The First and Second Books of Samuel," in his comments on 18:1–30. He refers to David M. Gunn, "David and the Gift of the Kingdom (2 Sam 2–4, 9–20, 1 Kgs 1–2)," *Semeia* 3 (1975) 14–45; see further David M. Gunn, *The Story of King David: Genre and Interpretation*, JSOTSup 6 (Sheffield: JSOT Press, 1978).

to someone's work for Yahweh. So whereas the regular spirit of Yahweh brought a positive energy that enabled Saul to function as king, his bad spirit from Yahweh was a negative energy that hindered his functioning. The implications of "assail" (bā'at) overlap with those of "overwhelm" (ṣālaḥ). This verb, too, suggests something taking hold of a person from outside, more or less irresistibly, but taking hold in an unequivocally disturbing way. The departure of God's spirit and the arrival of another spirit from God foreshadow the struggle between Saul and David that will feature prominently in the remainder of 1 Samuel,[44] when "the bounty of David's blessing was matched by the depth of Saul's misery."[45]

The bad spirit arouses Saul's anger, jealousy, and fear and makes him less and less capable of functioning, and "the more jealous and devious he became, the more successful David was."[46] While his behaving like a maniac reflects something coming upon him from outside, his fear, resentment, and jealousy are rational reactions to events in his family, court, and country, especially for someone lacking self-confidence. It would not be surprising or unreasonable if Saul had some negative inner feelings to be brought to the surface after the traumatic events recounted in 1 Samuel 13–15. But the narrative emphasizes the negative energy coming from outside. The coming of a bad spirit from outside can follow on anger and scheming, not lead to it (18:8–10). Yet we would be unwise to infer that the anger simply opens the way to the coming of the bad spirit, any more than to suggests that good qualities open up the way to the coming of God's spirit. Does sending the bad spirit mean

---

[44] Polzin, Samuel and the Deuteronomist, 158.
[45] Cartledge, 1 & 2 Samuel, 206.
[46] Klein, 1 Samuel, 191.

God compels Saul to act badly? Perhaps the bad spirit aroused potentials that were already present inside the person. There is a "delicate balance" between fate and fault in the Saul story.[47] From now on "Saul is continually and relentlessly active in his pursuit and retention of royal power. He is not a passive recipient of fate but is the agent of his own undoing. If we follow the account of the story itself, it will not do to portray Saul simply as a hapless victim of fate. That element of victimization operates in the narrative, but alongside it is Saul's own self-destructive effort."[48]

Saul prophesies away again (19:20–24). Translations such as "he fell into a prophetic frenzy" again obscure the significance of the statement as an indication of God's spirit bringing about something theologically, religiously, and ethically important.[49] "The same faculty for the numinous and the same sensitivity for suddenly being lifted into a higher state of consciousness which occurred there under the positive sign of election, appear here under the negative sign of being rejected."[50] It is not the bad spirit that has this effect, as it is when he gets his spear out (18:10). It is God's spirit, and it has the opposite effect. God's spirit is still capable of turning Saul (and his messengers) into another person, to protect David and even to protect Saul from wrongdoing by turning him into someone who declares Yahweh's message and/ or his praise.

[47] Yairah Amit, "The Delicate Balance in the Image of Saul and Its Place in the Deuteronomistic History," in Ehrlich with White, *Saul in Story and Tradition*, 71–79.

[48] Brueggemann, "Narrative Coherence and Theological Intentionality in 1 Samuel 18," 231.

[49] See the excerpt from Augustine's Sermon 162A in Franke, *Joshua, Judges, Ruth, 1–2 Samuel*, 287–88.

[50] Fokkelman, *Narrative Art and Poetry* 2:180; cf. Alter, *The David Story*, 122.

THE GOD OF DAVID

There is a further link between the bad spirit from God and the process whereby David came to replace Saul as king. It issued in David's being drawn into the life of the court in a way that would play a key role in his becoming king (16:14–23). Music helps Saul, and David can play guitar. One of Saul's boys also points out that David is a brave warrior with a gift of words and a presence. He is a real man.[51] This description sums up aspects of the way he is a better man than Saul and one whose mind, attitudes, and inner being match the destiny Yahweh is putting in front of him. It announces aspects of what will emerge as the David narrative unfolds.

Key to what will emerge is David's conviction about who Yahweh is, which comes out in the subsequent story in 1 Samuel 17. This story thus follows the anticipatory summary, but the narrative is actually backtracking and providing something of the basis for the summary. The Philistines and the Israelites are fighting again, and in his capacity as kid brother David takes provisions to his big brothers in the army. No one else knows him there, but he shows there both that he has a warrior instinct, that he can use words, and that he has a presence. And Yahweh proves to be with him (according to 2 Sam 21:19, actually Elhanan killed Goliath, but as told here, the story portrays further aspects of what David himself did turn out to be).

David's first words are, "What will be done for the person who strikes down that Philistine and removes the disgrace from upon Israel, because who is this foreskinned Philistine that he has

---

[51] See David J. A. Clines, "David the Man: The Construction of Masculinity in the Hebrew Bible," in David J. A. Clines, *Interested Parties: The Ideology of Writers and Readers of the Hebrew Bible*, JSOTSup 205 (Sheffield: Sheffield Academic Press, 1995), 212–41.

taunted the ranks of the living God?" (1 Sam 17:26). The series of ethnic comments and slurs (how primitive these Philistines are!) ends with a key theological statement. Yahweh is "the living God." The description does not mean that Yahweh is alive as opposed to dead, but that Yahweh is lively, vigorous, and active as opposed to sleepy, sluggish, and idle. The living God is the one who spoke out of the fire at Sinai in a way that no other people had heard (Deut 5:26), and who took the Israelites across the Jordan into Canaan and drove out its present inhabitants (Josh 3:10–11; cf. 2 Kgs 19:4, 16; Pss 42:2[3]; 18:46[47]; 84:2[3]; Jer 10:10; 23:36; Dan 6:20, 26[21, 27]; Hos 1:10[2:1]). David implies some shortfall in the Israelites' own assumptions about Yahweh. How could they be tolerating the taunts that are being put to them that reflect on their God who is quite capable of defeating these Philistines?

In this story, the words count. Arguably, the battle belongs to them.[52] Although the story is memorable, in a sense the narrator compromises the aim of telling a story by focusing on the words. David's statements would be more at home in the context of a psalm or the words of prophets such as Isaiah, Ezekiel, or Zechariah, where they recur. A story's nature is to carry the impact of the exercise in communication that it represents. Can theological statements compete? Do they inevitably lose impact? Yet communication in general, and the Scriptures in particular, incorporate direct statement as well as narrative. In this story, the words count.

David repeats his words to Saul, then adds his testimony to the experience that had proved the truth about Yahweh to him:

---

[52] J. Richard Middleton, "The Battle Belongs to the Word: The Role of Theological Discourse in David's Victory over Saul and Goliath in 1 Samuel 17," in James K. A. Smith and Henry Isaac Venema, eds., *The Hermeneutics of Charity: Interpretation, Selfhood, and Postmodern Faith. Studies in Honor of James H. Olthuis* (Grand Rapids, MI: Brazos, 2004), 109–31 (121).

Yahweh had rescued him from lion and bear. Therefore "he is the one who will rescue me from this Philistine" (17:36–37). The words also follow up a different kind of recollection. Rescuing (*nāṣal* hiphil) did not mean Yahweh striking the assailants down while David watched. When a lion or a bear carried off one of the sheep, "I would go out after it and strike it down and rescue from its mouth. And should it rise against me, I would take hold of it by the beard, strike it down, and kill it" (17:35). Rescuing is something David does. He does the striking down. So what does he mean by saying that God rescued him and will rescue him from Goliath? "The battle is Yahweh's, and he will give you [plural] into our hand" (17:47). Yet in the single combat that follows, nothing miraculous happens. David wins by a canny stratagem. "Yahweh will surrender you into my hand and I will strike you down" (17:46). But it is David's ploy that brings about the inescapable surrender. "You are coming to me with sword, with spear, and with javelin, but I am coming to you with the name of Yahweh Armies, the God of the ranks of Israel, whom you have taunted" (17:45). Well, yes, but the missing feature in the antithesis is "I am coming to you with a sling and some rocks," which will (with hindsight) turn out to be more practical to use and more effective than Goliath's weapons. In proffering David his armor (17:38), Saul shows himself doubly dimwitted: The offer ignores the importance of Yahweh and makes no allowance for the need of some strategy, of some "lateral thinking."[53] The Saul of 1 Samuel 17 is not the Saul of 1 Samuel 11, and David is indeed showing himself to be a better man than Saul.

While "there are no miracles in 1 Sam. 16–31,"[54] one could call what now happens a marvel or wonder (*pele'*). The story's

53 Campbell, *1 Samuel*, 189.
54 Murphy, *1 Samuel*, 167.

language and the thinking compare and contrast with that used when "Yahweh thundered," the Philistines "collapsed," and the Israelites "struck them down," and when, subsequently, "Yahweh's hand was against the Philistines," the towns that Israel had lost "returned" to Israel, and Israel "rescued" its territory (7:10–14). Whether the thunder was literal or metaphorical, the imagery suggests an event that was extraordinary and out of this world. So surely this one was.

The story ends with David depositing Goliath's head in Jerusalem (17:54) – anachronistically or anticipatorily, as he has not captured Jerusalem yet. But David's theological declarations addressed to Goliath are meant to be heard in Jerusalem. Yahweh of Armies is the God worshiped there (e.g., Pss 46:7, 11[8, 12]; 48:8[9]). The object of David's victory will be that "all the earth may acknowledge that Israel has a God, and that this entire congregation may acknowledge that it is not by sword or by spear that Yahweh delivers" (*yāšaʿ* hiphil, 1 Sam 17:47). While the word "congregation" (*qāhāl*) can denote an "assembly" in a looser sense (e.g., 1 Kgs 12:3), the only other occurrences of the word in Samuel–Kings denote the people assembled in the temple in Jerusalem, where Solomon is concerned "that all the peoples of the earth may acknowledge that Yahweh is God" (1 Kgs 8:60). Likewise Hezekiah, when Jerusalem is under pressure from the Assyrians and they have "taunted" Yahweh, bids Yahweh to act "so that all the kingdoms of the earth may acknowledge that you, Yahweh, are God alone" (2 Kgs 19:19, 22). All the earth needs to acknowledge it, but "this congregation" needs to acknowledge that Yahweh is the one who "delivers," that it is not by means of bow and sword that deliverance comes, and that it is with his name that it treads down its adversaries (Ps 44:3–7[4–8]). It is as Yahweh breaks bow and spear that he makes battles cease to the end of the earth (Ps 46:9[10]).

THE ROYAL FAMILY

Samuel began as the story of an ordinary family. It had its tensions and suffering, but it worshiped and it flourished. The same was true of the families of Kish and of Jesse. David now becomes a member of Saul's family, his adoptive son and Jonathan's adoptive brother.[55] David and Saul address each other as "father" and "son" even in 1 Samuel (24:11, 16[12, 17]). But Saul's family story is almost relentlessly gloomy, more like that of a mafia family, like the Sopranos' family.[56] David's family will not be an improvement. Such grimness, misfortune, and sadness can issue from the weaknesses of the head of the family, combined with the pressures and temptations of power and responsibility. Let no readers wish they were in positions of power. Let them hide as Saul did, or decline the opportunity to leave the sheep so as to come to a prophetic dinner, as David did not. The trouble is that the people in the Scriptures who seek to evade God's summons find they cannot. When a person therefore fails to evade responsibility, let them not leave go of a Samuel and a Nathan, and let God not leave go of them.

When David joins Saul's court, Saul loves him (16:21). Admittedly the translation is uncertain. While Samuel may refer to the king being fond of the young man, the words for love (ʾāhēb, ʾăhēbâ) are also political words. Hiram's "love" for David (1 Kgs 5:1[15]) meant he "was loyal to" David (CEB). Jerusalem's "lovers" (Lam 1:2) were her allies or friends. Maybe this narrative implies a form of political commitment on Saul's part.[57] But on any understanding of love, the reference to Saul's love will turn out to be an irony when Saul is

---

[55] Cf. Green, *David's Capacity for Compassion*, 56.
[56] Murphy, *1 Samuel*, 200.
[57] See McCarter, *I Samuel*, 281–82.

trying to get David killed. Love turns to envy, resentment, fear, and anger (1 Sam 18:8, 12, 15, 29; 20:30). "What an extraordinary degree of frenzy! What excess of madness," John Chrysostom comments. "For envy is a fearful, a fearful thing, and persuades men to despise their own salvation."[58] The anger extends to his birth son, an anger that expresses itself in a shaming of Jonathan and an attempt to kill him with his spear. Is it a half-hearted attempt? Instead of "threw" (*ṭûl*), LXX and Tg simply have "raised" (which suggests the verb *nāṭal*). Either way, the action foreshadows Saul's serious attempts on David's life that will follow. Not unreasonably, Saul's act issues in a responsive anger on Jonathan's part, an anger at the shaming as much as the threat (20:30–34).[59] The problem is that fact that Yahweh is with David. Saul fears that David is a rival for the throne. Even first-time non-Israelite readers of Samuel know that the story is going in this direction because they have read spoilers in 13:1–15:35, but Saul does not know it. Indeed, in a sense Yahweh does not know it. The future is still open for Saul. But giving in to his fears (18:8) will bring about their fulfillment.

David "remains a complete opacity in this episode, while Saul is a total transparency and Michal a sliver of transparency surrounded by darkness."[60] Even if Saul is not exactly manipulated by external forces to behave in a way he does not wish, Saul's internal life seems to be at the mercy of others, beyond his control.[61] Whereas

[58] *Homilies on Genesis 46–67*, Fathers of the Church 87 (Washington, DC: Catholic University of America, 1958), 11; and *Homilies on the Epistles of Paul to the Corinthians*, NPNF I, 12 (reprinted Peabody, MA: Hendrickson, 1995), 393 (cf. Franke, *Joshua, Judges, Ruth, 1–2 Samuel*, 278).

[59] See Jonathan Y. Rowe, *Sons or Lovers: An Interpretation of David and Jonathan's Friendship*, LHBOTS 575 (London: T&T Clark, 2012), 102–25.

[60] Alter, *The Art of Biblical Narrative*, 118.

[61] Malcolm Cohen, "The Transparency of King Saul," *European Judaism* 39 (2006): 106–15 (106).

First Testament narratives often leave people to infer characters' feelings from their words and actions, and "David is a cipher,"[62] the narrative is explicit about Saul's. It highlights the difference in the account of David, who "knows how to veil his motives and intentions – a veiling replicated in the narrative strategies used to present him."[63] In what sense was it "upright in David's eyes to be the king's son-in-law" (18:26)? When flight becomes a recurrent choice for David, crying when he knows he must definitively flee (20:41) is the nearest to a revelation of his feelings. There might seem little scope for trust in this family (*bāṭaḥ* comes only in 12:11 and *'āman* hiphil in 27:12, which prove the rule). In another sense, flight may be a strange expression of trust. Through 1 Samuel David makes no attempt to bring about his advancement (2 Samuel will be different). He hardly needs to; Saul and Jonathan do it for him. The bad spirit is at work; it is the nearest to a hint in the narrative that Yahweh is involved in bringing about David's advance, as if at this point he is concretely pursuing his purpose.

Elqanah's love for Hannah (1:5) finds a parallel in Michal's love for David (18:20, 28) which issues in her taking David's side over against her father, protecting him and telling lies for him (19:11–17). The First Testament has no hesitations about lying to intimidators, tormentors, and tyrants (cf. 6:1–7; 20:6; 21:2, 13[3, 14]; 27:10; 2 Sam 5:22–25; 15:34; 17:19–20; Exod 1:15–21), and John Chrysostom refers to Michal in justifying his engaging in deception so as to avoid being made a bishop.[64] Michal's deception recalls Rachel and the effigies (*tərāpîm*; Gen 31). Saul is a new Laban, Michal a new Rachel, David a new Jacob, "the new representative of the line

[62] Chapman, *1 Samuel as Christian Scripture*, 82.
[63] Alter, *The David Story*, 115.
[64] *Treatise on the Priesthood* 1:8, NPNF I, 9 (reprinted Peabody, MA: Hendrickson, 1995), 37.

of promise and the future hope of the nation."[65] That link hints that Michal's "love" might also be more multifaceted than simply the love of a woman for a man and an illustration of the interweaving of politics and relationship in a royal family. The broad potential in the Hebrew words for love helps facilitate expression of the point. Maybe Michal sees which way the wind is blowing and fancies being queen. Yet her countercultural action signifies that she recognizes she must commit herself to David and his kingship rather than to her father and his.[66] But she and her big sister pay a price for being princesses. In the context of the court, women are victims and political pawns (18:17–19; 25:44; 2 Sam 3:12–16), as are their children (21:8). They have no autonomy.[67]

That main narrative describing life at Saul's court begins as a story of love (1 Sam 18:1–4). "David and Jonathan are friends because they are both fighting Yahwists, with a common love of biffing Philistines…. 'When two such persons discover one another, when, whether with immense difficulties … or with … amazing and elliptical speed, they share their vision – it is then that Friendship is born. And instantly they stand together in an immense solitude.'"[68] Interpreters who read the story in the context of an approval of same-sex relationships may understand the relationship between Jonathan and David as a homosexual one, while interpreters who read the story in the context of disapproval of such relationships may not so understand it. Emically

---

[65] Keith Bodner and Ellen White, "Some Advantages of Recycling: The Jacob Cycle in a Later Environment," *BibInt* 22 (2014): 20–33 (33).

[66] See Jonathan Y. Rowe, *Michal's Moral Dilemma: A Literary, Anthropological and Ethical Interpretation*, LHBOTS 533 (London: T&T Clark, 2011).

[67] J. Cheryl Exum, *Fragmented Women: Feminist (Sub)versions of Biblical Narratives* (Valley Forge, PA: Trinity, 1993), 45, 55.

[68] Murphy, *1 Samuel*, 186, quoting from C. S. Lewis, *The Four Loves* (New York: Harcourt, Brace, 1960), 97.

rather than etically considered, the narrative's implications lie more with that other ambiguity over the nature of "love."[69] When "Jonathan's very self became bound up with David's, and Jonathan loved him as himself" (18:1; cf. 20:17),[70] his gift of clothing and battle equipment (18:4) hints at his surrendering his position to David. The gifts suggest regalia or insignia. They confirm that Jonathan is extravagant and uncalculating, as the story of his attack on the Philistine garrison suggested (14:1–15). He is not afraid of David ending up as king, as his father is (18:8). His self-confidence means he is not afraid of David, and he does not need to be king. Saul was small in his own eyes (15:17). He did not originally have any ideas of becoming someone big, but once someone is in that position, it is not surprising if it becomes important and becomes key to their self-identity.[71] Nicely, the verb for "became bound up with" (qāšar niphal) also means "conspire" (22:8, 13; 2 Sam 15:31).[72] A charge of conspiracy "hangs in the air between Saul and his 'two sons.'"[73] And Saul is not wrong that there is a conspiracy against him, but the conspirator is Yahweh.[74]

---

[69] Cf. McCarter, *I Samuel*, 342; Rowe, *Sons or Lovers*, 129; Markus Zehnder, "Observations on the Relationship Between David and Jonathan and the Debate on Homosexuality," *Westminster Theological Journal* 69 (2007): 127–74; Randall C. Bailey, "Reading Backwards: A Narrative Technique for the Queering of David, Saul, and Samuel," in Tod Linafelt et al., eds., *The Fate of King David: The Past and Present of a Biblical Icon*, LHBOTS 500 (London: T&T Clark, 2010), 66–81; James E. Harding, *The Love of David and Jonathan: Ideology, Text, Reception* (Abingdon: Routledge, 2014).

[70] Alter's translation, *The David Story*, 112.

[71] Paul S. Evans, "From Head above the Rest to No Head at All: Transformations in the Life of Saul," in Bodner and Johnson, *Characters and Characterization in the Book of Samuel*, 101–20 (103).

[72] McCarter, *I Samuel*, 305.

[73] Green, *How Are the Mighty Fallen*, 354.

[74] Brueggemann, *First and Second Samuel*, 171.

As is the case with Michal, it would be inappropriately cynical to confine Jonathan's love to a political commitment. Even David eventually speaks as if it is more (2 Sam 1:26), though it is harder to interpret his description of Saul and Jonathan as lovable and gracious (1:23). And most of the references to Jonathan's relationship with David can suggest both the personal and the political. They include Jonathan's delighting (*ḥāpēṣ*) in David (1 Sam 19:1; cf. 18:22; 2 Sam 20:11) and David's finding grace or favor in Jonathan's eyes (1 Sam 20:3; cf. 16:22; 20:29; 25:8; 27:5).

Jonathan's love for David issues in a loyalty expressed in a covenant or pledge, a *bərît* (20:8; 23:18; cf. the reference to "cutting" or solemnizing in 20:16). This word has a parallel breadth of meaning to that of "love." The last *bərît* in Samuel was the unpleasant one that Nahash tried to make with the people in Jabesh (11:1), and apart from the references to the covenant chest, all but one of the other occurrences of *bərît* in Samuel denote a treaty (we will wait until 2 Sam 23:5 for the exception). Here the covenant implies that "Yahweh [will be] between us for all time" as its guarantor (1 Sam 20:23, 42) and that David will show Jonathan Yahweh's commitment (*ḥesed*; 20:14–15). Only rarely do the image of covenant and the quality of commitment come together in the Scriptures. Linking them and associating them with references to love, delight, and binding mark the nature of the positive relationships. Within the family, the covenant means Jonathan mediates with his father on David's behalf (19:1–7). The friendship sealed in the covenant is an act of betrayal to the family, in the strict sense.[75]

Most people listening to the story in Samuel know that Saul dies and David succeeds him, and they perhaps know that kingship falls into David's lap like ripe fruit falling from a tree (unless they

---

[75] Cf. Rowe, *Sons or Lovers*, 54–76.

know other versions of the sequence of events). "That may tempt us to find the outcome self-evident." But "within the story, it is not at all self-evident that the hero's career will terminate in succession to the throne.... The superficial message is that David has one foot in the grave, in terms of power and political opportunities. But Jonathan is not misled by the moment," though neither does he want his sons to be victims of a change of dynasty when it comes.[76]

---

[76] Fokkelman, *Narrative Art and Poetry* 2:313, 314.

CHAPTER 5

Yahweh Who Protects a King
(1 Samuel 21:1[2]–2 Samuel 1:27)

The chapter title is deliberately ambiguous. Yahweh's rebuff of Saul and his commissioning of David introduce conflict into the royal family. David becomes a threat to Saul and Saul becomes a threat to David. Over subsequent chapters David has to run for his life, but Yahweh protects him. David twice has the chance to kill Saul, but he refrains. There are two reasons why David might have encouraged a ghost writer to include these stories in the narrative. They undermine any suggestion that David had brought about Saul's demise, so that he could succeed him. And it would be in David's interest to argue that killing the king was wrong. The prevalence of regicide in Kings would also mean that later monarchs might appreciate the inclusion of the stories, for this reason.

DAVID THE MAN OF ACTION

The ironic overwhelming by God's spirit that prevents Saul and his henchmen seizing David (1 Sam 19:19–24) does not put an end to Saul's preoccupation with David. David's tortuous involvement with the royal family apparently continues for a period of years, as conflict with the Philistines recurs and Saul betroths more than one of his daughters to David. Although "resealing his covenant with Jonathan gave David a single safe port in a sea of enemies,"[1] his involvement with the family comes to a conclusive end when Jonathan tells him of Saul's definitive decision to execute him (20:1–42). "David is a 'son of death' (20.31)."[2] He thus gives up on Gibeah in a final way and flees for his life (21:1, 10[2, 11]; 22:17). It is not the first time he has "fled" (19:12, 18; 20:1) and it will not be the last (27:4). The chapters that follow comprise a series of stories about flights, pleas, chases, lies, prayers, strategies, threats, commissions, slaughterings, revelations, miscalculations, and follies. David is thus on the run for a further period of years, mostly in Judah and some distance from Gibeah, until he comes to another decision about flight and escape that means abandoning Judah and settling in Philistia, never to see Saul again (27:1). "During these wilderness years his anointing to the kingship is contradicted detail after detail by daily events.... There are fifteen wilderness stories ahead."[3]

David is continuously active, never settling down for too long, and often taking initiatives, but there is no indication that he knows what he is doing when he takes flight, that he has a plan, here or later.[4] He leaves Gibeah without provisions or weapon, but he talks his way into obtaining them at Nob, not far away, which has apparently replaced Shiloh as Israel's main sanctuary (21:1–9[2–10]).

This story introduces auditors to the ambiguity of these wilderness years. Israelites were aware that they needed both to take seriously the metaphysical distinction between humanity and God (let alone the moral one) and also to affirm the reality of God's

[1] Murphy, *1 Samuel*, 214.
[2] Edelman, *King Saul*, 162.
[3] Peterson, *First and Second Samuel*, 109, 110.
[4] Green, *David's Capacity for Compassion*, 89.

approachability and of their connection with God. And Israel recognizes its differences from Yahweh as the holy one in the way it manages contact with sex, with death, and with blood – so Bathsheba makes herself holy from her taboo at the end of her period (2 Sam 11:4). Questions about taboo or defilement (*ṭum'â*) and about whether someone is clean or pure (*ṭāhôr*, 1 Sam 20:26) thus overlap with questions about holiness. When people are to meet with the holy one, they need to make themselves holy, and they may need someone to help them manage that transition (16:5).

The importance of food makes food one natural arena for marking the difference between humanity and God (as is implicit in the story in 2:12–17). One expression of that principle was the depositing each week of loaves of bread before Yahweh, the Presence Bread (traditionally, "showbread"). It thereby becomes holy rather than ordinary (*ḥōl*), and at the end of the week the priests would eat it. Possibly the rule at Nob is not quite so precise. Ahimelek is willing for David and his men to have it, but they need themselves to be holy (21:3–6[4–7]). The First Testament does not refer to "holy war," and it treats war as an ordinary thing, like food or buildings or times or possessions or people. But war can be made holy, as those other things can, by being given over to Yahweh so that (for instance) you surrender any rights to it. And making war in Yahweh's name, fighting Yahweh's battles (25:28), involves being holy in the sense of observing those separations. David can therefore plausibly claim that his men are holy and can eat the Presence Bread. One might wonder whether his claims about their holiness are true, but the First Testament would have little worry about his being "compelled to be a perfect liar" in some circumstances.[5]

---

[5] Hertzberg, *I & II Samuel*, 180.

David also acquires Goliath's sword, which would be "charged with symbolic meanings: a trophy of the unconquerable enemy conquered by faith; a token of the first great Davidic victory in the service of Saul, and now used in defense against Saul."[6] So equipped, David flees down from the mountain ridge, a day or two's journey west, to Philistine territory, to Gat (21:10–15[11–16]), to Goliath's town. People know about him there, and they intriguingly call him "king of the country," by which maybe they mean "the kind of person who could be ruler of a city state in Israel" like their "king" Akish. But auditors would catch another significance in the description.

It is a first indication of a potentially friendly relationship between Gat and David's Israel.[7] But David is afraid of the consequences of this recognition. He again gets by through deception, behaving like someone crazy or weird or "erratic."[8] We should not interpret this description too technically, though it does seem humiliating in light of the recognition of him as a king and his destiny to be king. But for an apparently crazy person, there is no future in Gat except life in a care home, so David "escapes," another important verb alongside "flee" (22:1; 23:13; 27:1; cf. 19:10, 12, 17, 18; 20:29). He moves halfway back towards the mountain ridge, to Adullam, to what is variously described as a cave and a stronghold there (22:1–5). Its location enables it to become a refuge for people who might be in danger and/or a gathering point for dissidents. It suggests another contrast with the Gittites' description of him as a king and the prestige, security, and salary of a position at Gibeah (22:7). But some "genius" is involved in the

---

[6] Peterson, *First and Second Samuel*, 111.

[7] See Daniel Pioske, "Material Culture and Making Visible: On the Portrayal of Philistine Gath in the Book of Samuel," *JSOT* 43 (2018): 3–27.

[8] Auld, *I & II Samuel*, 264.

way "David manages to throw in his lot with Israel's enemies, the Philistines, while retaining the affection of the Israelite populace."[9] For safety, he takes his parents to Moab, the home of Jesse's grandmother and the refuge of her original parents-in-law during a famine, according to Ruth 1:1–2; 4:14–22. Eventually he leaves for the Heret Forest in Judah, apparently further up the ridge. From there he ventures down to Keilah, a town nearer the Philistines' area, which is subject to Philistine raids on its threshing floors and thus on its grain supply for the next year. David "delivers" Keilah from the Philistines (arguably doing Saul's work),[10] and appropriates their livestock (provisioning his gang would be an ongoing challenge). Saul seeks him out there and the people of Keilah are going to surrender him. Had the livestock originally belonged to them?! For Keilah, was having David's gang around as much of a liability as an asset? Were they more scared of Saul than of David? David escapes and stays on the move for some time in the area south and east of Hebron, focusing on evading Saul. He has more than one fortunate escape.

The story of David, Nabal, and Abigail (25:1–42) incidentally opens another window on the means whereby David and his bandit group survive through this period. It hints that his men run a protection business. It is an activity about which he feels proud and honorable, through which he is arguably continuing to do Saul's business, and Nabal's staff accept its usefulness (25:7, 15–16, 21). Nabal, however, who might be seen as Saul's alter ego,[11]

---

[9] Rosenberg, "I and 2 Samuel," 133.
[10] Peterson, *First and Second Samuel*, 116.
[11] Cf. Robert P. Gordon, "David's Rise and Saul's Demise: Narrative Analogy in 1 Samuel 24–26," *Tyndale Bulletin* 31 (1980): 37–64 (43), reprinted in Gary N. Knoppers and J. Gordon McConville, eds., *Reconsidering Israel and Judah: Recent Studies on the Deuteronomistic History*, Sources for Biblical and Theological Study 8 (Winona Lake, IN: Eisenbrauns, 2000), 319–39 (324); he actually puts it the other way around.

does not see David as a king but as a runaway servant (25:10). When David determines to slaughter Nabal and his clan (25:22), Abigail maneuvers him out of his plan, "transcending the violence that marks her community ... through acts of hospitality ... to the hungry, to the landless, to the marginalized."[12] Nabal pays a price for his hard-heartedness;[13] he fortuitously drops dead. It enables David to add Abigail to his harem along with Ahinoam from elsewhere in the area, though he loses Michal (25:39–44). Perhaps Abigail brings Nabal's impressive estate with her into the marriage, easing David's economic position.

David's series of unplanned (and not always thought-through) ventures ends with a move back to Gat, which does make Saul give up chasing him (27:1–7). As in 20:1, it looks as if he is not relying on Yahweh but on "self-help."[14] With his large company, he would look more impressive than when he seemed a bit crazy. He persuades Akish to give him Ziklag, which is nominally a Judahite town anyway, apparently in reward for services about to be rendered concerning whose nature David consistently lies (27:8–12). "This time, David makes a fool of Achish."[15] With his braggadocio,[16] from Ziklag he raids, slaughters, and leaves no one alive, telling Akish that he has been raiding in Judah. Such was his rule (mišpāṭ). There is no talk of "devoting" here; it is just slaughter, ensuring that no reports get back

---

[12] L. Juliana Claassens, "An Abigail Optic: Agency, Resistance, and Discernment in 1 Samuel 25," in L. Juliana Claassens and Carolyn J. Sharp, eds., *Feminist Frameworks and the Bible: Power, Ambiguity, and Intersectionality* (London: T&T Clark, 2017), 21–38 (26).

[13] See Marjorie O'Rourke Boyle, "The Law of the Heart: The Death of a Fool (1 Sam 25)," *JBL* 120 (2001): 401–27.

[14] Edelman, *King Saul*, 232.

[15] Murphy, *1 Samuel*, 249.

[16] Cartledge, *1 & 2 Samuel*, 315.

to Akish. The profits apparently go to Akish, presumably with the cut for David and his men that they need. It is here that we get the only piece of chronological information in the narrative: David was at Ziklag for sixteen months, up until Saul's death. The well-founded suspicions of other Philistine leaders (presumably the rulers of the other Philistine towns) rescue David from having to fight for the Philistines against Judah. "Whether David, lacking this providential way out, would really have pitted himself against his own people is another imponderable in the character of this elusive figure."[17] One suspects that David would have found a way of making things work his way in such a battle (29:1–11).

DAVID THE MAN WHO ACKNOWLEDGES YAHWEH

The ambiguity of the David narrative points to another aspect of David's story. Woven into the reports of ventures and flights that claim no religious or ethical grounds or significance, and that may look as if they could have none, are notes of a religious or ethical kind. David has a capacity "for combining political savvy with a surprising morality and genuine devotion to God."[18]

Doeg reports that Ahimelek had inquired of Yahweh for David, and Ahimelek confirms it (22:10, 15). David's calling on Ahimelek issues in "the darkest passage in the story of David's rise to power,"[19] and David himself acknowledges some responsibility (22:22). The Talmud (*Yoma* 22b) nicely comments that Saul falls foul of both halves of Qohelet's exhortation (7:17) that one should neither be too righteous (in being merciful to Amalek) or too

---

[17] Alter, *The David Story*, 181.
[18] Borgman, *David, Saul, and God*, 79.
[19] McCarter, *I Samuel*, 365.

wicked (in the slaughter at Nob). When David takes his parents to find refuge in Moab it is "until I know what God will do for me" (1 Sam 22:3); we actually never hear of them again. Does David's wildly open phrase mean "until God gets Saul to stop pursuing me" or "until he makes me king"? There are no reports of such hopes on David's part, but do comments along these lines suggest that we should read between the lines here and elsewhere, or that on the contrary we should not? Is David's "until…" a statement of trust that stands in tension with the reports of decisive action?

References to David's inquiring of Yahweh interweave the account of the Keilah adventure (23:1–13). When David hears that its people are in trouble, he inquires whether to go and defend them. When his men raise questions about the wisdom of this plan, he checks out with Yahweh again. It is not clear how he does this inquiry, in that the story only subsequently reports Abiathar's arrival with a chasuble. But when Abiathar does arrive and Saul threatens to attack, David asks Yahweh whether Saul will do so and then whether the people of Keilah will surrender David and his men, which leads them to make scarce. David has access to information and direction from Yahweh; Saul works in ignorance.[20]

In the first account of David having a chance to kill Saul (24:1–22[2–23]), his men remind him that Yahweh had told him he would surrender Saul to him and that he could then do as he saw fit. The reminder (or invention) gives David a chance to show that what he sees fit is not to raise his hand against Yahweh's anointed. He repeats the phrase and utters it again later (and three more times in the second story). Anointing signifies being set apart by and for Yahweh. Anyone or anything anointed is off limits. David's attitude contrasts with Saul's at Nob. David does cut off a

---

[20] McCarter, *I Samuel*, 367.

corner of Saul's coat, after which his heart strikes him (cf. 2 Sam 24:10). That expression could suggest guilt, but David does not speak of guilt, and more likely the feeling is something like dread over what he has had a chance to do. Yahweh can decide on the rightness or wrongness of their action towards one another, David says. And yes, he will be faithful to Saul's descendants as well as to Saul himself.

On the second occasion (1 Sam 26:1–25), Abishay says something similar to David's men: Yahweh has given Saul into David's power. One lectionary nicely links this story with Luke 6:27–38. "The real sermon on the Sermon on the Mount is the way David dramatizes the divine injunction to be merciful, given to him in the signs of spear and jug. He plays the magnanimous king by taking the 'fool's' (1 Sam. 26:21) life in his hands and giving it back, because it belongs to the Lord."[21] This second story goes beyond the first, as one would expect (it works like parallelism).[22] David's profession of innocence in the relationship is even more profuse. He challenges Saul's staff about failing to look after Saul and protect him from assassination. He grieves over being driven away from his share in the country that is Yahweh's domain, as if to encourage him to go and serve other gods in the countries that belong to them, and to meet his death away from Yahweh's presence (we know that he knows Yahweh is in those other countries – he calls on them there).

In between the two stories is the account of David, Nabal, and Abigail. Here David swears by God that he will slaughter Nabal's

---

[21] Murphy, *1 Samuel*, 247.
[22] In a chapter titled "To Every Bad There Is a Worse," Sarah Nicholson argues that when Samuel has two accounts of something, regularly the second is tougher on Saul: see *The Three Faces of Saul: An Intertextual Approach to Biblical Tragedy*, JSOTSup 339 (London: Sheffield Academic Press, 2002), 53–74.

entire clan, but he then thanks Yahweh when Abigail prevails over him to do no such thing, and Yahweh brings Nabal's wrongdoing down on his own head. In buying David off, Abigail declares a particularly wide-ranging and systematic recognition of David and of Yahweh. She begins, "Yahweh will definitely make for my lord a trustworthy household" (25:28). The words take up a declaration of Yahweh's from way back (2:35) and they anticipate a promise that will come later (2 Sam 7:16; cf. also 1 Kgs 11:38). Here the reason is that "my lord is engaged in Yahweh's battles" with people such as the Philistines, whose final defeat will be one of David's most important achievements. "And nothing bad will be found in you through your days," she adds. It sounds like an exaggeration, whatever she means by "bad," but perhaps it is explained by what follows:

> When someone sets about pursuing you and seeking your life, my lord's life will be bound up in the bundle of the living with Yahweh your God, but the life of your enemies he will hurl away, in the middle of a sling's hollow. And when Yahweh acts toward my lord in accordance with everything good that he has spoken concerning you, and charges you to be ruler over Israel, this is not to be a cause of collapsing or stumbling of mind for my lord – to have shed blood for nothing and for my lord to have found deliverance for himself. (1 Sam 25:29–31)

The "this" is what she goes on to specify: shedding blood needlessly in order to find deliverance for himself. Such action is set over against leaving it to Yahweh, and leaving it to Yahweh would be the appropriate stance of a commandant (*nāgîd*), one who stands between Yahweh and his people and rules them as his appointee.[23] "Abigail functions as a prophet,"[24] though the

---

[23] Ellen van Wolde, "A Leader Led by a Lady: David and Abigail in I Samuel 25," *ZAW* 114 (2002): 355–75 (367–72).

[24] Van Wijk-Bos, *A People and a Land* 2, on the passage.

narrator imagines the speeches in the story, like the ones in the stories on either side, imagining what would or should or might be said. Abigail does not mention that Yahweh will make her husband drop dead (25:38), which could have aroused commentators' suspicions. But she is "a woman of good insight" (25:3), "a woman of wisdom and decisive action."[25] Though married to a stupid man (or perhaps through being married to a stupid man), she is able to counsel David in wise ways.[26] So Yahweh again protects David from his temptations here.[27]

The subsequent story about David and Ziklag (30:1–31) compares and contrasts. Returning to Ziklag after being ousted from the Philistine force, he and his men find that the Amalekites have been on a raid, burned the town, and taken the women and children captive. It is presumably a reprisal for the raids reported earlier (27:8). The Amalekites are not people you can mess with, even when they have been eliminated, but fortunately they do not practice "devoting." Taking people captive is economically more sensible than killing them. David's men turn on him; he is under pressure (*ṣārar*), like Saul (28:15), who had prayed for Yahweh to deliver David from pressure (26:24). But "David strengthened himself through Yahweh his God" (30:6). Like the earlier comment that Jonathan had "strengthened his hand" through Yahweh (23:16), the expression suggests a reinforcement that makes a down-to-earth material difference, through reminders of Yahweh's commitment and promises. While the verb (*ḥāzaq*) is sometimes translated "encouraged," because it suggests building

---

[25] Philip F. Esler, "Abigail: A Woman of Wisdom and Decisive Action," in Bodner and Johnson, *Characters and Characterization in the Book of Samuel*, 167–82.

[26] McCarter, *I Samuel*, 401.

[27] Cf. Polzin, *Samuel and the Deuteronomist*, 208.

up morale and giving new energy (e.g., Neh 2:18; Ezek 13:22), it is an encouragement that makes a practical difference. When David strengthened himself, it means he got a grip of himself and gained the strength to take the action that was needed (cf. 2 Sam 2:7).

David then proceeded to inquire of Yahweh through Abiathar with the chasuble. Should he pursue the Amalekites? Will he catch up with them? Yes, he will, and he will rescue the women and children (30:6–7). They march as far as Wadi Besor, which flows roughly east from Beer Sheba towards the Mediterranean. Although it wouldn't take long, many of the men are exhausted, perhaps because they have not had chance to recover after the trek from further north. But most of them have got their breath back; they locate the Amalekites enjoying the proceeds of their adventures, slaughter them, rescue the women and children, appropriate the flocks and herds, and march back to the wadi.

Here, the question whether they should "devote" the Amalekite herds does not arise. David does not ask, and the prophet Gad does not take an initiative and tell him, as Samuel did in relation to Saul. Yahweh can operate in different ways in different contexts, and the Torah as we have it did not exist in David's day. Even when it does exist later, it does not have to be understood like a law code, as David had assumed already back at Nob (21:3–6[4–7]), and as Jesus will note (Mark 2:23–27). The era of devoting is over for Israel, even if other peoples do it (e.g., 2 Kgs 19:11; 2 Chr 20:23), and even if Yahweh does (Isa 43:28).

The question at Wadi Besor is rather, do the men who were too tired to proceed get a share in the gains? Against the view of some of the men who fought, David's answer is, "Of course they do." It is "what Yahweh has given us." David makes it a rule that stands "until today" (though this rule also does not make it into the Torah) that "the share of the person who goes down in battle is the same as the share of the person who stays with the stuff" (30:24–25). The profits of the venture do also provide him with resources to make himself more popular with his "friends" in Judah. As the narrative emphasizes attitudes implying he was not implicated in Saul's death, it is open about actions that will stand him in good stead in the future (cf. 2 Sam 2).

Like the first story of David's wilderness years, this final David story in 1 Samuel epitomizes David's ambiguity. He is the man of action, the man who can act without thinking about right and wrong, the man who can undertake appalling deeds, but also the man who can seek Yahweh's advice and will, who can resist temptation, who can act with generosity. This man cannot be grasped. As "we are never given a hint of what Samuel thinks of David,"[28] and Samuel never speaks to David, the narrator wisely declines to sum him up. "We know so much about David – and yet so little."[29] These dynamics continue through 2 Samuel. The image of David that dominates many readers' minds is constructed from the Psalms. It is simpler, more comprehensible, and more obviously edifying, yet it may not truly come even from the Psalms but rather be built up from them on a basis of a false inference.

The image in Samuel is theologically more profound. We cannot explain David as a great hero or a man of deep spirituality, and we cannot therefore explain why he rather than Saul should have been God's choice. He simply is, in his complexity, contradiction, and inconsistency. If there is an "elliptical path taken by divine providence to guide David toward his monarchic role,"[30] we cannot see why it should be. God's choice of him and his

---

[28] Peter D. Miscall, *The Workings of Old Testament Narrative*, Semeia Studies (Chico, CA: Scholars, 1983), 99.

[29] Campbell, *1 Samuel*, 221.

[30] Murphy, *1 Samuel*, 209.

perseverance with him emerges from God's freedom rather than David's deserve. Living with God's working with David requires belief in God's freedom and grace.

THE FOG OF FLIGHT AND PURSUIT

The story of David and Saul is "a cat-and-mouse game" played in the dark.[31] We do not know how long a time period it covers. There is no order about the narrative of these years; one could rearrange it without making a difference to the impression it conveys. There are short stories and longer stories, large and small repetitions. In 1 Samuel:

> History, as this narrator construes it, is not simply driven and shaped by grand themes. It works much more concretely by an heir giving away his robe (18:4), by women singing glad songs and (unwittingly?) intensifying the second numeral which applies to David (18:7), by a musical therapist driving Saul further away from sanity (18:10–11), by a military man being banished from court and becoming even more popular (18:12–16), by a daughter who loves a man who must be killed for reasons of state (18:20, 28), by a boldness that secures two hundred foreskins when only one hundred are required (18:25, 27), by a deference that self-abases and waits and can wait forever (18:18, 23).[32]

Perhaps the chapters collect a variety of existent stories and assemble them in a random way. Or perhaps the author created them that way to convey deliberately the impression they give, of events unfolding in a meaningless fashion that gets no one anywhere, except that it keeps David alive and gives Saul manifold opportunity to evade the fate that 13:1–15:35 has laid out for him.

---

[31] Brueggemann, *First and Second Samuel*, 163.
[32] Brueggemann, "Narrative Coherence and Theological Intentionality in 1 Samuel 18," 239.

It's never over until it's over, for David, for Saul, and for God. Meanwhile, the narrative recalls Daniel 11 with its account of one thing following another, one human initiative following another, but nothing getting anywhere. In Daniel and in 1 Samuel, eventually the narrative will get somewhere, but for the time being,

> Tomorrow, and tomorrow, and tomorrow,
> Creeps in this petty pace from day to day,
> To the last syllable of recorded time;
> And all our yesterdays have lighted fools
> The way to dusty death. Out, out, brief candle!
> Life's but a walking shadow, a poor player,
> That struts and frets his hour upon the stage,
> And then is heard no more. It is a tale
> Told by an idiot, full of sound and fury,
> Signifying nothing. (Macbeth, in Shakespeare's *Macbeth*, Act 5, Scene 5)

As the narrative offers no hint that David has a plan and is pursuing it, except that of staying alive, it offers no hint that Yahweh has a plan and is pursuing it, except that he intends for David to become king. The only question is how will Saul meet his end and how will David reach the throne,[33] and in this connection Yahweh is engaged in events. But he is not orchestrating everything or behind everything. He takes no initiatives like the ones in 9:15–17 and 16:1. As the narrative is quiet about David's thinking, so it is quiet about Yahweh's. It does not hint that Yahweh is pursuing a plan that is mysterious to us but nevertheless real.

> Samuel (and most of the OT) is wrestling with a more radical thesis that renders God's role, his will and plan, undecidable. It is not just that we cannot fully know his will and plan, for 1 Samuel

---

[33] Barbara Green, "Enacting Imaginatively the Unthinkable: 1 Samuel 25 and the Story of Saul," *BibInt* 11 (2003): 1–23 (3).

gives us no assurance that there is any such thing as a divine will and plan.... Divine statements and comments on divine activity are very limited in their information and in their relevance to the context.... Throughout the remainder of 1 Samuel, David will generally succeed, but we can only ask, and then ask again, why? Is his success due to the Lord's intervention, and, if so, does this have anything to do with David's character or behavior? Or is it due to his own ability and sagacity, to Saul's incompetence, to the help of others, or to just plain luck? The same applies to Saul's failure.[34]

Why are these stories about David and Saul in the Scriptures? Commentators work hard to suggest how they offer positive or negative examples for life, or wisdom for life, or insights on spirituality. And they do offer pointers in these directions, but the principles for discerning the instruction they offer often come from modern Western principles and priorities, and the narrative interweaves stories that may offer instruction of this kind with stories that offer no such pointers. The implication is that the focus of the narrative does not lie here. The narrative rather constitutes an account of a chaotic sequence of events involving a series of conflicts between two confused and confusing people whose lives are not offered for analysis on the basis of insight or morality or spirituality, any more than it portrays the sequence of events as one in which God is systematically pursuing a purpose behind the scenes.

By the end of chapter 26, the matter of Saul's death has been ominously raised three times, but what neither character nor reader yet knows is its manner. Will God strike him as he did Nabal? Will he die of natural causes? Or will he fall in battle? Whatever turns out to be the case, one puzzling aspect of the story will remain: why is it taking so long to dispose of Saul? We

---

[34] Miscall, *1 Samuel*, 129, 123.

already suspect that there is something of a providential delay in this deferred denouement. But what does the providential delay itself signify?[35]

It anticipates the story of Israel, which will also go on so long from Moses's day to the fall of Jerusalem. For Israel, too, it's never over until it's over. And God will wait a long time for events to turn out in a way that fulfills his purpose, while giving his people a chance to determine their destiny.

For Saul, was it over before he went to see the medium, or afterwards? It may never be too late for God, but it may be too late for Saul. When Nebuchadnezzar came to besiege Jerusalem, was it too late for the city? Did the lifting of the siege give the city one last chance? When Nebuchadnezzar resumed the siege, was it too late for the city? When the food was totally gone, was it too late? Even if it is never too late for God, it may be too late for Jerusalem. Jeremiah half-implies that it is too late to prevent the city's fall, yet it is not too late to surrender. But it was too late for Zedekiah. Perhaps it is now too late for Saul, and he will indeed have to join Samuel (28:19), with neither of them aware that they are awaiting resurrection day. But the narrative's interest lies more in the story of Israel. And in MT it continues straight into what we call 2 Samuel 1.[36]

SAUL DESPERATELY SEEKING

Saul's story is a riddle, an enigma, a *mashal*.[37] Over against David with his initiatives and decisions is Saul with his initiatives and decisions, in the context of "the crossing fates" of the two characters.[38]

[35] Polzin, *Samuel and the Deuteronomist*, 212–13, 214.
[36] Cf. Firth, *1 & 2 Samuel*, 283.
[37] Green, *How Are the Mighty Fallen*, 55.
[38] Fokkelman, *Narrative Art and Poetry* 2:17.

Compared with David, Saul is not much of a "man."[39] One could get the impression that he spends hardly any time being king (e.g., fighting the Philistines).[40] Perhaps actually relationships with the Philistines were generally friendlier than Samuel's reports of periodic battles may seem to imply.[41] As the dominant feature of David's story is his need to evade Saul (he must have been doing other things in between), the dominant feature of Saul's story is his pursuit of David. He is obsessed by this quest.

The horrific implications emerged immediately, when Saul discovered about David going to Nob on the way to Gat. Saul slaughters the priests there, and slaughters the entire town (1 Sam 22:6–23). Ahimelek had trembled when David came. Did he tremble for David's sake,[42] or for the same reason as the Bethlehem elders when Samuel arrived?[43] If the latter, his "apprehension" at David's arrival is "grimly vindicate[d]."[44] Ahimelek speaks straight to Saul, but Saul makes no allowances and asks no questions about the truth or untruth of Doeg's testimony. There is no "devoting," but it is an almost complete elimination. In his paranoia,[45] "the king who has lost his kingship and kingdom … is demonstrating the loss by acting in a way unbefitting

[39] Marcel V. Măcelaru, "Saul in the Company of Men: (De)Constructing Masculinity In 1 Samuel 9–31," in Ovidiu Creanga and Peter-Ben Smit, eds., *Biblical Masculinities Foregrounded* (Hebrew Bible Monographs 62; Sheffield: Sheffield Phoenix, 2014), 51–68; cf. Rowe, *Sons or Lovers:*, 32–53.

[40] Campbell, *1 Samuel*, 251.

[41] See Siegfried Kreuzer, "Saul – Not Always–At War: A New Perspective on the Rise of Kingship in Israel," in Ehrlich with White, *Saul in Story and Tradition*, 39–58.

[42] Cf. Campbell, *1 Samuel*, 226.

[43] Fokkelman, *Narrative Art and Poetry* 2:353–54.

[44] McCarter, *I Samuel*, 349.

[45] Halbertal and Holmes, *The Beginning of Politics*, use the words paranoid and paranoia twenty-four times of Saul.

any king."⁴⁶ It is the logical action of a man with power who
looks at things the way Saul does, and it is a way of getting at
David, or the action of a truly mad man frustrated by a pretend
mad man.⁴⁷

Ironically, the elimination again lets one man escape and thus sur-
renders to David the priesthood, its means of guidance, and in due
course the continuance of the priestly line through David's reign.
In the short term, when Saul discovers that David is at Keilah and
gives chase, Abiathar can be the means of David getting the guidance to evade Saul (23:1–13). Saul subsequently prays for Yahweh's
blessing on people from Ziph for having mercy on him by telling
him David's whereabouts (23:21). The odd reference to mercy pairs
with the puzzling reference to people not feeling hurt for him (22:8,
ḥālâ). Along with the cry he will shortly utter and the tears he will
shortly shed (24:16[17]), are they among the signs that Saul is a morally injured person?⁴⁸ The Philistines "accidentally" force him to
give up that pursuit of David (23:19–28). It is not the only time that
they are the means of David's deliverance, by accident or by David's
maneuvering. "Saul's career has been marked by seeking and not
finding or by seeking one thing and finding another."⁴⁹

He chases David to En-gedi (that will mean the mountain area
above the oasis rather than the oasis itself). When David declines
the chance to kill him, Saul cries and responds:

> You are more in the right [ṣaddîq] than me ... in that Yahweh
> surrendered me into your hand and you didn't kill me....

⁴⁶ Miscall, *1 Samuel*, 136.
⁴⁷ Green, *How Are the Mighty Fallen*, 352.
⁴⁸ Brad E. Kelle, "Moral Injury and the Interdisciplinary Study of Biblical
War Texts: The Case of King Saul," in John J. Collins et al., eds. *Worship,
Women and War: Essays in Honor of Susan Niditch*, Brown Judaic Studies 357
(Providence, RI: Brown University, 2015), 147–71.
⁴⁹ Miscall, *1 Samuel*, 144.

Yahweh – he will recompense you with good things on account
of this day, for what you have done for me. And now, there, I
hereby acknowledge that you will definitely become king and the
kingship over Israel will be firm in your hand. So now, promise
me by Yahweh, if you cut off my offspring after me and if you
eliminate my name from my father's house… (24:18–21[19–22];
it is the kind of curse that runs out in an ellipsis)

Once again, 24:1–22[2–23] tells the whole story of Saul and David,
and after this acknowledgment, Samuel can die (25:1).[50] The whole
story repeats in 26:1–25, with Yahweh causing a deep sleep to fall
on Saul's company (it does not stop David from rebuking them).
Samuel had told Saul he had been stupid; he now says it himself
(*sākal* niphal, then hiphil, 13:13; 26:21). He contrasts with David,
who has been smart and successful (*śākal* hiphil, then qal, 18:5, 14,
15, 30).[51] He promises never to harm David again and prays, "may
you be blessed, my son David, yes, you will indeed act and yes, you
will indeed be successful" (26:21, 25). They are the last words they
will ever speak either to the other; 27:1 marks a new beginning, the
moment when David finally abandons Judah. Once more there
follows, not long after, a report that Samuel had died, though not
finally (28:3).

We do not hear of Yahweh speaking to Saul. Some irony
attaches to the prophesying in 19:20–24, because no prophet
speaks to Saul as to David (22:5), until the prophet who comes
back from the dead to say nothing new except to name David as
the "neighbor" who will succeed Saul (28:6, 17). Yahweh does not
respond to Saul's inquiries as he does to David's (23:2, 4, 11, 12),
not least in connection with Saul's attempts to capture him. But

---

[50] Auld, *I & II Samuel*, 294.
[51] Klaus-Peter Adam, "Nocturnal Intrusions and Divine Interventions on Behalf
of Judah: David's Wisdom and Saul's Tragedy in 1 Samuel 26," *VT* 59 (2009):
1–33 (31).

then, Saul had slaughtered the vehicles of inquiry except for the one who escaped to David. Saul's son strengthens David's hand through Yahweh, and declares that Saul will not capture him and that David will become king with Jonathan second to him. A crucial new nuance thus attaches when David and Jonathan again confirm a covenant or pledge before Yahweh (23:16–18).[52] But it is their last contact.

Saul faces his final battle (28:1). On notable earlier occasions (13:1–15:35), Samuel had mediated Yahweh's message to him, though there had been problems in the outworking of this role. But anyway, Samuel is dead. Saul has now killed off the priests except for the one who escaped to David and took the chasuble with him. He has expelled from the country the mediums who might be able to engage in divination on his behalf. Previous references to effigies (15:23; 19:11–17) hint at the prevalence of such forms of divination in Israel, and if Saul has abolished them, it is an impressive achievement. Saul asks Yahweh what is going to happen or what to do ("asks" is *šā'al*, the verb that resonates with Saul's name). But Yahweh does not answer by dreams, by "Urim," or by prophets. Saul is reduced to the resources of the Philistines themselves (6:2).[53] It is a sad end for one who once prophesied.[54] At Endor, 10 miles or so across the Jezreel Plain from the Israelite camp, Saul's staff find a medium, a ghost-mistress, who can channel voices from people who have passed (the practice is not just a recourse for people in traditional societies but one

[52] Van Wijk-Bos, *Reading Samuel*, 124.

[53] Auld, *I & II Samuel*, 327.

[54] Matthew Michael, "The Prophet, the Witch and the Ghost: Understanding the Parody of Saul as a 'Prophet' and the Purpose of Endor in the Deuteronomistic History," *JSOT* 38 (2014): 315–46; cf. also Dolores G. Kamrada, *Heroines, Heroes and Deity: Three Narratives of the Biblical Heroic Tradition*, LHBOTS 621 (London: T&T Clark, 2016), 105–73.

that is common in the West today,[55] and not least among Israeli women).[56]

The story that follows presupposes some nuancing of the regular First Testament understanding of death and its aftermath, which it shares with other traditional societies. The human person is not a combination of a body and soul in which the body is a dispensable shell for the body, and death means the two simply separate ("John Brown's body lies a-moldering in the grave, but his soul goes marching on"). Body and mind or spirit or personality are indeed distinguishable and semiseparable, so that the body can be in one place but the spirit somewhere else (e.g., 1 Cor 5:3–4; 2 Cor 12:2–4). But in their normal state, they are two aspects of one whole. Death does not bring their separation but the departure of life from the whole person. On the basis of Jesus's resurrection, people who belong to him can look forward to the resurrection of their whole person in the future; it will require a miraculous reconstituting of the person they once were, their bodies having totally perished. Meanwhile, they await that event, and the grave or Sheol are the two sides to the place where they wait. Body and spirit, they continue to exist, but they are lifeless. Sleep provides a useful analog for their position.

---

[55] See Ora Brison, "The Medium of En-Dor and the Phenomenon of Divination in Twenty-First Century Israel," in Athalya Brenner-Idan and Archie C. C. Lee, eds., *Samuel, Kings and Chronicles I*, Texts@Contexts (London: T&T Clark, 2017), 124–47.

[56] See Tali Stolovy et al., "Dissociation and the Experience of Channeling: Narratives of Israeli Women Who Practice Channeling," *International Journal of Clinical and Experimental Hypnosis* 63 (2015): 346–64. Suzie Park also looks at the story against a Korean background in "Saul's Question and the Question of Saul: A Deconstructive Reading of the Story of Endor in 1 Sam. 28:3–25," in Uriah Y. Kim and Seung Ai Yang, eds., *T&T Clark Handbook of Asian American Biblical Hermeneutics* (London: T&T Clark, 2019), 241–51.

HOW OR HOW NOT TO DIE A KING

Saul and two other men travel across the plain and arrive at night; it is sometimes said that contact with dead people happens more at night. Saul asks the woman to make contact with Samuel's ghost (*'ôb*). Samuel appears, apparently having had a kind of interim physical reconstituting, though only the medium sees him. His appearance both scares her and makes her realize who Saul is. Perhaps part of the background is that a medium may profess to hear and transmit voice and words (cf. Isa 29:4), but not to see the physical person. And maybe the actual appearance of a figure such as Samuel would confirm a hunch that her visitor was more than just an ordinary person. She calls Samuel an *'ĕlôhîm*; the word can denote any figure who is more than merely natural.[57]

Saul needs Samuel to tell him what he should do. The wording is the same as Samuel's before the Gilgal event (10:8).[58] The Philistines are making war against him and God has turned away from him. "It is a moment of great intensity in this long narrative, and I think Saul's most exposed, most honest, moment."[59]

Samuel does not appreciate being awakened from his sleep in Sheol. Presumably a medium could not generate an appearance by Samuel against God's will, but on this occasion it suits God to allow it, and typically, he does not mind very much whether the prophet whom he calls is happy to be drafted. Indeed, "death has not mellowed Samuel."[60] Further, Samuel "refuses to be an alternative to Yahweh, who has already made his position clear (v. 16). There is no space between Yahweh and himself that can be

---

[57] See Tsumura's comment, *The First Book of Samuel*, on 28:13.
[58] Auld, *I & II Samuel*, 328.
[59] Green, *How Are the Mighty Fallen*, 429.
[60] Brueggemann, *First and Second Samuel*, 194.

exploited." A prophet's vocation can be to encourage a king before a battle and tell him not to be afraid (cf. Isa 7:4), and Jonathan once gave David that kind of encouragement (1 Sam 23:17). Samuel will not fulfill the role.[61] He reaffirms the message he gave Saul after the Amalek event, and tells him that he and his sons will die in the battle next day. "He returns from the dead to cut through all the events that have occurred since 1 Samuel 15."[62] The one thing he adds to his earlier messages is the identification of the neighbor to whom God will give the kingship (28:17). It constitutes a prophetic confirmation of what Akish's men have said (21:11[12]), Jonathan has said (23:17) and Saul himself has said (24:20[21]).

> Why should Saul ask the witch to call up Samuel, of all people? Because Saul knows that Samuel can be relied upon to speak the truth to him; Samuel is the plumb line of truthfulness, in the narrative, and Saul knows it: "With Samuel, Saul is forced back to brutal reality, away from brutal illusion. He has been battling David all this time, as he thought, but in reality he has been battling Yahweh."... This meeting between Saul and Samuel ... is like an inverted version of their first, divinely guided meeting. In the first encounter, Saul did not intend to meet Samuel, but does, and is involuntarily offered the kingdom; in their last meeting, he wills to meet Samuel and is told that his army will fall "into the hand of the Philistines" because the "kingdom" has been given by God "to David." (1 Sam. 28:19, 17)[63]

The story can be read as sympathetic to Saul and to the medium. The woman is not so much a witch as a seer who brings the word

---

[61] Auld, *I & II Samuel*, 328, 329.

[62] Miscall, *1 Samuel*, 172.

[63] Murphy, *1 Samuel*, 268, 257. The first internal quotation is from Edwin R. Good, *Irony in the Old Testament* (London: SPCK, 1965), 77–78. On the notion of an inverted version of the first meeting, see Grenville J. R. Kent, *Say It Again Sam: A Literary and Filmic Study of Repetition in 1 Samuel 28* (Cambridge: Lutterworth, 2012), 148–51.

of Yahweh to Saul in a way that maybe he finally hears,[64] and afterwards she makes a meal for him before he sets off on his journey back to the camp; a meal is perhaps part of the séance process. The narrative takes a matter-of-fact form and raises no questions about the possibility of contacting dead people. It thus compares with the attitude taken elsewhere in the First Testament (e.g., Lev 19:31; 20:6, 27; Deut 18:11; 2 Kgs 21:6; Isa 8:19), which does not question the possibility but does forbid such activity. After Second Temple times, the story became more puzzling, partly because Jews and Christians had come to assume the existence of Satan, of resurrection, and of heaven and hell. Like many modern readers, Jewish and Christian readers might from then on be disinclined to take the story literally. While Samuel in general did not attract the attention of Jewish and Christian writers over the centuries as Genesis, Psalms, or Isaiah did,[65] Saul and the medium did draw their attention. Nicely, Origen insists on a literal interpretation against people such as Tertullian who read the story figuratively and believed that Satan generated an apparition of Samuel.[66]

---

[64] See Esther J. Hamori, "The Prophet and the Necromancer: Women's Divination for Kings," *JBL* 132 (2013): 827–43; Daewook Kim, "Saul, the Dead Samuel and the Woman (1 Sam 28,3–25)," *Biblische Notizen* 178 (2018): 21–34. J. Kabamba Kiboko, *Divining the Woman of Endor: African Culture, Postcolonial Hermeneutics, and the Politics of Biblical Translation*, LHBOTS 644 (London: T&T Clark, 2017), 191–216.

[65] But for selections from early Christian and Reformation writers, see Cooper and Lohrmann, *1–2 Samuel, 1–2 Kings, 1–2 Chronicles*.

[66] The texts from Tertullian and Origen, the substantial treatise of Eustathius, and works of other writers appear in Rowan A. Greer and Margaret Mary Mitchell, eds., *The "Belly-Myther" of Endor: Interpretations of 1 Kingdoms 28 in the Early Church*, Writings from the Greco-Roman World 16 (Atlanta, GA: SBL, 2007); cf. the quotations in Franke, *Joshua, Judges, Ruth, 1–2 Samuel*, 320–23; also K. A. D. Smelik, "The Witch of Endor: I Samuel 28 in Rabbinic and Christian Exegesis till 800 A.D.," *Vigiliae Christianae* 33 (1977): 160–79; Patricia Cox, "Origen and the Witch of Endor: Toward an Iconoclastic

In the sixteenth through the nineteenth centuries attention focused more on the medium/witch/prophetess.[67]

The Torah gives no reason for its prohibition. It is an aspect of repudiating aspects of traditional religion and spirituality such as the use of images of God and tattoos. They can give a misleading impression of God and of the nature of a relationship with God, and they can carry implications associated with alien religious beliefs and draw people into sharing those beliefs and practices. Paul takes a similar view of meat sacrificed to other gods (1 Cor 10:14–32). Outside that context, some practices associated with other religions such as tattooing might be unobjectionable. As regards recourse to mediums, seeking contact with family members who have passed is not inherently incompatible with faith in Yahweh. But Isaiah 8:19–20 (admittedly an enigmatic passage) declares that there actually is something wrong with seeking messages from Yahweh that way, and a central implication of 1 Samuel 28 is similar. Israel had other ways of being in touch with Yahweh and he had other ways of speaking to Israel, but Yahweh has made it clear that he has nothing else to say to Saul. Saul's recourse to the medium confirms the point. Samuel simply says what Yahweh regularly gave him to say to Saul. The challenge to

Typology," *Anglican Theological Review* 66 (1984): 137–47; and for the view that the Samuel figure was actually a demon, Johannes Bugenhagen, *Annotationes ... in Deuteronomium. In Samuelem prophetam, id est, duos libros Regum* (Nuremberg: Petri, 1524), 276–77 (cf. Cooper and Lohrmann, *1–2 Samuel, 1–2 Kings, 1–2 Chronicles*, 129); Willet, *An Harmonie upon the First Booke of Samuel...*, 313–14 (cf. Cooper and Lohrmann, *1–2 Samuel, 1–2 Kings, 1–2 Chronicles*, 130); Grenville J. R. Kent, "'Call up Samuel': Who Appeared to the Witch at En-dor? (1 Samuel 28:3–25)," *Andrews University Seminary Studies* 52 (2014): 141–60; Murphy, *1 Samuel*, 261–71.

[67] Christopher James Blythe, "The Prophetess of Endor: Reception of 1 Samuel 28 in Nineteenth Century Mormon History." *Journal of the Bible and Its Reception* 4 (2017): 43–70.

Saul was to respond to what Yahweh had said to him already. Jesus will make a similar point in a parable about two people who have died. The well-to-do man wants Abraham to send the poor man back to warn his family about the fate that awaits them, to which Abraham's response is that they need to listen to Moses and the Prophets (Luke 16:19–31).

In the battle that duly follows, the Philistines win a victory, kill Saul's sons, and wound Saul. He commits suicide rather than be captured, killed, and further humiliated. The Philistines decapitate him and fasten his body to the wall of Bet-shean, the Philistine town nearby. They thereby make even his last act a failure, and attempt to ensure that he does not find rest in the tomb and thus in Sheol. But the people of Jabesh-gilead whom Saul had once delivered send a company to bring the bodies of Saul and his sons back home and give them a proper burial. So Saul's life does end not in humiliation but with dignity,[68] and "the curtain falls where his reign began."[69] Indeed, "it is perhaps a more generous portraiture toward Israel's first king than we have heard narrated elsewhere."[70] In *City of God* 17:7, Augustine has a version of the LXX text of Samuel's words that speaks of God taking the kingdom from Israel, not just from Saul, which Augustine interprets in a troubling direction: It denotes the replacement of the Jewish people by the church. The honoring of Saul rather fits with Saul's preparing the way for David in a strange sense; "David is chosen for Saul and for the people he represents."[71]

---

[68] Klein, *1 Samuel*, 290.

[69] Hertzberg, *I & II Samuel*, 234.

[70] Green, *David's Capacity for Compassion*, 131.

[71] Murphy, *1 Samuel*, 286, adapting thinking from Karl Barth, Hans Urs von Balthasar, and Joseph Ratzinger.

The sequence of events in 1 Samuel 31 repeats in 2 Samuel 1 in a way that maintains the irony characterizing this narrative. On his return to Ziklag, David surely flops, draws breath, and makes love to Abigail one night and Ahinoam the next. Except that David is not a flopper, and not much of a lover (he does not get around to fathering children for some while: see 3:2–5). He knows that the Philistines and the Israelites were getting ready for a battle, so the two days are moments of suspense, until an Amalekite who is a resident alien in Israel arrives. At least, the Amalekite says that is what he is, though it might be not the kind of thing you make up. But he gives a different account of Saul's death from the narrator's account, which we are presumably invited to take as the true one. The Amalekite thinks that David will like his version (and will perhaps promote him to full citizen),[72] but David does not. At least, David says he does not, though the narrator does not tell us what David is thinking, here or in his subsequent lament for Saul and Jonathan. The man says he killed Saul but did not. Does David, who might have killed Saul but did not, and yet profits from his death, meet his alter ego in him, and then execute him?[73]

Anyway, through him "the symbols of [Saul's] kingship are transferred to David…. The confirmation of David's kingship by the people governed by that crown still lies in the future. But the crown has arrived."[74] And no doubt it suits David to continue to emphasize to anyone listening that you do not attack "Yahweh's anointed," and that doing so is a capital offense (1:16). The expression "Yahweh's anointed" comes otherwise only in Lamentations

[72] Cf. Alter, *The David Story*, 197.

[73] Cf. Robert Polzin, *David and the Deuteronomist: A Literary Study of the Deuteronomic History*. Part Three: 2 Samuel (Bloomington: Indiana University Press, 1993), 5–8.

[74] Craig E. Morrison, *2 Samuel, Berit Olam: Studies in Hebrew Narrative and Poetry* (Collegeville, MN: Liturgical Press, 2013), 24.

4:20, where it is glossed as implying that he is "the breath of our nostrils ... in whose shadow we said we would live among the nations." The implication is that "on the death of the king, the very life of the nation is under threat."[75] And at the end of the first king's reign, "Israel is once again occupied by the Philistines, returning to the position it had been in prior to Saul's reign."[76]

Irony and ambiguity continue in David's elegy for Saul and Jonathan. Why would David want it taught (2 Sam 1:18)? An elegy belongs at someone's funeral. Why would he want it taught specifically to Judahites (1:18)? Is that requirement another affirmation that he, the Judahite, does not rejoice in the death either of the anointed king or of his son and potential successor, and neither should they, and everyone else should note the fact? On the other hand, when the Philistines already know about these deaths because they brought them about (1:20; cf. 1 Sam 31:9), why avoid letting the Philistines know about them?[77] But rhetorically, the exhortation functions as an expression of sorrow at the fact that the Philistine women will indeed rejoice.[78] Were Saul and Jonathan great shedders of blood and piercers of bodies (2 Sam 1:22)? The person talking is the great killer David! Were they always victorious, equally speedy and strong (1:22–23)? Actually, 1 Samuel 14:47–52 did imply something along those lines. Were they both lovable and gracious (2 Sam 1:23)? Were they parted neither in life nor in death (1:23)? What about the conflict between them, over David!?[79] David speaks

---

[75] Auld, *I & II Samuel*, 359.

[76] Edelman, *King Saul*, 288.

[77] Birch, "The First and Second Books of Samuel," in his comments on 1:20.

[78] Anthony F. Campbell, *2 Samuel*, FOTL 8 (Grand Rapids, MI: Eerdmans, 2005), 23.

[79] J. Cheryl Exum, *Tragedy and Biblical Narrative* (Cambridge: Cambridge University Press, 1992), 93.

with "elegiac generosity."[80] Did Saul deck the Israelite women in crimson luxury and gold ornaments (1:24)? The elegy is a eulogy,[81] and eulogies do not tell the whole truth. David's words have a "calculated eloquence," an "intended rhetorical effect on an audience."[82] Who, then, knows what feelings lie behind them? But the elegy parallels the honoring of Saul and his sons by the Jabeshites, as the Amalekite's story parallels the narrator's account. "Although the Lament might serve David, it serves the memory of Saul and Jonathan more."[83]

[80] McCarter, *II Samuel*, 76.

[81] Polzin, *David and the Deuteronomist*, 13.

[82] Tod Linafelt, "Private Poetry and Public Eloquence in 2 Samuel 1:17–27: Hearing and Overhearing David's Lament for Jonathan and Saul," *Journal of Religion* 88 (2008): 497–526 (500).

[83] K. L. Noll, *The Faces of David*, JSOTSup 242 (Sheffield: Sheffield Academic Press, 1997), 116.

CHAPTER 6

Yahweh Who Establishes a King
(2 Samuel 2–10)

Like Samuel as a whole, 2 Samuel 2–10 works in a rough chronological order but also groups related events within that broad framework. These chapters cover the positive side to David's reign before coming to David's affair and his killing of Uriah, with its grim aftermath. They raise issues concerning key aspects of the nation's life: government, family, a capital city, defense, the main place of worship, and Yahweh's promises to David's dynasty. In each case, the narrative may bring out the theological ambiguity of the subject, or the wider First Testament context may do so.

GOVERNMENT: DAVID'S KINGSHIP

The auditors, the narrator, and David himself know what is due to happen after Saul's death. David needs no prophetic anointing; Samuel performed it long ago. But Saul's anointing and David's anointing were private or family affairs. Humanly speaking or politically speaking, they did not bring about recognition or enthronement. Samuel organized that for Saul. David now asks Yahweh what to do, implicitly in order to bring it about (2:1–4a). Consulting Yahweh can be what he does when there is or could be conflict between him and his clan (1 Sam 23:1–13; 30:1–10), and this moment is a key one for them all. He does not ask about Benjamin, where

Saul was based, but about Judah. He himself came from there and he has links there, partly through his marriages: Jezreel (the Jezreel in Judah) and Carmel are both in the Hebron area. Otherwise, he leaves it to Yahweh to offer instructions. The narrative does not tell us whether he was still a client of the Philistines or whether the people of Hebron had any say in his move there ("going up" has military connotations in 2 Sam 5:17, 19).[1] But his clan does settle in Hebron, the natural capital of Judah, and the Judahites do publicly anoint him there. Was a priest such as Abiathar their agent in this action?

David goes on to thank the Jabeshites for the commitment to Saul expressed in burying him. He prays for Yahweh to show them commitment and steadfastness, and promises that he will bring good things to them in return for what they did. "Oh, and by the way, the Judahites have anointed me king" (2:4b–7). While it might seem that the Jabeshites are too far north and east to be of immediate political use to him, Saul's cousin and commander-in-chief, Abner (1 Sam 14:50), is about to crown Saul's son Ish-boshet over Israel as a whole at Mahanaim (2 Sam 2:8).[2] The precise location of both towns is uncertain, but both are east of the Jordan. Mahanaim's location there as the place to crown Saul's successor hints at Israel's reduced state, weakened by the Philistines. "Israel" (2:9) apparently comprises Gilead, Benjamin, Ephraim, and one or two other miscellaneous places, which further conveys a telling impression of what the diminished "Israel" means.

There follows ongoing conflict between Saul's people and David's people, through which David's people get consistently

---

[1] Arnold A. Anderson,. 2 Samuel, WBC 11 (Dallas, TX: Word, 1989), 23.

[2] 1 Chr 8:33; 9:39 have Esh-baal for Ish-boshet; here, bōšet (shame) replaces ba'al, which in later usage would sound like a reference to Baal, but in origin will refer to Yahweh as Master. Either 'îš ba'al, "Man of the Master" or 'ēš ba'al "The Master Exists" might be the original form.

stronger and Saul's frailer (*dal*, 3:1). The narrator has noted that David inquired of Yahweh before making his move, whereas for Ish-boshet, Abner just takes action. Given that Yahweh of course intends David to become king over Israel as a whole, the only question is the human means by which this aim will come about. It is characteristic of the way the Scriptures see God's relationship with events that God has a long-term aim that he is intent on fulfilling, but the process whereby it will be fulfilled depends on an ongoing interaction with everyday coincidences and human decision-making. David's story is an illustration of and an episode in that dynamic. At the moment, Abner is the real power in Israel. His significance is suggested by Ish-boshet's accusation that he has bedded Rizpah, the mother of two of Saul's children (2 Sam 21:8) and Saul's "secondary wife" or "servant-wife" (*pilegeš*, 3:7). Translations commonly describe her as a "concubine," but the word does not imply an extramarital relationship, though she, with her children, does not have the same status or rights as a primary wife. Whether Ish-boshet's accusation is true or not, it implies a suspicion that Abner, a member of Saul's family, has aspirations to the throne.

The strength of Abner's position in Israel is then suggested by his proposing that David should solemnize an agreement in which Abner would turn over Israel as a whole to him (3:12). Abner describes it as a fulfillment of Yahweh's word (3:18), which of course it is. Samuel has not recorded a word that precisely expresses what Abner says, but it would not be surprising if Abner had political considerations in mind in putting it that way. Perhaps the agreement would entail Abner acquiring the position of commander-in-chief. But his move becomes an ironic part of the way Yahweh's ultimate will is indeed put into effect. Abner contributes to the fulfillment of Yahweh's word through losing his life in an act of violence that constitutes redress for a killing he undertook but tried to avoid. He had killed the brother of Joab, one of David's henchmen and eventual commander-in-chief (8:16). And Joab slew his brother's killer of whom he could also be suspicious as his potential rival as commander.[3] Should Abner have died as a fool dies? "Abner is a prime example of *hubris* that never comes to know its limits," so the answer is "Yes."[4] Actually, "there is not room for both Abner and Joab in David's camp; one or the other must die."[5] The fulfillment of Yahweh's purpose comes about through misunderstanding and waywardness and by means of random, misguided, and willful human acts, through bloodshed and betrayal. Killing begets killing as "the road to kingship is strewn with violent and murderous encounters, and funerals are the order of the day."[6]

When Ish-boshet heard of Abner's death, "his hands became weak" (4:1: Contrast the phrase in 1 Sam 23:16 about a hand becoming strong). Abner's death had worked in David's favor, and he had lamented Abner (2 Sam 3:31–39), again with the implication that he was not behind the death. I am soft/tender/gentle (*rak*), David claims, implausibly, and he prays for Yahweh to requite Joab (3:29, 39). But Yahweh did not, and David left the task to Solomon for after his death (1 Kgs 2). Meanwhile, it did not stop David making good use of Joab as commander-in-chief, in his aggressiveness and ruthlessness, nor stop Joab, "a skilled fighter and a bold talker,"[7] making good use of his capacity to confront David (2 Sam 10–12;

---

[3] Anderson, 2 *Samuel*, 57–58.

[4] Exum, *Tragedy and Biblical Narrative*, 106, 107.

[5] Campbell, 2 *Samuel*, 43.

[6] Van Wijk-Bos, *Reading Samuel*, 155.

[7] Barbara Green, "Joab's Coherence and Incoherence: Character and Characterization," in Bodner and Johnson, *Characters and Characterization in the Book of Samuel*, 183–204 (186).

14; 18–20; 24). In due course two Benjaminites assassinate Ish-boshet (4:2–12). "For David to secure power in the north, some carefully placed killings must occur – Saul and Jonathan, Abner, and now, in this chapter, Ish-boshet."[8] Then representatives of the northern Israelites come to David:

> "Here, we are your flesh and blood. Further, in previous days, when Saul was king over us, you were the one who took Israel out and brought Israel in. Yahweh said to you, 'You're the one who will shepherd my people Israel. You're the one who will be ruler over Israel.'" So all Israel's elders came to the king at Hebron, King David solemnized a pledge to them at Hebron before Yahweh, and they anointed David as king over Israel. (5:1–3)

The monarchy falls into David's lap. The Saulide Israelites are not literally David's flesh and blood, like Abimelek when he speaks thus to the Shechemites (Judg 9:2), and the point of the comment lies in that fact. They are making a declaration of commitment, a performative statement: We hereby pledge ourselves to being one people with you. Once again there is no talk of Yahweh's involvement. Their approach, their pledge or covenant, and their anointing are human actions, though they, too, refer to an alleged message to David.[9] They, too, describe themselves as fulfilling Yahweh's word, but they, too, may be mentioning Yahweh chiefly as part of their political maneuvering, yet speaking more truly and theologically than they realize. So do their actual words as they pick up the word "commandant" (*nāgîd*) rather than using the word "king." Yahweh's term was "commandment" when he commissioned Samuel to anoint Saul (1 Sam 9:16; 10:1). It suggests someone appointed by Yahweh who rules under Yahweh's direction. "The elders apparently do not wish to overlegitimize or

---

[8] Brueggemann, *First and Second Samuel*, 232.
[9] Auld *I & II Samuel*, 392–93.

excessively exalt David in office."[10] They perhaps imply that they are not the only ones: Yahweh is happy for David to be *nāgîd*, but not so enthusiastic about his being king.[11] The people also quote Yahweh as commissioning David to "shepherd" them, which contributes further to a reframing of the notion of kingship.[12] It is the first occurrence of the verb "shepherd" since the beginning of David's story (1 Sam 17:15). David knows that a shepherd looks after sheep, provides for them, directs them, and protects them from attack (cf. Ps 23).

The related, less metaphorical Hebrew expression for the king's remit is that he is responsible for the exercise of faithful authority or right decision-making, for *mišpāṭ ûṣǝdāqâ* (2 Sam 8:15). This phrase can be seen as the Hebrew term for social justice, though that notion in English is vague, and one has to allow for differences in the notion of justice in different cultural contexts in accordance with the different conceptual schemes within which it functions.[13] The First Testament understanding can usefully be seen against the background of other Middle Eastern understandings.[14] The Hebrew hendiadys combines the ideas of legitimate power and authority (*mišpāṭ*) and obligation to do the right thing by people in one's community to whom one is bound (*ṣǝdāqâ*). The king's responsibility is to govern in a way that expresses *mišpāṭ ûṣǝdāqâ* and to see that the nation as a whole works on that basis, as people

[10] Brueggemann, *First and Second Samuel*, 238–39.
[11] Donald F. Murray, *Divine Prerogative and Royal Pretension: Pragmatics, Poetics and Polemics in a Narrative Sequence About David (2 Samuel 5.17–7.29)*, JSOTSup 264 (Sheffield: Sheffield Academic Press, 1998).
[12] Peterson, *First and Second Samuel*, 157.
[13] See Alasdair C. MacIntyre, *Whose Justice? Which Rationality?* (London: Duckworth, 1988).
[14] See Richard G. Smith, *The Fate of Justice and Righteousness During David's Reign: Narrative Ethics and Rereading the Court History according to 2 Samuel 8:15–20:26*, LHBOTS 508 (London: T&T Clark, 2009).

such as a community's elders and the heads of its households exercise their responsibility.

FAMILY: DAVID'S WIVES AND CHILDREN AND BROTHERS

When David made his move on Hebron, his "men" came with him, with their "households" (*bayit*; 2:3). These chapters do not refer to extended families (*mišpāḥâ*; cf. 1 Sam 9:21; 10:21; 18:18; 20:6, 29; 2 Sam 14:7; 16:5), which might be a sign of the breakdown of such structures in a body that has been on the move and on the run. A household would suggest a unit such as could in more settled circumstances fit in a house, not so different from what Western people might call a nuclear family. Brothers are prominent in 2 Samuel 1–4, usually as the agents or victims of violence.[15] Deuteronomy especially emphasizes that the community needs to see itself as a brotherhood, though monarchy seems to encourage fratricide.

David took Ahinoam and Abigail with him to Hebron (2:2), and he acquired four more wives there (3:2–4). The Hannah story presupposed that for ordinary people the essence of marriage lies in providing a context for developing love and for sexual expression, for generating a family, and for partnering in work, though marriage would also seal relationships between extended families. Being in leadership reworks such assumptions. Having several wives is a sign of a man's status and significance. Marriage's potential for sealing relationships also becomes a paramount consideration, as Ish-boshet's suspicion of Abner's relationship with Rizpah implies (3:6–7). Ahinoam and Abigail regularly appear as

---

[15] Polzin, *David and the Deuteronomist*, 47–53.

"the Jezreelite" and "the wife of Nabal the Carmelite"; their origins would undergird David's identity as a Judahite, encourage his relationship with Judahite clans further south than Bethlehem, and stand him in good stead as he moves to Hebron. Likewise, wife number three's being the daughter of King Talmay of Geshur suggests a healing of the relationship implied by 1 Samuel 27:8. The narrative tells us nothing about the background of David's other three wives. Maybe they were just means of making David look impressive.

It does tell us that between them the six wives gave birth to six sons in Hebron (3:2–4). The notes about wives and children are marks of David's flourishing and eminence, though "the list bristles with potential disasters,"[16] as will emerge. In Jerusalem, David acquires more full wives and secondary wives, and fathers eleven more sons and some daughters (5:13–14). "This listing of David's wives clashes with any romantic stereotypes that may have accrued to David in our imaginations."[17] While the First Testament does not express general disapproval of polygamy but accepts it as an aspect of the way things are, like divorce and multiple marriages in Western societies, it regularly notes the trouble in which it issues. Deuteronomy 17:17 does specifically prohibit kings from multiplying wives. A king could argue that the context there suggests multiplying foreign wives who served other gods; but would David's Jerusalem wives be Jebusites?

Then there is Michal. "Instead of receiving validation from her loved one, Michal has, it seems, married a man much like her father."[18]

---

[16] Alter, *The David Story*, 208.

[17] Peterson, *First and Second Samuel*, 150.

[18] Lilian R. Klein, "Michal, the Barren Wife," in Athalya Brenner, ed., *Samuel and Kings*, A Feminist Companion to the Bible (Second Series) (Sheffield: Sheffield Academic Press, 2000), 37–46 (39).

David expresses no affection for Michal (actually he expresses no affection for any of his wives). She is the wife that he acquired "at a price," … and she is rightfully his as part of a deal that Saul breached. Later when David will transfer the ark of the Lord to Jerusalem, Michal, "daughter of Saul," will spy her husband dancing (2 Sam 6:16) and despise him (by then her affections for him have diminished). She probably realizes that her restitution to David in this scene expresses the new king's political eclipse of Saul, her father, which the transfer of the ark of the Lord to David's city later solidifies. Her return to court also strengthens David's legitimacy as Saul's successor. Thus, we should not expect the narrator to present on stage the tender reunion of husband and wife after years of separation. David's demand for Michal's swift return was driven not by his affection for her but by his desire to signal to his court that he has supplanted her father's house.[19]

Michal had loved David (1 Sam 18:20), and as with Saul and Jonathan it might be overly cynical to take this love as simply the hard-headed, practical kind of allegiance. But it looks as if David left her behind when she facilitated his flight from Gibeah, which led to Saul's passing her on to Paltiel/Palti ben Laish (19:11–18; 25:44). Claiming her back (2 Sam 3:12–16) might be quite legal and in keeping with the Torah.[20] The political consideration overrides Paltiel's tears too.[21] The juxtaposition of Rizpah and Michal (3:6–16) draws attention to their sharing the fate of being "politically charged symbols."[22]

While the narrative does not tell us Michal's reaction to this sequence of events, her closing scene in the narrative hints at it (6:16–23). "At the beginning of their story a loving Michal helped

[19] Morrison, *2 Samuel*, 39.
[20] McCarter, *II Samuel*, 115.
[21] Robert Barron, *2 Samuel*, Brazos Theological Commentary on the Bible (Grand Rapids, MI: Brazos, 2015), 62.
[22] Peterson, *First and Second Samuel*, 151.

David escape 'through the window' from her father's henchmen while now she looks at him from a distance 'through the
window,' in seething contempt."[23] "Through the window" conveys a further irony: It is the position of a woman looking for
the man she is preparing to welcome (Judg 5:28; cf. Cant 2:9).
Whereas Ahimelek could describe David as honorable, speaking
to Michal's father (1 Sam 22:14),[24] only sarcastically could Michal
now describe David as showing himself honorable (2 Sam 6:20).
As she sees it, his honor has gone, as happened to Israel when
the covenant chest that is now returning first departed (1 Sam
4:21, 22).[25] "This is the only time that the two exchange words, a
meager harvest for a union that began, at least on Michal's side,
with love."[26]

Her story closes with the laconic footnote, "Michal the daughter of Saul had no child until the day of her death" (6:23). Because
Yahweh closed her womb? The story does not say so, as it did
with Hannah. Because David never came near her? Because she
did not wish to go near David? One way or another, her story
ends with sadness and expresses the price a woman pays for
being born into the royal family. "The animosity between the
house of David and the house of Saul is played out in 2 Samuel
6 as a marital conflict."[27] "Michal's union with David had promised the possibility of keeping the Saulide line alive, but her failure to produce children removed the last brick supporting the
house of Saul."[28]

[23] Alter, *The David Story*, 228.
[24] Auld, *I & II Samuel*, 414.
[25] See Gary Stansell, "Honor and Shame in the David Narratives," *Semeia* 68 (1994): 55–79 (65–68).
[26] Van Wijk-Bos, *Reading Samuel*, 177.
[27] Exum, *Tragedy and Biblical Narrative*, 87.
[28] Cartledge, *1 & 2 Samuel*, 442.

CAPITAL: JERUSALEM, DAVID'S CITY

Jerusalem is significant both as a city and as a capital. In the Scriptures, the city comes into existence in Genesis 4. It takes this place in among the first murder, the first instance of polygamy, the development of cattle raising, and the invention of musical instruments and tools, which hints at the city's ambiguity. The context of Cain's fear suggests an aspect of its significance. It is potentially a place of security, at least in relation to outsiders, though modern city life may seem a place of insecurity, in relation to insiders. A major difference between a city (*'îr*) and a village (*pərāzâ*) is that a city has walls (cf. 1 Sam 6:18), which offer protection and the possibility of refuge in a time of invasion for people who live in the region in villages and homesteads. In peaceful times, the city can live symbiotically with the villages and homesteads around it. Specialists in tool-making, pottery, and jewelry can focus on their work in the city, and farmers and shepherds who are in surplus can bring their surplus to the city and exchange it for these specialists' wares. At least, it would be a neat theory. Among the Canaanites and the Philistines, the land comprised a collection of city-states, of which the Jebusites' Jerusalem was an example, so that there is no distinction between a city and a capital. But when the Israelites as a collection of clans become a nation organized as a state with a king, a city comes to accompany the throne.[29]

Jerusalem straddled the border of Judah and Benjamin. Long ago, the Judahites took Jerusalem (Judg 1:8), but evidently could not hold onto it. "The Jebusites living in Jerusalem, the Judahites could not dispossess, and the Jebusites have lived with the

---

[29] J. P. Fokkelman, *Narrative Art and Poetry in the Books of Samuel, Volume III: Throne and City (II Sam. 2–8 & 21–24)* (Assen: van Gorcum, 1990), 16; compare the volume's subtitle.

Judahites in Jerusalem until today" (Josh 15:63). In yet another comment, "the Jebusites living in Jerusalem, the Benjaminites did not dispossess, and the Jebusites have lived with the Benjaminites in Jerusalem until today" (Judg 1:21). We have heard nothing of the city since Judges 19, when a Levite with his wife and servant thought with terrible irony that it was a less safe place to stay than an Israelite town. The Israelites' failure to take possession of the city presumably reflects the strength of its position, on a bluff of land with steep slopes on three sides. That strength would also underlie its antiquity as a city or city-state. It features in a number of documents from the second millennium, including an Egyptian curse and some letters from officials in Canaan to the Egyptian king at el-Amarna,[30] though the name of the Jebusites (and Jebus), like Hivites and Perizzites, does not occur outside the First Testament.

It is now apparently the only city in the mountains that is still occupied by Canaanites, and David determines to capture it. It represents a completion of Israel's occupation of the highland, and in its strong position and its location between Judah and Benjamin it would make an excellent site for a capital. Thus "the king and his men went to Jerusalem against the Jebusites ... and David captured the stronghold of Zion" (2 Sam 5:6–7). The Jebusites were confident that they could resist David's forces, but they were wrong (5:6–9). Exactly how the city fell is unclear, but its conquest was an achievement of human bravery and ingenuity. It issues in the town becoming "David's City," equivalent to "Gibeah of Saul" as the state's administrative center. David subsequently builds it up on all sides. Zion was perhaps the high point and the

---

[30] James B. Pritchard, ed., *Ancient Near Eastern Texts Relating to the Old Testament* (3rd ed. Princeton, NJ: Princeton University Press, 1969), 328–29, 483–90.

citadel within the city. While Deuteronomy 20:17 requires that the Israelites should devote the Jebusites, Samuel does not indicate that they did so. Araunah the Jebusite is still farming nearby in 2 Samuel 24, and those other references in Joshua and Judges note that the Jebusites are living with the Judahites and Benjaminites in Jerusalem "until today." Subsequently, 1 Kings 9:21 has Solomon turning them into a conscript labor force.

Thus "David kept getting bigger as Yahweh the God of Armies was with him" (2 Sam 5:10). It is the first occasion since David's going up to Hebron (2:1) that the narrative has commented on Yahweh's involvement in events; these two references mark the beginning and end of the story of David's becoming king in Hebron and in Jerusalem. And he is now an important player on the regional scene. "A foreigner ... writes a fitting climax to the story of David's rise to power as king of Israel": The king of Tyre provides him with timber and craftsmen to build him a house in Jerusalem.[31] "And David acknowledged that Yahweh had established him as king over Israel and that he had exalted his kingship, on account of his people Israel" (5:12).

It is sometimes said that David was in the habit of consulting Yahweh before any significant undertakings, but the narrative does not give this impression. He did consult Yahweh before making his move on Hebron (2:1) and in connection with the battles against the Philistines (5:17–26), as he did on a few earlier occasions (1 Sam 23:1–12; 30:7–8), but more often he makes up his mind what to do and does it, and Yahweh is with him as he does so. Christians often speak of seeking the Lord's guidance about some action, but only one time in a thousand does the Lord send an answer by means of some prophetic word; usually, people pray and then go on and decide what to do using their own insight. It looks as if David does the same, though Saul got in trouble for acting in something like that way (1 Sam 13:8–14). We may guess at the rationale for David's capturing Jerusalem, but the narrative gives neither a practical nor a theological rationale. In due course Solomon, Yahweh, and the narrator will refer to Jerusalem as the city that Yahweh chose (e.g., 1 Kgs 8:44, 48; 11:13, 32, 36; 14:21; cf. Ps 132:13), but it seems that David chose it first. Subsequently, its significance was vastly enhanced through its marvelous escape from conquest by Sennacherib (cf. Isa 36–37; Pss 46; 48), then imperiled through its abandonment by Yahweh and its destruction in 587 BC. And its choice by Yahweh will be the basis of hopes for the future when he seems to be ignoring its needs (Zech 1:17; 2:12[16]; also 3:2)

The puzzling account of its capture (2 Sam 5:6–8) includes the report that the Jebusites had told David he would not get into the city because "the blind and the disabled will turn you back." David had then challenged his men to find a way to take the city. He disdainfully described "the blind and the disabled" as people "he dismisses" or as people who "dismiss him" (the participle can be understood either way). The verb (śānēʾ) is usually translated "hate," but like its antonym "love" it suggests more an attitude and commitment than an emotion. Were the Jebusites simply saying that even blind or disabled people could hold the city? But the narrative then adds, "so that's why people say, 'someone blind or disabled will not come into the house.'"

Now the Torah says that the blind and disabled cannot be priests (Lev 21:18). Is the "house" the temple that will eventually be built here? Or is it the "house" whose building the narrative goes on to relate (2 Sam 5:11)? In the context, part of the background to this question lies in another puzzle. Just before its account of the capture of the city, the narrative introduced us to Saul's grand-son, Jonathan's son, Mephiboshet (4:4),[32] who had "become dis-abled" through a fall. The puzzle is why the narrative mentioned Mephiboshet at that point; the subsequent references to the blind and disabled provide a clue. Can someone like Mephiboshet not be king because he is disabled? The story might also link with the only other reference to blindness in Joshua–Kings, in 2 Kings 25:7, when Zedekiah loses the throne and is blinded.[33]

We await more clarification, which comes when David wants to know if there is anyone still alive from Saul's household (9:1–13). One could, as usual, ask whether politics lies behind David's ques-tion and behind the action he goes on to take. If so, what follows suggests it might be possible for "compassion to co-exist with political expediency."[34] David actually asks whether there is any-one to whom for Jonathan's sake he should show "commitment." That word (*ḥesed*) combines the implications of love and loyalty, of grace and faithfulness. Like grace, it suggests a generosity or willingness or dedication that emerges from the heart of the per-son who shows it, rather than being deserved by the person who receives it. And like faithfulness, it suggests an unwavering stead-fastness and consistency, one that persists even if the other per-son forfeits any right to it. The word comes more in Samuel than any other book in the First Testament apart from Psalms, and it occurs three times in 9:1–13. It also came three times in the story of David and Mephiboshet's father, where Jonathan got David

---

[32] The name looks like a contracted from of *mippî bōšet*, "Out of the Mouth of Shame"; contrast *mippî yhwh* in Jer 23:16 (cf. McCarter, *II Samuel*, 439). In 1 Chr 8:34; 9:40 he is Merib-baal or Meri-baal, "The Master Contends" or "He Contends with the Master" or "Rebellion of the Master."

[33] Anthony R. Ceresko, "The Identity of 'the Blind and the Lame' ('iwwēr ûpissēaḥ) in 2 Samuel 5:8b," *CBQ* 63 (2001): 23–30.

[34] Birch, "The First and Second Books of Samuel," in his reflection on 9:1–13.

to promise to maintain a commitment to Jonathan's household, even if Jonathan were dead and even if Yahweh had wiped out all David's enemies and therefore David no longer needed to keep his commitments (1 Sam 20:14–17).

David now lets Jonathan cash his check postmortem. David summons Mephiboshet from the place where he is staying, across the Jordan. Mephiboshet bows right down, which might be difficult for him, and calls himself not only David's servant but also a dead dog. He will know that anyone associated with his father tends to end up deceased. But David passes on Saul's assets to Mephiboshet via a surviving member of Saul's staff, Ziba, while insisting that Mephiboshet should eat at David's table in Jerusalem. The last line in the chapter notes again that he was disabled; 2 Samuel 5:8 "echoes in the background."[35] Whatever those puzzling phrases in 2 Samuel 5:6–8 meant, they do not denote that David dismisses a disabled person or that a disabled person dismisses David or that a disabled person cannot come into the house. (There will be more foreground in 2 Sam 16 and 19.)

DYNASTY: DAVID'S PROMISE AND PRAYER

Meanwhile, Yahweh has spoken of David's house(hold) in another connection.

> Yahweh will make a house(hold) for you. When your days are full and you lie down with your ancestors, I will set up your off-spring after you, who will come out from inside you, and I will establish his kingship. He is the one who will build a house for my name. I will establish his royal throne for all time. I myself will become a father to him and he will become a son to me. When he goes wrong, I will reprove him with a club in the hand

---

[35] Morrison, 2 *Samuel*, 84.

of human beings, with the blows of human hands, but my commitment will not depart from him as I removed it from Saul, whom I removed from before you. Your household and your kingship will be trustworthy before you for all time. Your throne will be established for all time. (7:11–16)

Britain has the "the House of Windsor," Spain has "the House of Borbón," the Netherlands has "the House of Orange-Nassau." A "house" is a dynasty. Dynastic monarchy was a regular feature of Middle Eastern states, and Saul had thus once expected that Jonathan would succeed him; Abner had then presumed that Ish-boshet should do so. David had not assumed that it would be that way in Israel. He knew that Yahweh had designated him as king, even though he had no direct familial links with Saul. He almost gained a link through a marriage to Merab and he temporarily gained one through a marriage to Michal, which might have helped politically insofar as people made that dynastic assumption. Here Yahweh declares that he himself will make a household for David. It is an odd promise in a way, in that David already has a substantial household, but here the word "house" suggests "dynasty." Yahweh will set up his offspring, his physical son; that is, establish him in a position of authority. Initially, Yahweh's words simply suggest a reference to David's own successor, who we know was Solomon. He would already have become king by the time the earliest version of this promise was put into writing. Maybe his time was already past. The promise that he will build the material house that David desired further makes clear that Solomon brings this promise's fulfillment.

The promise is that this successor will have a son–father relationship with Yahweh. Only occasionally does the First Testament speak of Yahweh as father, and it never speaks of an ordinary individual as his son. It does assume that Yahweh relates to Israelites in the manner of a father who has compassion for his children (Ps 103:13), and it expresses regret that people did not call on Yahweh as father (Jer 3:19). The implication is not that the Israelites could not relate to Yahweh with the confidence of children relating to their father. The Psalms make clear that Israelites were freer in their relationship with Yahweh than Christians may be in relation to their earthly father or their heavenly father. But the First Testament does not use that image to convey this reality. It does speak of a father–son relationship between Yahweh and the king in passages where the point is that a son is heir to his father's beneficence (Pss 2:7–8; 89:26–27[27–28]), which might be part of the point in 2 Samuel 7:12–14. More explicit is the link between fatherhood and chastisement,[36] a significant feature of references to fathers and sons in Proverbs. Fathers discipline their children. Fatherhood denotes authority, and sonship denotes obedience (e.g., Matt 21:28–31). Yahweh's promise, then, is that he will discipline this son, but he will not cast him off. He will be like the prodigal father (Luke 15:11–32).

In light of the observation in Hebrews 1:5 that God never said to an angel, "I will be his Father and he will be my Son," Martin Luther declares that this promise in 2 Samuel 7:14 refers to "Christ alone."[37] Tertullian comments, "if you explain this simply of Solomon, you will send me into a fit of laughter," apparently because it makes David sound like a woman giving birth,[38] though David uses the same language of Absalom as his son (16:11). Actually, Hebrews 1:5 does not quite say that 2 Samuel 7:14a is a

---

[36] Anderson, 2 Samuel, 122.

[37] Lectures on Titus, Philemon, and Hebrews (St. Louis, MO: Concordia, 1968), 114 (cf. Cooper and Lohrmann, 1–2 Samuel, 1–2 Kings, 1–2 Chronicles, 176).

[38] Against Marcion, Book III, 20 (cf. Franke, Joshua, Judges, Ruth, 1–2 Samuel, 351).

prophecy of which Jesus is the fulfillment, and the New Testament nowhere else refers to the passage. If it did, Menno Simons has the better of the argument in noting that the whole promise cannot refer to Jesus, because it envisages sin on the part of David's son. Indeed, he comments,

> that this is spoken of Solomon literally, he himself testifies in plain words. (I Kings 3:6; 8:20). Solomon, without doubt, represented in figure Christ Jesus, as in His glory, wisdom, building of the temple, etc. You see, very dear sirs, we should not take the letter for the spirit, and the spirit for the letter. But that the promise according to the Spirit had reference to Christ is incontrovertible; for this the holy prophets of God plainly show.[39]

He refers to Isaiah 9:6[5]; Jeremiah 23:5; 33:15.

The antithesis of letter and spirit does not work very well, but we can begin recasting Menno's point by noting that the framework of Yahweh's promises is long term. They speak of a name, of a "place" for Israel, of freedom from foes, and of a continuing dynasty. They use the expression "for all time" (*'ad-'ôlām*) on three occasions; it comes at five more points in 2 Samuel 7 (and 1 Chr 17), more times than any other chapter in the First Testament apart from the exceptional Psalms 119 and 136. And Psalm 2 assumes that the father–son relationship applies to "his anointed," to "my king," whoever it is at any particular moment. Psalm 89 is more specific, in appealing to Yahweh's pledge that he would establish David's offspring for all time and not let his commitment depart from his sons even though he would chastise them if they abandoned his teaching; it therefore protests that he has gone back on his covenant or pledge (*bərît*, the word that does not occur in 2 Sam 7).

---

[39] "Brief Confession on the Incarnation 1544," in *The Complete Writings of Menno Simons* (Scottdale, PA: Herald, 1986), 419–54 (436) (cf. Cooper and Lohrmann, *1–2 Samuel, 1–2 Kings, 1–2 Chronicles*, 177).

On their arrival at Sinai, Yahweh had said to the Israelites, "If you really listen to my voice and keep my pledge, you will be for me personal treasure from among all the peoples" (Exod 19:5). It has been suggested that Yahweh's words to David now bring to an end the time when Yahweh's commitment to Israel is governed by such an "if."[40] On this understanding, 2 Samuel 7 marks a transition "from law to grace." Up to now "God's relationship with Israel was a *conditional* relationship in which God was faithful, but his blessings were dependent on Israel's obedience."[41] Here Yahweh makes "an *unconditional* promise of undeserved grace."[42]

But there are several problems with this view. First, Yahweh's relationship with Israel was based on grace from the beginning of Israel's story as the First Testament tells it. Yahweh's promises to Abraham (Gen 12:1–3) were not based on law or on obedience; they came out of the blue. The "if" in Exodus 19:5 has something preceding it, the reminder that "You yourselves saw what I did to Egypt. I lifted you on eagles' wings and brought you to me. So now...." (Exod 19:4–5). The Israelites did not escape from Egypt on the basis of fulfilling an "if."

Second, on the other hand an "if" continues to be intrinsic to God's relationship with his people in both Testaments. If you forgive other people, you get forgiven (Matt 6:14–15). If you keep my commands, you will remain in my love (John 15:10). There is no difference in God's way of relating to his people before David, after David in the First Testament, or in the New Testament. The language of "conditional/unconditional" does not appear in the Scriptures, but in terms of this framework, one might say that God's relationship with his people is unconditioned (it did not

[40] Brueggemann, *First and Second Samuel*, 257.
[41] Cartledge, *1 & 2 Samuel*, 458.
[42] Cartledge, *1 & 2 Samuel*, 459.

come about because they fulfilled conditions), but it is conditional (its continuance depends on their keeping up their commitment, as God keeps up his). Even that way of putting it makes the matter more quasi-legal than it is. God's relationship with his people is covenantal rather than contractual. It is at this point that English is fortunate to have the two expressions that spell out possible implications of the Hebrew word *bərît*. A covenant is a relationship like the mutual commitment of David and Jonathan, a solemnly expressed and formally ratified pledge to which the two parties promise to be faithful. It is not a legal concordat with sanctions that can be the subject of a court case, but a personal bond that nevertheless carries at least as much weight. In Western thinking, marriage is a covenant of this kind, though it is also a legal bond. When two people marry, they do not say "I will marry you on condition that you do the following...." Yet their marrying does presuppose that they are making a binding mutual commitment. Such is the relationship between God and his people before David, after David, and in the New Testament. It is not a contract.

Third, while both the priority of grace and the necessity of obedience are intrinsic to the covenant between God and his people, one or other may need more emphasis in different contexts. Genesis emphasizes grace, Exodus (and even more Deuteronomy) the need for obedience. Romans emphasizes grace, James the need for obedience. So Yahweh's message to David might have marked this time as one when grace needs the emphasis. But that possibility is not the implication of Yahweh's words. Yahweh does not draw a contrast between Sinai and Zion or between Moses and David. He draws a contrast between Saul and David – or rather between his commitment to Saul and his commitment to David. His promise reworks and nuances the message of Samuel (1 Sam 13:13–14; and even more 15:28–29). He had chosen Saul out of his grace, not because he had deserved it through his obedience, but he had subsequently rebuffed him because of his disobedience. He had transferred his allegiance to David but he would not change his mind about David, even though he no more deserved it because of his obedience than Saul did. And persisting with David will no more reflect David's deserving. Maybe Yahweh has let the negative point about kingship be demonstrated through Saul and needs now to let the arrangement continue. He will thus operate on the basis of mercy and grace to Israel and to David, and maintain his commitment not to change his mind about David by not abandoning his son as he abandoned Saul. Solomon's story will prove the point: Like David, Solomon is more wayward than Saul, but he gets away with it.

In what sense that commitment is to hold "for all time" is not clear. The future will continue to see interaction between Yahweh's will and the religious and moral stupidity of kings and people. For four centuries, descendants of David will reign in Jerusalem, which at least avoids most of the assassinating and deposing that goes on in Ephraim. But after Solomon their realm will become pathetically smaller, and yet smaller over the centuries until the last Davidic king flees the city to be made blind, in 587 BC. Yahweh does promise that this calamity will not be the end of the story (e.g., Jer 23:5–6), and as a descendant of David, Zerubbabel governs Jerusalem under the Persians. Subsequently, Hasmonean kings reign there after Jerusalem sees off Antiochus Epiphanes, but they were not descendants of David, and no descendant of David sits on the throne in Jerusalem ever again. Jesus ben Joseph reigns there metaphorically, but he is not very enthusiastic about being designated as the anointed of Yahweh who was to come (e.g., Luke 7:18–23; 9:18–22). Some Jews and Christians believe that in due course God will fulfil his promise to David and a descendant of David will reign as anointed king in Jerusalem, but after

2,500 years or so it is questionable whether such an event could count as the fulfillment of a promise made "for all time."

Actually, it had already become clear in 1 Samuel 2:30 that "for all time" (*'ad-'ôlām*) might not mean "forever." One way or another, Yahweh evidently did change his mind about his promise to David's household, as he did about the promise to Eli's household. Perhaps "for all time" always presupposes "until there is reason for me to stop." The general poor effectiveness of the Davidic monarchy over the centuries might provide reason. Perhaps Yahweh presupposes "until I decide to try something better," which would fit with Jesus's comments. The symbolic significance of David and of the idea of being the anointed one would mean that Jesus could hardly say "I'm not the anointed one," but the literal implications of the idea would also give a misleading impression. So Jesus avoids the question. For parallel reasons, it was both appropriate for his followers to declare, "he is the anointed one" and to say, "but there are other things to say about him that are more important." Maybe it is therefore useful that "Christ" came to be more of a name than a reminder of David.

Such considerations lie outside the framework of 2 Samuel 7. Within its framework, what follows is a prayer of David's in which he first expresses wonder at the contrast between who he is and who Yahweh is and what Yahweh has done with Israel.

> Thus you are great, Lord Yahweh, because there is no one like you, no God except you, in all that we have heard with our ears. And who is like your people, like Israel, a nation on the earth that God went to redeem for himself as a people, to make for himself a name, and to do big and awe-inspiring things (for you all) for your country, before your people whom you redeemed for yourself from Egypt (nations and their gods). You established your people Israel for yourself as a people for all time, and you Yahweh became God for them. (7:22–24)

He then goes on to urge Yahweh indeed to do as he says. Why does David so urge Yahweh?

> When, therefore, we pray to God, it is not that we are doubting whether he is already inclined to do us good; or whether he watches out to support us in all our necessities; or whether he knows them well; or that when he has spoken, he does not want to carry out his Word. Rather, the fact is that our faith ought to be exercised, and that God, in offering us his mercy and grace, invites us to have the boldness to call on him (Eph 2:18).[43]

David assumes that God's promises do not make prayer unnecessary. They make prayer possible.

DEFENSE: DAVID'S WAR-MAKING

Describing one's military as defense forces is a euphemism, but the war-making in 2 Samuel does start as defensive (5:17–25). The Philistines might have been fine with David reigning over Judah in Hebron, where he could have been vaguely their underling or client. His being crowned king over wider Israel would be different, especially with a capital just up the valley from their heartland. So they invade. It is the kind of occasion when David inquires of Yahweh. Inquiring via the chasuble (see Chapter 2, on "Ministry") can generate only a yes or no, as it does on the occasion of the first incursion (5:17–21). On the occasion of the second, David gets a battle plan (5:22–25), which suggests he receives a word from Yahweh via a priest or prophet. He will hear the sound of marching in the treetops, the message says, which perhaps implies a rustling that is a sign that Yahweh's forces are on the march.

---

[43] John Calvin, *Sermons on 2 Samuel* 1:387, as quoted in Cooper and Lohrmann, *1–2 Samuel, 1–2 Kings, 1–2 Chronicles*, 180.

Further collections of battle reports (8:1–14; 10:1–19; 12:26–31) recount further victories over the Philistines, Moabites, Arameans, and Ammonites. The reports follow a description of Yahweh having settled David down in his house, untroubled by enemies all around (7:1), but that description looks like an oversimplification, as it has been in other contexts (see Josh 22:4; 23:1). There is more settling with enemies that needs doing,[44] and/or this sequence provides a particularly clear example of the chapters following a dramatic rather than chronological order. Indeed, the narrative later reports more conflicts with the Philistines (2 Sam 21:15–22), when David's men discourage him from getting involved because they do not want to risk the quenching of Israel's "light" (*nēr*; cf. *nîr* in 1 Kgs 11:36; 15:4; 2 Kgs 8:19). Maybe they are afraid David is past it. Even in his heyday he apparently starts leaving the fighting to Joab (2 Sam 11:1), and Samuel almost closes with a list of other warriors, through some of whom "Yahweh brought about a great deliverance" (23:10, 12).

As a result of his accomplishments, David becomes the dominant power between Egypt and Mesopotamia. It is a time of Egyptian weakness during the Twenty-First Dynasty, but his achievement is astonishing. The battles are evidently not just defensive wars like his earlier battles with the Philistines, nor wars undertaken to protect other people who were under attack, like Saul's attack on the Ammonites, nor wars to put down Yahweh's enemies, like Saul's attack on the Amalekites. They include expansionist wars and wars of redress. They fulfill political aims, foster national pride, create an international reputation for David, establish a small empire, and they will bring economic gains; David paid for the materials in 5:11–12 somehow. He also dedicated (*qādaš* hiphil) a substantial

---

[44] Gilmour, *Representing the Past*, 77–78.

amount of the spoils to Yahweh, which might contribute to the cost of offerings in the tent sanctuary and in due course to the building of the temple. Those ends were achieved with the accompaniment of cruelty to animals and inhumane treatment of prisoners (8:1–8).[45] There was no inquiring of Yahweh before these campaigns, though there was a prayer by Joab, who has not struck one as the praying type (10:12).[46] But in these ventures, "Yahweh delivered David wherever he went" (8:6, 14). The victories do not imply a recognition of David's faithfulness; Yahweh was often delivering Israel in Judges when the people were not faithful.[47] But once again, there is a synergy of human activity and divine activity in what happens. The achievements would not come about without David's activity; they would not come about without Yahweh's activity. They resemble the conceiving and birthing of a child.

Modern readers of the David story may be inclined to contrast his military activity with the imperative to love one's enemies. Yet David recognizes the obligation to love one's enemies; he does so in relation to Saul and to Shimei (16:5–14). Conversely, the Jesus who tells people to love their enemies (Matt 5:44) also looks forward to repaying everyone for what they have done (Matt 16:27; cf. Rom 2:6–11; Rev 22:12) as well as to arranging the eternal punishment of people who have not looked after his brothers and sisters (Matt 25:31–46). Can we resolve the tension between these two stances?

One aspect of the teasing out lies in noting the difference between people who act with enmity to us and people who act wrongly towards other people, between enemies within our own family or people and enemies within other families or peoples, between

---

[45] Anderson, 2 Samuel, 134.
[46] Cartledge, 1 & 2 Samuel, 493–94.
[47] Polzin, David and the Deuteronomist, 91.

personal enemies and national enemies, or between individuals and nations. Paul speaks of not taking redress from one's enemies but rather feeding them (Rom 12:19–20), picking up from Proverbs (20:22; 25:21–22), but he goes on to note that it is the imperial authorities' job to wield weapons that will execute wrath on wrongdoers (Rom 13:1–4). While it may require extravagant courage and hope to tell individuals to love their enemies, it may require even more unreasonable courage and hope to tell nations to do so.[48]

That consideration offers a clue to the difference in scriptural attitudes to questions about national violence and questions about individual violence. Israel gets into trouble in Samuel for wanting a central government, but one should be sympathetic to the dilemma they feel. Surviving and succeeding in their relationships with other nations worked fine when Yahweh was killing Egyptian children, drowning the Egyptian army, and making the walls of Jericho collapse, but such intervention was not Yahweh's regular way of operating. More usually, the Israelites had to fight their battles. Sometimes people pray and God does something miraculous; sometimes he enables an infertile woman to get pregnant; sometimes he resuscitates someone who has died. More often, he lets matters in the world unfold on the basis of the dynamics he wrote into the world when creating it and on the basis of his making humanity responsible for the world. And the way nations relate to each other is the way they do when someone like David is their leader. Yahweh brings up the Philistines from Caphtor and the Syrians from Qir (Amos 9:7); but they get there by fighting. It is in the same way that the Israelites gained initial possession of Canaan, and David completes that possession.

---

[48] See Reinhold Niebuhr, *Moral Man and Immoral Society: A Study in Ethics and Politics* (New York: Scribner's, 1932).

The First Testament story recognizes that this process does not work well. The story that reaches a high point in Samuel and in the opening chapters of Kings marches steadily downhill until both Ish-boshet's Israel and David's Judah lose their national existence and never regain it within the First Testament. Within the story in Kings, Israel and Judah come under the control of bigger empires and stay that way. The visions in Daniel note how directionless is these empires' history, and the New Testament does not give the impression that things change with the transition from the Assyrian, Babylonian, Persian, and Greek Empires to the Roman Empire. Nor have things progressed under succeeding imperial powers. Working with the people of God as a nation turned out not to work in the First Testament. The New Testament does not show much indication of a different perspective, notwithstanding Luke 1:53–55, 68–75; Acts 1:6–8, which prove the rule as they reaffirm some such hopes but give no indication that the hopes lead anywhere. David is the highpoint of an experiment whereby Yahweh engages in history with his usual energy that holds nothing back, and demonstrates that this experiment fails. The monarchy eventually ceases to exist, and so does Israel as a nation.

David pays a price for being used in this way. Given the job that he wanted to be undertaken, Yahweh knew what he was doing when he chose David. He chose someone with a trust in Yahweh and a killer instinct, a person who would advocate for the saving power of the God of Israel and then not only put Goliath to death but cut his head off and take it to Jerusalem. What David advertised himself to be as a child soldier remained his way of operating and being over a decade or two or three.[49] He surely did pay a price. It is possible that Saul was a morally injured and

---

[49] David A. Bosworth, "David, Jether, and Child Soldiers," *JSOT* 36 (2011): 185–97.

traumatized person.[50] It must be the case that David would be. People come back from battle traumatized, and David has more battle experience than most. How could he not be injured by what he has done? Is it significant that he now gives up leading Israel into war (2 Sam 11:1; 12:26–31)? It is hardly surprising that the peak of his story as king is also the beginning of the story of his own moral folly. He not only commits adultery, as many leaders do, but arranges for Uriah's killing, an action comparable to those of some other leaders ("history books are full of many other murderous adulterers").[51] His heroic masculinity unravels.[52]

So the story of David's warmaking is the peak of his story as a leader and of Israel's story as a nation, and it marks the beginning of the downfall of both. The twofold story invites twenty-first-century nations to a realism about our national lives and our warmaking, and about the wars from which we have prospered. Britain and the United States, for instance, enjoy the life that we do because we created empires and annihilated native peoples. The story might also encourage a more serious acceptance of an obligation to give resources for the healing of the trauma of the people who fight for us.[53]

SANCTUARY: DAVID'S TEMPLE

Whereas Saul had apparently not thought of bringing the meeting tent and the covenant chest to Gibeah to consolidate its position

---

[50] See the sections on "Saul Desperately Seeking" in Chapter 5.
[51] So the seventeenth-century Venetian nun Arcangela Tarabotti, *Paternal Tyranny* (Chicago, IL: University of Chicago Press, 2004), 112.
[52] Sara M. Koenig, "Make War Not Love: The Limits of David's Hegemonic Masculinity in 2 Samuel 10–12, *BibInt* 23 (2015): 489–517.
[53] On the broad question with consideration of Saul, David, and Uriah, see Jan Grimell, "To Understand and Support Contemporary Veterans Utilizing Biblical Combat Veteran Types," *Journal of Pastoral Care & Counseling* 72 (2018): 232–40.

as the nation's center, David makes this move. The account of his establishment as king reaches a further high point with the inter-related narratives of his bringing the covenant chest to Jerusalem and his proposition concerning the building of a temple there. While both initiatives may have a political side, like everything he does, and while both initiatives relate to worship, both also move in the realm of symbolism, and both relate to the reality of Yahweh's presence in the city.

"Presence" is a rich and complex idea. In English translations, "presence" commonly renders the word for "face" (*pānîm*). When you are in someone's presence, you see their face. Further, the English word "before" translates the Hebrew expression "to the face of." At the sanctuary Hannah was praying "to the face/presence of Yahweh," and Samuel ministered there to his face/presence (e.g., 1 Sam 1:12, 15, 19, 22; 2:11, 18; 3:1). The same expression can be used of situations outside the sanctuary. Abraham stood to the face/presence of Yahweh at Mamre (Gen 18:22; 19:27), and his servant bowed to his face/presence in Laban's house (24:52). Statements about Yahweh being "with" David also indicate his dynamic and active presence.

But most references to Yahweh's face or presence denote the reality of his presence in the sanctuary; he has committed himself to being there. David dancing "before" Yahweh (2 Sam 6:5, 14, 16, 21) proves the rule: He is not in the sanctuary, but he is dancing before the covenant chest. People know that they can go and see Yahweh in the sanctuary, ask him things, thank him for things, and honor him there. In a sense, it is odd to speak of the face and presence of Yahweh in this way. The language more literally fits a deity who has an image, with a face that one can see. Yet Israel knows that Yahweh metaphorically but really has a face that looks at people and smiles at them, as he metaphorically but really has eyes, ears, mouths, noses, hands, and feet that work, in the way that those of other so-called deities do not (Pss 115:5–7; 135:16–17). In English we can speak of a blind person going to "see" someone; "sight" becomes a metaphor, but it denotes a reality of being in the person's presence.

The question of the origin and history of the sanctuary where the covenant chest resided is convoluted, but the Samuel narrative presupposes that Yahweh had commissioned its construction and undertaken to be invisibly but really present above the covenant chest there, between or above the two griffin-like statues. While Samuel mostly refrains from using the image of covenant to describe the relationship of Yahweh and Israel, it frequently refers to the covenant chest containing the rocks inscribed with the Decalogue, the basic covenant obligation that Yahweh laid upon Israel at Sinai in light of his deliverance of the people from servitude to Egypt (cf. 1 Kgs 8:21).

Israel had managed without the chest for a decade or two or three since its depositing at Qiryat-yeʿarim/Baʿalê yəhûdâ. The people had been able to gather "in the presence of Yahweh" in sanctuaries other than Shiloh (e.g., 1 Sam 7:5–6; 10:17–25; 11:14–15; 12:7). Maybe the dominance of the Philistines, controlling the Geba/Gibeon area (2 Sam 5:22–25) would have made retrieving it problematic (6:11 notes that Obed-edom from Gat, who is presumably therefore a Philistine, is still there). The vivid poetic account of the chest's retrieval in Psalm 132 almost suggests that no one could remember where it was. The psalm may link with an annual celebration of the retrieval, and the story in 2 Samuel 6 might link with it too. Victory over the Philistines perhaps now opens up the possibility of the chest's retrieval,[54] and the new context of David's settling in

---

[54] McCarter, *II Samuel*, 159–60, 168.

Jerusalem makes the retrieval desirable. Recovering it will establish a link between exodus, Sinai, Jerusalem, and (in due course) temple. It will be a political act, a religious act, and a theological act. Whereas the city is something new, the covenant chest will give it a link with the old. Jerusalem will succeed Shiloh, though it will not (yet) become the only legitimate sanctuary; Solomon will go to Gibeon, described as "the biggest shrine" (1 Kgs 3:4).

David has a tent ready for the chest (2 Sam 6:17). It is the first allusion to a sanctuary tent since the reference to the one at Shiloh (1 Sam 2:22). It is not clear whether it counts as "the meeting tent" (see 1 Kgs 1:39; 2:28–30; 8:4; 2 Chr 1:3–6, 13; 5:5). The title "Yahweh [of] Armies" (2 Sam 6:2) also makes the connection with the covenant chest and Shiloh (1 Sam 1:3, 11; 4:4). David's leading the procession dressed in a linen chasuble makes another link with Shiloh; Samuel wore one there (1 Sam 2:18; cf. 22:18). It was common Israelite practice to take over Canaanite sanctuaries and transfer them to Yahweh's service; it happened to sanctuaries such as Bethel. So it would make sense if the place where David puts the tent for the chest is the site of the Jebusite sanctuary in whose context David would be priest-king "after the manner of Melchizedek" (Ps 110:4).[55]

There is some overlap between the celebratory liturgical bringing in of the chest and the ritual for inaugurating temples, palaces, and cities that is recorded in some Assyrian inscriptions from the time of kings such as Sargon II, Sennacherib, and Esarhaddon.[56]

---

[55] And where Nathan and Zadoq had once ministered? (so, e.g., Gwilym H. Jones, *The Nathan Narratives*, JSOTSup 80 [Sheffield: Sheffield Academic Press, 1990]).

[56] Victor A. Hurowitz, "The Inauguration of Palaces and Temples in the Assyrian Royal Inscriptions," *Orient* 29 (2014): 89–105; cf. David Toshio Tsumura, *The Second Book of Samuel*, NICOT (Grand Rapids, MI: Eerdmans, 2019), 83.

But things go wrong when the chest threatens to fall off its wagon, Uzzah reaches out to steady it, and Yahweh angrily strikes him dead. The narrative offers no explanation for the anger that this event generates. As Qohelet again notes, sometimes we do not know why Yahweh brings disaster to people. What happens recalls the calamity the chest brought at Bet-shemesh, as well as among the Philistines. It implies a warning about the chest's dangerous nature; one might take Exodus 19:21–24 as an anticipatory commentary on the event. It reminds people (as the New Testament puts it) how dangerous it is to fall into the living God's hands (Heb 10:31). But the narrative focuses more on David's responsive anger (it uses the same expression of him as of Yahweh, but it does not indicate the object of his anger), his responsive fear or awe in relation to Yahweh, and his decision to leave the chest where it is in the care of Obed-edom. "In view of the circumstances it is doubtful that Obed-edom was overjoyed to receive the custody of the awesome ark."[57]

Whereas the chest's time with the Philistines brought trouble on them following their desecration of it, here the chest's time with another Philistine, following the Israelites' desecration of it, brings blessing on him, which encourages David to complete the project. Further dancing and rejoicing follow, more enthusiastic than the first time, perhaps more like cartwheeling or acrobatics.[58] People are dancing before the Ten Commandments![59] David in particular manifests himself full of life on this second attempt at the retrieval (though his whirling is the lead in to the Michal

---

[57] Anderson, 2 Samuel, 104–5.
[58] Sarah Schulz, "The Dancing David: Nudity and Cult in 2 Sam. 6," in Christoph Berner et al., eds., Clothing and Nudity in the Hebrew Bible (London: T&T Clark, 2019), 461–76 (467–69).
[59] Barron, 2 Samuel, 59–60.

scene).[60] "He was a Palestinian, I confess, from a people that is more emotional and unrestrained than our European people."[61] While Irenaeus did not quite say (as he has been quoted) that "the glory of God is a human being fully alive,"[62] the story does enthuse over someone being full of life in worshiping God – not just David but everyone. The sacrifices offered on the way continue in the tent: Like most First Testament sacrifices, they are not offerings for sin but expressions of commitment (whole offerings) and of a joy shared between God and people ("well-being" or "fellowship" offerings).

So the covenant chest brings a new representation of Yahweh's presence to Jerusalem. David has been able to inquire of Yahweh before (2 Sam 2:1) and Yahweh has been with David before (5:10). Now David can come in and "stay" in Yahweh's presence in this sanctuary (7:18; in other contexts one would take *yāšab* to mean "sit," but there are no other references to sitting in Yahweh's presence, and the verb means "stay" or "live" in 7:1, 2, 5, 6).

And now David wants to build Yahweh a proper house rather than having him live in a home that is made only of "curtaining" (*yərʿîâ*, 7:2). The Shiloh sanctuary was already described as both a house and a palace, and it had a doorpost and doors (1 Sam 1:7, 9; 3:3, 15), but evidently David has in mind something more substantial and impressive. He himself has a palace after all, and building a temple for the deity is something else that kings do.

---

[60] See the section on "Family" earlier in this chapter.

[61] Martin Bucer, *De regno Christi Iesu seruatoris nostri: Libri II* (Basel: Oporinus, 1557), 207, as translated in Cooper and Lohrmann, *1–2 Samuel, 1–2 Kings, 1–2 Chronicles*, 171.

[62] Irenaeus, *Against Heresies* Book Four, 20:7; cf. Barron, *2 Samuel*, 64. Irenaeus actually says, "The glory of God is a living human being, and a living human being consists in beholding God."

The prophet Nathan (who appears for the first time, out of the blue) recognizes that it is wise to affirm the king's bright ideas. He then experiences Yahweh tapping him on the shoulder during the night to ask whether he himself might be allowed an opinion on the king's idea. He is, after all, the one who will have to live in this house. "Even when directed by God's prophet ... the king could still act against his and Israel's best interests."[63] Traditional critical theory sees the simultaneously entertaining and frightening aspect to this story as the result of Deuteronomistic redaction. If it is, it brings credit to the redactors.

Yahweh raises a number of questions with David about the project. First, "Are *you* the one to build a house for me, for my living in?" (2 Sam 7:5). Although the narrative does not wholly follow a chronological order, even on its order there are battles ahead (8:1–14; 10:1–12:31) as well as behind (5:17–25).[64] The Chronicles theory that David cannot build the temple because he is too busy shedding his enemies' blood (1 Chr 22:8; 28:3) is not far wrong.[65] Yahweh will give David relief, but the time has not yet come (2 Sam 7:11). It is David's son who will build the house "for my name" (7:13; cf. 1 Kgs 5:3–5[17–19]). That expression recurs in the account of the temple dedication in 1 Kings 8–9, where it picks up from Deuteronomy 12–16. It does not otherwise appear in Samuel, and even here the idea of the name "dwelling" does not feature. The expression is thus not as technical as it is elsewhere. It is one of a number of images by which one may speak of God's presence. When Christians mutter the name "Jesus," especially in the "Jesus Prayer," the uttering of

---

[63] Polzin, *David and the Deuteronomist*, 74.

[64] McCarter, *II Samuel*, 241, 251.

[65] Cf. Gregory Goswell, "Why Did God Say No to David? (2 Samuel 7)," *JSOT* 43 (2019): 556–70.

the name conveys a sense of the presence. In Israel, the uttering of Yahweh's name in the sanctuary suggests the reality of
Yahweh's presence there; even when there is no one else there,
the name is there, and Yahweh is there. Speaking in terms of
the name being present affirms the reality of that presence, but
takes account of what 2 Samuel 6 has recognized: The actual
presence of God could be so electric or so nuclear that no one
could survive it.

Second, regarding "a house for me, for my living in," Yahweh
adds: "I have not lived in a house from the day I brought the
Israelites up from Egypt until this day. I have been going about in
a tent-dwelling. Whenever I went about among all the Israelites,
did I speak a word with one of the chiefs ... saying 'Why have
you not built me a house of cedar?'" (7:6–7). Whatever the precise nature of the house at Shiloh, again the assumption is that
it was more like a Bedouin tent than a proper building. And the
narrative in Joshua through Samuel has implied that the meeting tent has been at several places, in continuity with its being
on the move during the Israelites' journey before their arrival
in Canaan. Yahweh has liked it that way. Yahweh's objection
has far-reaching implications. It hints that the temptation of the
people of God is to want to get God to settle down, whereas
he always wants to be on the move. It coheres with the First
Testament narrative's portrayal of the tent sanctuary as preceding the building of the temple. Temple, like kingship, is an
institution that Yahweh will now allow to Israel, but it is not
his preference. When the church turns the word "church" into
a word for a building and builds "sanctuaries," the pattern
continues.

Third, Yahweh says that while David has spoken about building Yahweh a house, "a house is what Yahweh will make for you"

(7:11). In effect, Yahweh says, "I took hold of you, I appointed you, I have been with you wherever you have gone, I intend to give you a great name, and in this relationship I am the one who does the house-making" (7:8–11).[66] The reminder harks back to the process whereby Yahweh took hold of David long ago (1 Sam 16:1–13).

---

[66] See further the section on "Dynasty" earlier in this chapter.

CHAPTER 7

Yahweh Who Watches a King
(2 Samuel 11:1–24:25)

The story of David, Bathsheba, and Uriah, and its immediate after-math, is the great turning point in David's story.[1] "There are not many places in the Bible where a character's reputation is so suddenly and effectively demolished as in 2 Samuel 11." Yet "at the center of the story of David we find something much more akin to the bursting of a bubble than to the relaxed deflation of a balloon. The tragic turn of events that follows chapters 11–12 is but a consequent reverberation of the explosive events of … earlier chapters," 1 Samuel 16–2 Samuel 10. "The success and adulation that have constantly accompanied David up to now were only questioned by the Deuteronomist's subtle hints, which, here or there, helped us to wonder whether there was more – or less – to David than met the eye."[2] Nevertheless what now happens comes as a sudden and ongoing revelation, shock, and horror in different ways to the auditors, and perhaps to David, and perhaps to Yahweh. Yahweh summoned Samuel and commissioned him to anoint Saul, commissioned him to anoint David, made extravagant promises to David, but now declares that he will cause dire events to arise from his household. Then for the most part he simply watches them do so.

---

[1] Alter, *The David Story*, 249.
[2] Polzin, *David and the Deuteronomist*, 117, 119.

DAVID'S VICTIMS

The story of David, Bathsheba, and Uriah links with a number of ways of thinking about ethics. Ethics involves rules; its basic principles are written into human nature; it is tied up with theology; it can find expression in narrative; and it involves personal moral qualities that manifest themselves in actions and are also developed by actions.

Given that ethics involves rules for life, there is some irony in David's installing the covenant chest in Jerusalem. It contained the rocks inscribed with the basic rules of Israelite spirituality and ethics, of relationships with God and with other people. He now ignores at least half of the latter. He has sex with someone else's wife and he has someone murdered; these acts involve him first wanting someone else's wife and then stealing her.

Secondly, in light of the way David ignores an ethic of rules, Nathan's eventual challenge to him has several significant features. Nathan does not quote the rules, as other prophets rarely allude to the Decalogue though they presuppose its expectations. Nathan's parable about the man with big flocks and the man with one sheep implicitly appeals to a sense of right and wrong that David has in his heart and mind, by virtue of being human. His assumptions compare with Paul's in Romans 1–3. But a person can quash this sense of right and wrong, as Paul also implies. It turns them into a foolish and worthless person (*ben bəliyyaʿal*) like Nabal (1 Sam 25:25). David is neither foolish nor wise, but something in between.

In addition, thirdly, Nathan accuses David of despising Yahweh (2 Sam 12:10). If one is to relate David's actions to the ten rules for life, then David has ignored the ones about spirituality and relationship with God as well as the ones about other people. Or rather, Nathan presupposes (like the Decalogue itself) that the two are inextricably linked. Dishonoring one's neighbor is an expression of dishonor to God; we honor God by honoring our neighbor. Ethics and spirituality, relationships with other people and with God, cannot be separated. Ethics is theological; theology is ethical. Nathan also expresses the point in another way, accusing David of despising Yahweh's word (12:9). The charge recalls Samuel's confronting Saul for flouting Yahweh's word of command (1 Sam 15:13, 23, 24, 26), though on that occasion Saul was ignoring a concrete command. It recalls the description of the Decalogue itself as Yahweh's word (Deut 5:5).[3] Closer in implication and nearer to hand is Nathan's own declaring of Yahweh's word of promise concerning what Yahweh intended for David (2 Sam 7:4, 21, 25). In this respect, too, ethics is tied up with spirituality and theology. The point emerges in the forms of expression Yahweh uses: "I am the one who anointed you ... and I am the one who rescued you," but "Uriah the Hittite you struck down with the sword, and his wife you took for yourself as wife, and him you killed" (12:7, 9). The point is implicit in David's acknowledgment that he has "done wrong in relation to Yahweh" (12:13), even if this admission is worrying in its omitting mention of Uriah, Bathsheba, and the other victims of Joab's stratagem.

Fourthly, the principle finds yet earlier expression in the punchline of the preceding chapter: "the thing that David did was dire in Yahweh's eyes" (11:27), "the only unambiguous statement in the narrative."[4] The chapter relating the (un)ethical actions of David is a narrative, and narratives generally "show" rather than "tell." They leave implications, feelings, and motivations unstated. While

---

[3] Auld, I & II Samuel, 466–67.

[4] Gale A. Yee, "'Fraught with Background': Literary Ambiguity in II Samuel 11," Interpretation 42 (1988): 240–53 (244).

the narrative in 11:1–27 thus does finally comment on Yahweh's feelings about the events, it leaves ambiguous the feelings of the people involved.[5] Why does David stay behind in Jerusalem? Why does he want Bathsheba when he has all those other wives? Is something political going on?[6] What does Bathsheba feel about David's summons, their sexual relationship, and her pregnancy?[7] What do David's staff think? What does Uriah think, and what is his motivation in his response to David, and what is the significance of his being repeatedly labeled a Hittite?[8] What does Joab think about the task required of him? What does Bathsheba think about Uriah's death ("mourning" denotes simply the formal process) and about her marriage to David and her baby's death? Why does Yahweh stay uninvolved until he sends Nathan? Interpretations of the story give a variety of plausible answers to these questions that reflect the perspectives of the interpreters (e.g., feminist, postcolonial). Their variety underscores the story's inherent ambiguity. This ambiguity is an aspect of its ethical significance. Not knowing the answers to those questions means finding ourselves in the

[5] See Menahem Perry and Meir Sternberg, "The King through Ironic Eyes: Biblical Narrative and the Literary Reading Process," *Poetics Today* 7 (1986): 275–322; cf. Meir Sternberg, *The Poetics of Biblical Narrative: Ideological Literature and the Drama of Reading* (Bloomington: Indiana University Press, 1985); John Ahn, "Murder, Adultery, and Theft," in John Ahn, ed., *Landscapes of Korean and Korean American Biblical Interpretation*, International Voices in Biblical Studies 10 (Atlanta, GA: SBL, 2019), 73–97.

[6] So Randall C. Bailey, *David in Love and War: The Pursuit of Power in 2 Samuel 10–12*, JSOTSup 75 (Sheffield: Sheffield Academic Press, 1990).

[7] See, for example, Lilian R. Klein, "Bathsheba Revealed," in Brenner, *Samuel and Kings, A Feminist Companion to the Bible* (Second Series), 47–64; Winfred Omar Neely, "The Wife of Uriah the Hittite: Political Seductress, Willing Participant, Naive Woman, or #BathshebaToo? The Preacher as Sensitive Theologian," *The Journal of the Evangelical Homiletics Society* 20 (2020): 51–63.

[8] See Uriah Kim, "Uriah the Hittite: A (Con)Text of Struggle for Identity," *Semeia* 90/91 (2002): 69–85.

stories and making ethical judgments about them, which tell us something about ourselves through our reflection on our reading of them, on the interpretation we bring to them, and on the different interpretations offered by other people.

Fifthly, however, the ambiguity about the characters in the story contrasts with a further aspect of its ethical implications. Ethics involves the personal qualities of a community or an individual. Behavior expresses moral character, in virtues and vices. Even where it leaves unclear whether David manifested different qualities, the story implies a positive evaluation of some (and a negative evaluation of their opposites).

- Attentiveness or focus as opposed to lethargy or apathy (11:1–2, 9–13). While David is enjoying a long siesta at home, the covenant chest and the army are on the battlefield. David's attitude contrasts with his earlier discomfort about being at ease (7:1–2) and with the attitude implied by Joab's later exhortation (12:27–28). David "has ceased to be the king requested by Israel who would 'go out before us and fight our battles'" (1 Sam 8:20);[9] indeed, eventually he is "lampooned as a pagan king" (2 Sam 12:26–31).[10]
- Resistance to "fleshly" inclinations as opposed to indulgence of them (11:2–3).
- Using one's power to protect rather than to dominate (11:4, 6–21). Further, idealizing David's "hegemonic masculinity" brings "an ethical cost,"[11] and simply describing his relationship with Bathsheba as adultery understates the significance of the power differential between them.

---

[9] Brueggemann, *First and Second Samuel*, 273.
[10] Smith, *The Fate of Justice and Righteousness During David's Reign*, 141.
[11] Koenig, "Make War Not Love," 517.

- Giving as opposed to taking. With the narrative's took, took, took, took (11:4; 12:4, 9, 10), compare Samuel's take, take, take (1 Sam 8:11–16). "David has become … the king of whom Samuel warned."[12]
- Restraint, in recognition of religious commitments as opposed to ignoring them, in connection with sex (2 Sam 11:4, if she was still purifying herself) and war (11:6–8), since engagement in battle on Yahweh's behalf requires one to abstain from sex (as David knows: 1 Sam 21:5[6]).
- Smartness as opposed to folly (2 Sam 11:4), if Bathsheba's washing implies the completion of her purifying after her period (when she was therefore particularly liable to conceive).[13] Much more significant is the smartness in following what is good in Yahweh's eyes (11:27b).
- Recognition of the ease with which one thing can lead to another (11:6–15). At the beginning David would hardly have been able to imagine where the story would end.
- Resistance to immoral expectations as opposed to obedient implementation of them (11:14–25).
- Authenticity as opposed to cynicism (11:25).[14]
- Gratitude for and recognition of God's giving as opposed to ignoring it and focusing on taking (12:7–8).
- Respect for Yahweh's word as opposed to despising it (12:9).
- Respect for Yahweh as opposed to despising him (12:10). "Arrogance is more basic than adultery. David has become contemptuous of God."[15]

---

[12] Firth, *1 & 2 Samuel*, 418.

[13] Though it may more likely refer to purification after having sex: See Tikva Frymer-Kensky, *Reading the Women of the Bible* (New York: Schocken, 2002), on the passage.

[14] Cf. Brueggemann, *First and Second Samuel*, 277–78.

[15] Green, *David's Capacity for Compassion*, 201, 203.

- Commitment (*ḥesed*) to a person such as Uriah (cf. the appearance of this motif in 9:1, 3, 7; 10:2) as opposed to disdain for his rights and person (12:9–10). "Hierarchically organized power is defined by the powerwielder's capacity to act from a distance."[16]
- Transparency in relationships with one's community as opposed to a secrecy that needs to conceal dishonor (12:12).
- Giving Yahweh's enemies reason to honor Yahweh as opposed to reason for feeling contempt for Yahweh (12:14). "There is no crime deserving of greater guilt than to give to the heathen a reason for blaspheming."[17]

HOW YAHWEH RESPONDS TO DAVID'S WRONGDOING

"David sent Joab ... sent to inquire ... sent aides ... sent to Joab ... sent by the hand of Uriah ... sent and collected" (11:1–27). But then, "Yahweh sent Nathan"(12:1).[18] David may not have tried hard to conceal his affair, but he had kept the second half of the story a secret (12:12). Army gossip had apparently not exposed the truth about how Uriah died. And on earlier occasions David has acted in secret with impunity (1 Sam 19:2; 20:5, 19, 24; 23:19; 26:1). But Yahweh somehow knew the whole of what had happened and did not need to ask David embarrassing questions. It is the second time Yahweh has sent Nathan to see David (see 2 Sam 7:4). Their third meeting (see 1 Kgs 1:11–40) will be different again.[19]

---

[16] Halbertal and Holmes, *The Beginning of Politics*, 82.

[17] Salvian the Presbyter, "The Governance of God," 122 (cf. Franke, *Joshua, Judges, Ruth, 1–2 Samuel*, 366). NRSV and other modern translations think the original reading was "definitely felt contempt for Yahweh"; Rashi (in *miqrā'ôt gədôlôt*) describes MT's expression as a euphemism.

[18] Peterson, *First and Second Samuel*, 182–83.

[19] Auld, *I & II Samuel*, 464.

Nathan's parable has a devastating effect. Part of its force lies in the background of the king's responsibility to oversee the faithful exercise of authority (2 Sam 8:15). The rich man's faithless exercise of power (he "took") needs confronting. So "David the royal judge condemns David the rich oppressor."[20] Yahweh's reaction to David's killing of Uriah sits alongside his apparently not faulting him for executing one in every three of the Moabite military (8:2). Uriah, too, was not an Israelite. Is the reason for the repeated note of his Hittite ethnicity that it gave David an excuse both for appropriating his wife and for having him killed?[21] Yet Uriah was in the Israelite military (indeed, he was one of the elite "Thirty" in 23:39) and his name means "Yahweh is my flame/light"; he was a foreigner who served Yahweh.

Yahweh's strategy worked. When Nathan told the parable, "David's anger flared" (12:5). It is his first expression of feelings. And Nathan condemns him both in respect of Uriah and in respect of Uriah's wife.

> God's reproof of adulterous King David is ample testimony that men deserve greater punishment than women in violating the marriage bed. He said nothing to Bathsheba, who fell on being tempted by the king. Your lying insulting tongues never cease preaching that the *fons et origo* of all fornication and adultery is woman. As they are supposedly cunning and shrewd in hiding their desires, they inveigle men to their dooms with charms and flattery – at least, this is how your evil minds would have it. Many of you are enemies of our sex, and still you know how to go to extremes, without opposition, or any fault on woman's part, in a way that deserves the most burning outbursts of God's anger, since only Heaven's fire is a fitting scourge for them.[22]

---

[20] McCarter, *II Samuel*, 305.

[21] Cf. van Wijk-Bos, *Reading Samuel*, 195.

[22] Tarabotti, Paternal Tyranny, 112; cf. Cooper and Lohrmann, *1–2 Samuel, 1–2 Kings, 1–2 Chronicles*, 203.

Issuing the rebuke implies that Yahweh wants David to recognize his wrongdoing. The pattern follows a regular one in the Prophets, where indictment leads into a "therefore." Perhaps it implies that the recognition will benefit David as a human being. Yahweh's confrontation honors him as a person. It will benefit the readers of Samuel. It will vindicate Yahweh himself in David's eyes and in their eyes. And it will affirm the moral integrity of the way things work out in the world, which can often raise questions (as they will in a moment in this story, at least for Western readers).

Yahweh wants to tell David about the consequences that will follow his wrongdoing (12:10–12). The principle concerning chastisement enunciated to David in connection with Solomon applies to him too. Actually, if the man in Nathan's parable deserves to die (he is a *ben māwet*, a son of death; 12:5), how much more does David (to whom Saul applied that expression in 1 Sam 20:31). But instead of David dying, the dire consequences that will follow from his dire action will affect him by affecting his wives and the rest of his household.

Events will see a "natural" working out. "The sword will not depart from your household for all time." Typically, Yahweh combines that idea with the idea that he himself will act: In response to David's dire deed, Yahweh will take dire action (*ra'*; 2 Sam 12:9, 11). "What do you say to this, you who believe that God does not judge our actions?"[23] There will be some poetic justice about what happens:[24] It will involve sword, wives, and public exposure. There is a moral and theological link between the natural and the deliberate action. The "natural" result will issue from the fact that "you

---

[23] Salvian the Presbyter, "The Governance of God," in *The Writings of Salvian, the Presbyter* (reprinted Washington, DC: Catholic University of America, 2008), 62 (cf. Franke, *Joshua, Judges, Ruth, 1–2 Samuel*, 361).
[24] Cf. Hertzberg, *I & II Samuel*, 314.

despised me." The words about the natural outworking also make for a grievous link with David's offhand comment that "the sword devours this one and that one" (11:25).[25]

David duly acknowledges, "I have done wrong in relation to Yahweh" (*ḥāṭā'tî lyhwh*; 12:13). The verb is traditionally translated "sin," but its implications are more relational than this rendering implies; Samuel uses it about wrongdoing in human relationships (e.g., 1 Sam 2:25; 19:4–5). "Offended" is closer, though that expression could imply merely a point about Yahweh's feelings and not about objective wrongdoing. The stark simplicity of David's words, without excuses and without appeal, emerges more clearly when set alongside the confession in Psalm 51. The two confessions are not incompatible. Either could be uttered in words but not in reality, and linking the two could make for some irony. But for David, "the subsequent history indicates that this moment of self-recognition does not mark any fundamental change."[26]

Meanwhile, Nathan's response is: "Indeed, Yahweh has passed on your wrongdoing – you will not die. Nevertheless, because you definitely made Yahweh's enemies feel contempt through this thing, indeed the son born to you will definitely die" (2 Sam 12:13–14).

"Passed on" or "removed" (*'ābar* hiphil) is an unusual expression, and not a regular term for forgiveness or pardon, though David himself later uses it (24:10). To "forgive" (*nāśā'*) is literally to carry; Saul spoke of Samuel's carrying his wrongdoing (1 Sam 15:25), which would mean absorbing the consequences and not making him carry them. To "pardon" (*sālaḥ*) is a creative, almost miraculous, act whereby a person with proper authority makes a

[25] Cartledge, *1 & 2 Samuel*, 517.
[26] Davis, *Opening Israel's Scriptures*, 191.

wrongdoing effectively cease to exist. The verb Nathan uses can
mean "transfer" (cf. 2 Sam 12:31). Its frightening implication could
be that Yahweh transfers the wrongdoing to David's son along
with its punishment. But the other occasions when the verb relates
to dealing with waywardness (Job 7:21; Zech 3:4) do not suggest
passing it onto someone. Yet on both occasions when David is the
wrongdoer, here and in 2 Samuel 24, taking away the wrongdoing
is accompanied by calamity coming on people other than David.
David does wrong not simply as a private individual but as a father
and a king.

And although the First Testament forbids the punishing of
children instead of their parents (Deut 24:16; Jer 31:29–30; Ezek
18:20), it also speaks of Yahweh "attending to" (*pāqad 'al*) children
as well as their parents in connection with the parents' wrongdoing (Exod 20:5; 34:7; Num 14:18; Deut 5:9; Jer 29:32), or "requiting"
(*šālam* piel) children as well as parents (Jer 32:18). The second kind
of statement may presuppose that the children are adults continuing in their parents' wrongdoing. Yet it may also see children as
"bound up in the bundle of the living" with their parents (1 Sam
25:29), and parents with their children. Emotionally and physically, parents and children are mutually dependent at different
stages of their life. In David's case, it also applies politically.

Here and elsewhere Yahweh recognizes these realities. They are
aspects of the way he created the world and the way he makes it
work. He has already affirmed it in connection with the rest of
David's household, and the ensuing narrative will portray it working out in connection with his children as well as his wives. Tamar
will be raped, Absalom will attempt a coup, and Amnon, Absalom,
and Adonijah will die violently. Bathsheba's child is thus not the
only one who will die as a result of David's wrongdoing bringing trouble on his family and nation. "The violence he had earlier

avoided" in his relationship with Saul "spirals out of control in his own life."[27]

So Yahweh afflicted the child (*nāgap*), as he afflicted Nabal (1 Sam 25:38). The child got ill, in the way that children do, but in a premodern society they often then die. David therefore inquires with God (*bāqaš* piel) concerning the child. The First Testament knows that Yahweh's declarations of intent do not close down conversation with him about a matter, any more than they do for children in relation to parents. "Crying out to God is advantageous for a person both before the issue of a decree and after the issue of a decree" (*b. Rosh Hashanah* 16b). Yahweh can relent of dire trouble he has said he would do, as he did at Sinai. "Who knows" (cf. Joel 2:14; Jonah 3:9) whether Yahweh may be gracious (*ḥānan*; 2 Sam 12:22)? This verb also appears in the Sinai narrative, in a context noting that one cannot know whether Yahweh will act that way: "I decide who to be gracious to," he says (Exod 33:19). So who knows? Prayer means taking the risk of asking for things without knowing whether God will grant them. Like the Sinai narrative, the David story walks around the mystery and complexity of Yahweh's response to his people's waywardness, in the way that narrative can.

David fasted, as one may fast in penitence and prayer (1 Sam 7:5–6), and for some days he would come in (to the sanctuary, the tent he had erected for the covenant chest, in the former Jebusite sanctuary?),[28] stay the night, and lie on the ground (2 Sam 12:16). But after a week the child died. Then David got up, bathed, smartened himself up, changed his clothes, came into Yahweh's house (the same place?), and bowed down there. Then he went home and

---

[27] Birch, "The First and Second Books of Samuel," in his introductory comments to 2 Samuel 11.
[28] See the section on "Sanctuary" in Chapter 6.

ate. David's behavior is logical but unconventional: He looks as if he is mourning when the child is still alive, then he stops mourning when it has died. The combination of logical and remarkable sums up aspects of David.

Why would David care so much about this baby among the umpteen he has fathered, a number of whom have presumably died in infancy (his second son, Kileab, certainly seems to have died at some point)? This child's death somehow becomes a symbol of the grim nature of this turning point in David's story. Yes, the man who acted as David did is "a son of death," almost "a dead man" (12:5).[29] "I am going to him," David says (12:23). From now on, David is on his way to dying.

He consoles Bathsheba (no one consoles him), they make love, and she gets pregnant with Solomon. And "in that Yahweh loved him" (Solomon), he sends again by means of Nathan and calls the baby Yedidyah (loved by Yahweh), "on account of Yahweh" (12:24–25). Several subtleties combine to underscore the positive nature of the paragraph, before the narrative returns to conclude the account of the battle with the Ammonites within which this story has been a huge interruption. That first clause ("in that…") has an unusual word order, with the subject before the verb, which points to its leading into what follows. In referring to "love" ('āhēb) it uses the verb that can also suggest affirming and being loyal to, and that often has political implications. It is a significant and prophetic comment on Solomon. But Nathan's new sending that contrasts with the earlier sending to confront also brings a new name for the child. This second name does not occur anywhere else, and the functional interrelationship of the two names is not clear, but the second name may safeguard against any possibility

---

[29] Cf. Auld, *I & II Samuel*, 466.

that the first refers only to a political commitment. Further, the element that apparently means "loved" (*ydyd)* is close to "David" (*dwd)*. The child is "Yahweh's David." The grimness of David's deeds is not the end of the story, and Bathsheba will be instrumental in bringing this replacement child to the throne in succession to David.[30]

WHAT'S LOVE OR SMARTNESS GOT TO DO WITH IT

The narrative that follows (13:1–14:33) is a kind of palimpsest of the preceding story, though a heightened one.[31]

- Amnon takes David's place, though he "loves" (as David did not) and also rapes and repudiates.
- Tamar takes Bathsheba's place, though she suffers more and more explicitly.
- Jonadab takes the place of David's staff, though he is (supposedly) smarter.
- Joab plays himself, acting (he thinks) in David's interests and in the people's interests.
- The smart woman takes Nathan's place, though she follows Joab's script rather than Yahweh's.
- In the parable, the widow and the surviving son take the places of the rich and the poor man.
- In reacting to the parable, David plays himself.
- As a mourner, the smart woman also takes Bathsheba's place and David's place.
- Absalom takes the place of the sword.

---

[30] Cf. Cheryl You, "The Historian's Heroines: Examining the Characterization of Female Role Models in the Early Israelite Monarchy," *Journal of Biblical Perspectives in Leadership* 9 (2019): 178–200 (192, 193).

[31] Smith, *The Fate of Justice and Righteousness during David's Reign*, 149.

"Tamar's rape is unbearable to read. Because the narrator provides us with so much preliminary information about Amnon's scheme, we watch in dread."[32] Tamar is the daughter of David and the sister of Absalom. Like them, she is beautiful, and "beauty causes an awful lot of mayhem in this cycle of stories."[33] For her, it means she becomes "a woman of sorrows and acquainted with grief" (cf. Isa 53:3).[34] Her story begins with a recurrence of that verb for "love," used here with a meaning that suggests emotion rather than allegiance. Indeed, it errs on the other side of this range of meaning (NRSV has "fell in love," NJPS "became infatuated"). "Every time we read or hear the word "love," we do well to be alert to what is going on.... No word in our language is in more need of probing and testing of the kind that this story gives it."[35]

The person who suggests to Amnon the ploy by which he can seduce or rape Tamar is their cousin Jonadab. As David's nephew, Jonadab counts in a broad sense as a member of David's household, from which Yahweh has warned David that dire trouble would arise (12:11). To describe Jonadab, the story also introduces the word "smart" or "wise" (ḥākām, 13:3), for the first time in Samuel, again used with negative connotations. Jonadab is either smart in a bad sense, or not really smart in light of what happens. He is "a smart man for faithlessness" (riš'â).[36]

Threatened with rape, Tamar suggests (desperately but plausibly?) that David would not be legalistic about her being Amnon's half-sister if Amnon raises the question of marrying. She is beside

[32] Morrison, 2 Samuel, 109.
[33] Robert Barron, 2 Samuel, 123.
[34] Phyllis Trible, Texts of Terror: Literary Feminist Readings of Biblical Narratives, Overtures to Biblical Theology 13 (Philadelphia, PA: Fortress, 1984), 36.
[35] Peterson, First and Second Samuel, 194.
[36] B. Sanhedrin 21a; cf. Rashi, in miqrā'ôt gədôlôt.

herself to avoid being raped and also forced to have illicit sex. Such a thing "is not done in Israel" (13:12). It "would run counter to the accepted values of the whole nation" and be an outrage (*nǝbālâ*); the word commonly refers to sexual wrongdoing (hence Tg's *qālān*) and to acts that cost the perpetrators their death.[37] LXX and Vg have terms denoting "folly," which vastly understates the enormity of the kind of action to which the word refers. Forcing Tamar to have sex will be the kind of thing done by dissolute and morally blind people (*nǝbālîm*, people such as Nabal), people who do not care if they outrage the entire community and imperil their relationship with it. And like the words of a person such as Nabal in relation to David (1 Sam 25:39), it would bring reviling on Tamar (2 Sam 13:12–13).

Tamar has a lot more to say than Bathsheba,[38] who uttered only the two words "I'm pregnant." But "her rational argument was designed to appeal to the mind, and in that moment Amnon was not thinking with his mind."[39] Amnon's not being open to persuasion raises more sharply the question whether in any sense his feeling for Tamar was actually love. "He was too strong for her and overpowered her and laid her" (13:14). The question about his supposed "love" is underlined when he then "repudiates" her (*śānē'*; 13:15). This word is the antithesis of the word for love; whereas it is conventionally translated "hate," it is also an attitude and action word as much as an emotional one (as in 5:6–8). It is thus expressed in sending her off (*šālaḥ* piel, the word for

[37] Shimon Bar-Efrat, *Narrative Art in the Bible*, JSOTSup 70 (reprinted Sheffield: Sheffield Academic Press, 1997), 262, 263.

[38] A Graeme Auld, "Contexts for Tamar: Samuel and the Song of Songs," in David J. A. Clines and Ellen van Wolde, eds., *A Critical Engagement: Essays on the Hebrew Bible in Honour of J. Cheryl Exum* (Sheffield: Sheffield Phoenix, 2011), 21–31 (29).

[39] Cartledge, *1 & 2 Samuel*, 537.

divorce), which she sees as an even more dire action than raping her. She is quite incoherent about it: "No, the cause…. This big dire thing…. More than the other thing that you did with me, sending me off…" (13:16). After having sex with her, he would be morally and socially obliged to marry her, not send her off (Exod 22:16[15]; Deut 22:28–29). He will not even do the right thing in that sense. Thus, she is desolate (*šāmēm*; 2 Sam 13:20), someone abandoned and left on her own like a town that has been attacked, conquered, devastated, and depopulated, with a desolation a little like Michal's childlessness.[40] Crying out (*zā'aq*), shouting something like "rape!" or "woe" or "somebody do something" as she walks,[41] she goes back to the house she apparently shares with her full brother Absalom.

Tamar's story anticipates the way rape still works.

- Tamar was sexually assaulted, not by a stranger, but by someone she knew.
- The violation took place not in a dark alley or in a desolate park, but by a member of Tamar's own family in his home.
- Tamar was exploited through one of her most vulnerable traits – her kindness and her upbringing to take care of the other.
- Tamar said no; her no was not respected.
- When Tamar sought help, she was told to keep quiet.
- The process for achieving justice and restitution was taken out of Tamar's hands entirely and carried forward by her brother – it became men's business.

---

[40] Karla G. Shargent, "Living on the Edge: The Liminality of Daughters in Genesis to 2 Samuel," in Brenner, *A Feminist Companion to Samuel-Kings*, 26–42 (35).

[41] Van Wijk-Bos, *A People and a Land 2*, on the passage, following Tikva Frymer-Kensky, *Reading the Women of the Bible* (New York: Schocken, 2002), 165–66.

- In the end, it was Tamar's perpetrator for whom her father mourned, not her.
- Tamar's story comes to a close without her.[42]

When she gets home, Absalom tells her to keep quiet and not set her mind on the thing for now (13:20), but his words hint that this urging will not be the end of the matter, and Jonadab will later tell David that Absalom is plotting action over the next two years (13:23–36). On hearing of the rape, David is very angry (13:21), but he does not do anything. Nor does Yahweh send someone, as he sent Nathan.[43] But when no one would still be suspecting him, Absalom has Amnon killed. In the execution of this event, "David is … set up as an accomplice to the murder of his son, just as Amnon had previously set him up to be an accomplice to Tamar's rape."[44] Perhaps Absalom maneuvers David into taking the action he should have taken anyway, like the other Tamar in relation to David's ancestor Judah (Gen 38).

Absalom flees and takes refuge with his grandfather (2 Sam 13:37). Knowing that David's mind was on Absalom (though the implications of that statement are unclear),[45] Joab gets a smart woman (the second time the adjective occurs in Samuel and in this story) to tell David another parable about someone killing his brother. The recurrent expression "put words in her mouth" means telling her the kind of thing to say (e.g., Ezra 8:17); her skill means she can formulate the words, as is required by the

[42] Pamela Cooper-White, *The Cry of Tamar: Violence against Women and the Church's Response* (Minneapolis, MN: Fortress, 1995), 4–5.

[43] Barron, *2 Samuel*, 128.

[44] Barron, *2 Samuel*, 129.

[45] See the discussion of David's heart/mind in Marti J. Steussy, *David: Biblical Portraits of Power, Studies in Biblical Personalities of the Old Testament* (Columbia: University of South Carolina Press, 1999), 53–70 (esp. 65–66).

conversation in which she keeps interrupting the king.[46] If anything, "she shows that she might have been trained by Abigail,"[47]
who was not described as "smart" but was "good in her insight"
(1 Sam 25:3). The parable again portrays a situation that requires
the king to take action, in this case restraining an executioner
(whose action would be quite proper; to speak in terms of "blood
revenge" gives a misleading impression). David fails to see that the
parable is about him in a more personal sense, that he is colluding
with a sort of execution in the form of Absalom's self-imposed
banishment. "You're smart, too," the woman tells David. If only
he had been. "Just as her phony widowhood duped David, her flat-
tery obstructs David from interrogating her further. She is indeed
wise."[48]

David gets Absalom brought back, confines him to his own
house, and only after two more years summons him. He bows to
the ground before David, and David hugs him.

THE SWORD NEVER DEPARTS

The story of Tamar has a significance in its own right. But it
starts with Absalom and a reference to Tamar as his sister, and it
leads directly into the account of Absalom's coup that occupies
2 Samuel 15–20. "David's strategically motivated marriages have
resulted in numerous offspring, initially symbols of his power,
who become a gravely destabilizing force."[49] The Tamar story has
portrayed the enormity of Amnon's wrongdoing, Tamar's suffering and loss, Absalom's hardnosed cunning, Joab's manipulative

---

[46] Birch, "The First and Second Books of Samuel," in his comments on 14:8–11.
[47] Auld, *I & II Samuel*, 492.
[48] Morrison, *2 Samuel*, 123.
[49] Rosenberg, "I and 2 Samuel," 135.

shrewdness, and David's simple-minded naivety. "The bitterness of David's tragedy is that he not only cannot spare his children misery, but he even plays an unwitting role in the tragic fates they suffer."[50] He does not know what to do, and Joab wants to get a grip of the situation.[51] The narrative has not necessarily implied that Absalom acted outrageously. Given David's softness, he too might seem to have taken proper redress (not mere revenge) on Amnon. Nevertheless, "if the death of Bathsheba's firstborn to David began the fulfillment of Nathan's dark prophecy, the actions of Amnon and Absalom brought it to a full flowering that would ultimately bear even more bitter fruit in Absalom's revolt."[52] The account of his popularity and further ruthlessness (14:25–33) forms the background to what will follow. The narrative thus hints that Absalom's restoration will not be the end of the story, as 11:1–12:31 hinted that the death and birth of the two sons would not be the end of its story. Perhaps even "David's failure to address the rape of Tamar and his unwillingness to acknowledge the justice of Absalom in executing Amnon for this crime were the chief factors that pushed Absalom to the point of usurping his father's throne."[53] It is questionable whether Joab was acting in David's interests or in Israel's, and whether the woman was being smart with Joab's message, like Nathan. Joab is always problematic in the way he "serves" David. She/he say that David is acting against the people, while she/he are doing the opposite – and it looks as if they love Absalom and would agree with the popular assessment of him (14:25–27).

---

[50] Exum, *Tragedy and Biblical Narrative*, 130.
[51] Jeremy Schipper, *Parables and Conflict in the Hebrew Bible* (Cambridge: Cambridge University Press, 2009), 57–73.
[52] Cartledge, *1 & 2 Samuel*, 544.
[53] Smith, *The Fate of Justice and Righteousness during David's Reign*, 146.

The narrative goes on to portray the fulfillment of Nathan's threat that dire trouble would arise out of his own household, that someone else would bed his wives, and that a sword would be whirling through his household for all time (*'ad-'ôlām*; 12:10–11). The story of Tamar and Amnon has not referred to Yahweh's activity (though the smart woman and David speak of him). It has points of comparison and contrast with 1 Samuel 25, and this lack of reference to Yahweh is one of the contrasts (see especially 25:38).[54] In the chapters that follow, Yahweh does not need to intervene to make things happen, as he did to bring Saul to the throne and then bring David to the throne. Things happen by the natural course of events as human beings (especially Absalom) make their decisions. Does trouble regularly arise naturally – is it grace that needs divine intervention?

"David is ultimately decrowned by Absalom"; in Samuel as a whole, "as a dialogic hero, David is crowned and decrowned."[55] It is impossible to make coherent sense of his successive attitudes after Absalom's return and then in light of his coup. There is negligent administration of justice, if Absalom's insinuations are justified (2 Sam 15:1–6). There is careless ingenuousness that suggests David is affected by "middle-aged torpor,"[56] when Absalom is taking Yahweh's name in vain (15:7–12). There is panicked disarray and retreat that involves David's leaving his wives behind for Absalom, unwisely and coldly (15:13–18). There is generous concern for a Gittite (15:19–23). There is tentative hopefulness in Yahweh and prayerful calculation, both hinting that David still has

---

[54] Cf. Auld, *I & II Samuel*, 484.

[55] SuJung Shin, "A 'Dialogic' Hero David from the Perspective of 'Internally Persuasive Word' in the Narrative of Samuel," in Ahn, *Landscapes*, 59–72 (70, 71).

[56] Barron, *2 Samuel*, 141.

something of his old trust in Yahweh (15:24–37). There is unquestioning credulity (16:1–4). There is charitable forbearance with someone who sees him as guilty for the death of various members of Saul's household, who have lost their lives in connection with David's becoming king (16:5–14).

In contrast, Absalom's actions manifest a coherent but ineffective logic. Things begin with his ongoing preparing of the way (15:2–6).[57] Then he asks if he may go to Hebron to fulfill a vow (15:7–12) – but that rationale is "padding."[58] He accepts the support of his father's aide, Hushai, who is actually a spy (16:15–19). He consults a renowned adviser, who bids him publicly bed his father's wives and formulates a smart plan to kill David that gives himself a key role (16:20–17:4). But he follows the bad advice of the aide who also gives Absalom a prominent role, is secretly still supporting David, but is a more skilled persuader (17:5–14).[59] He uncovers an intelligence operation, but fails to silence it and loses impetus, while the smart adviser hangs himself in anticipation of events confirming the wisdom of his rejected plan (17:15–23). Absalom leads a huge force in pursuit of David across the Jordan, but loyalists provision David's company and David regroups (17:24–29). When David proposes to lead his forces out in battle and they urge him to leave the battle to them, David bids his commanders spare Absalom. They defeat Absalom's forces but take no notice and kill Absalom (18:1–15). Absalom had set up a monolith for himself near Jerusalem for his burial, but the troops bury him in the forest under a heap of rocks (18:16–18).

---

[57] With two past *yiqtol* verbs and six *weqatal* verbs (J. P. Fokkelman, *Narrative Art and Poetry in the Books of Samuel, Volume 1: King David (II Sam. 9–20 & 1 Kings 1–2)* [Assen: van Gorcum, 1981], 165).

[58] Fokkelman, *Narrative Art* 2:170.

[59] Bar-Efrat, *Narrative Art*, 223–37.

David still does not know what he is doing. He is so distraught about Absalom that he threatens to demoralize the troops (18:19–19:8a[9a]). He gets the Judahites (who had presumably supported Absalom) to conduct him back across the Jordan, but he sacks Joab in favor of Abner and thereby signs Abner's death warrant (19:8b–15[9b–16]). He pardons Shimei (19:16–23[17–24]), operating by Proverbs 26:4–5,[60] though Shimei would be wise to read the small print in the pardon (see 1 Kgs 2:8–9). He throws up his hands over Ziba and Mephiboshet in a way that has still not resolved the questions about what had actually happened (2 Sam 19:24–30[25–31]).[61] He expresses his appreciation to Barzillai for his provisions (19:31–40[32–41]) and is then faced with conflict and rivalry between Judah and the northern clans (19:41[42]–20:2). He sequesters the wives he had unwittingly surrendered to Absalom and commissions Abner to deal with the northern clans' rebellion under Shebna. He then panics and intervenes in a way that leads to Abner's death. But it also leads to Joab sorting out Shebna with the help of another smart woman, who does not mind causing some violence (20:3–22).

The narrative from 13:1 to 20:26 makes many references to Yahweh and includes many statements that people attribute to Yahweh, but in themselves the chapters' meaning is "more than usually elusive."[62] It is on the basis of what precedes that one can see the narrative as describing how David pays "the wages of sin."[63] And everything in the sorry story is humanly explicable. It

---

[60] Willet, *An Harmonie upon the Second Booke of Samuel...*, 98.

[61] On interpretations of who is telling the truth between these two, see Jeremy Schipper, *Disability Studies and the Hebrew Bible: Figuring Mephibosheth in the David Story*, LHBOTS 441 (London: T&T Clark, 2006), 49–60.

[62] Campbell, *2 Samuel*, 135; cf. Gilmour, *Representing the Past*, 198–99.

[63] See Gillian Keys, *The Wages of Sin: A Reappraisal of the "Succession Narrative,"* JSOTSup 221 (Sheffield: Sheffield Academic Press, 1996).

issues from decisions and actions that are intelligible in light of who the people are.

There is one crucial exception, the decision by Absalom and his forces to follow Hushai's plan rather than Ahitophel's. Arguably, the very fact that Absalom was asking his staff for advice is cause for concern. "A plan of Ahitophel's that he gave, in those days, was like when one would ask for a word of God – so was every plan of Ahitophel both for David and for Absalom" (16:23). Actually, we have not ever heard of David asking for a plan, but we have often heard of him asking for a word from Yahweh (e.g., 2:1; 5:19, 23), which was how to discover the wise thing to do. There was no talk of counsel or counselors before Absalom's coup. Sayings such as Proverbs 20:18 do commend the taking of counsel,[64] but this narrative half-implies that "the very introduction of the practice of royal counsel, like the introduction of royalty itself, contaminated Israel and turned its Yahwistic spirit into foolishness."[65] And only in connection with this one decision does the narrative report that Yahweh did something, commanding the nullification of Ahitophel's battle advice (2 Sam 17:14) and answering David's prayer (15:31). Ahitophel's plan was "good." Perhaps it was obviously good, and it is therefore a mystery why Absalom turned it down, or perhaps Hushai had massaged his ego, or perhaps only the way things worked out showed that it would have been a good plan. With hindsight, at least, rejecting it did not make sense, and this mistake is the turning point in this narrative.

Why would Yahweh act in order to deliver David and bring a "dire fate" on Absalom, which in light of subsequent events

---

[64] Van Wijk-Bos, *A People and a Land 2*, on the passage.
[65] Polzin, *David and the Deuteronomist*, 176–77.

likely implies bringing about his death?[66] Once more, it was not because David was a better or wiser man than Absalom, any more than he had been a better or wiser man than Saul. He was simply the man after Yahweh's heart, the man Yahweh had decided to use. Presumably Yahweh could have chosen to intervene to stop Absalom's coup at some earlier point, but he had already decided not to do so. He will let the sword have its way, and no one urges him to relent over that decision. He has already concluded that "something is rotten in the state of Denmark."[67] As had happened with Eli's priesthood and Saul's monarchy, and will in due course happen with Ephraim and with Judah, there can come a time when Yahweh says, "That's it," and lets events take their natural course. Much of the time, all Yahweh does is watch. Perhaps that fact links with the Samuel narrative's holding back from condemning Ahitophel for taking his own life, just as it did not condemn Saul, nor will the Gospels condemn Judas. They were acts of self-assertion illustrative of regular human self-assertion rather than being the acts of distinctively wicked people.[68]

A summary of David's administration, restating an earlier one from happier times (8:15–18), brings 2 Samuel 13–20 to a close (20:23–25).

A FAMINE AND AN EPIDEMIC

At some point in David's reign, there was a famine (21:1). Actually, there likely were a number; the vagaries of Middle Eastern rainfall

[66] Smith, *The Fate of Justice and Righteousness during David's Reign*, 187–88.
[67] William Shakespeare, *Hamlet*, Act I, Scene 4.
[68] See Karl Barth, *Church Dogmatics* III/4 (reprinted London: T&T Clark, 2010), 81.

mean failure of the harvest from time to time. And generally the First Testament's accounts of famine treat it as "just one of those things." So it was with the famines that affected the families of Abraham, Isaac, Jacob, and Elimelek and caused them to migrate (Gen 12:10; 26:1; 42:5; Ruth 1:1). These stories show that people do not take a famine as an indication that God is angry. But this famine continues for three years, and David therefore asks Yahweh what is going on. Literally, he "inquired of Yahweh's face," as one inquires of a king's face (1 Kgs 10:24); the expression suggests going to the sanctuary rather than consulting the "Urim and Thummim."

The answer is that there is bloodshed (*dāmîm*, literally "bloods"), bloodguilt, hanging over the nation from the time of Saul. Saul had apparently slaughtered some Gibeonites, breaking the Israelites' promise to spare them (Josh 9). David asks the Gibeonites how to put things right, how to bring about cleansing or expiation (*kāpar* piel), the verb's only occurrence in Samuel. It suggests eliminating something that stands as an obstacle between two parties, usually Israel and Yahweh. But it sometimes relates to two human parties (Gen 32:20[21]; Prov 16:14), which could make sense here. In effect, the Gibeonites say they believe in capital punishment (cf. Num 35:30–34),[69] and they want to see seven of Saul's sons killed to compensate for the Gibeonite deaths, to level things out. Their assumption is that the king's entire household shares in responsibility for the king's actions, as it shares in the privileges of belonging to his household. And execution is the recognized consequence of breaking a solemn pledge, as the pledge-making ceremony suggests (Gen 15:10–18; Jer 34:18).[70] They say they want

---

[69] Michael Widmer, *Standing in the Breach: An Old Testament Theology and Spirituality of Intercessory Prayer* (Winona Lake, IN: Eisenbrauns, 2015), 229.

[70] Anderson, *2 Samuel*, 249.

to execute the men "for Yahweh," though the narrative says they execute them "before Yahweh" (2 Sam 21:6, 9).[71]

David agrees. The narrative does not comment on whether he was wise or whether he might have gone back for a further consultation with Yahweh.[72] Ironically, the story is a little reminiscent of the story of Saul and Jonathan, which almost issued in Jonathan's death (1 Sam 14), and of other unwise promises such as Jephthah's (Judg 11). But perhaps David the powerful king was right not to refuse some form of redress to people who had been treated in the way the Gibeonites had been treated.[73]

The story is more interested in the aftermath of David's action. One of the mothers of the dead men is Rizpah, already (allegedly) the victim of Abner's political sex act (2 Sam 3:7). She takes action to stop the vultures attacking the bodies of the dead men, so that in due course they can be properly buried and can find their rest. While David is the person who has all the political and judicial power in this situation, Rizpah has some moral power as the mother of some of these men.[74] "Emotionally and dramatically, Rizpah commands the center of this story.... Her defiance of convention sets her apart from and above the world in which she suffers."[75] "Although Rizpah's protest, unlike Antigone's, is silent, it is not without its own literary eloquence.... Impassioned

[71] Cf. László T. Simon, *Identity and Identification: An Exegetical and Theological Study of 2 Sam 21-24*, Tesi Gregoriana Serie Teologia 64 (Rome: Gregorian University Press, 2000), 70; LXX and Vg make this distinction, but Tg and modern English translations do not.

[72] Cf. You, "The Historian's Heroines," 194.

[73] Cf. the South African response to the story, recorded by Gerald West, "Reading on the Boundaries: Reading 2 Samuel 21:1-14 with Rizpah," *Scriptura* 63 (1997): 527-37 (529).

[74] Birch, "The First and Second Books of Samuel," in his reflections on 21:10-14.

[75] Peterson, *First and Second Samuel*, 243.

pleas and angry outbursts would lessen the impact of the story and detract our attention from the act itself. Silence gives Rizpah a preternatural magnitude and underscores the gravity of the ritual she performs."[76] Her action leads David not only to collect up the men's remains but also to fetch the remains of Saul and Jonathan from Jabesh-gilead and bury them all in Saul's family tomb. And it is after she has taken her action and inspired David to take his action (not just after the executions) that "God let himself be petitioned ('ātar niphal) for the country" in connection with the famine (21:14).[77] Thus "Second Samuel 21:1–14 brings to a close the chain of tragic events which has beset the house of Saul."[78] The story has "brought to a conclusion the contorted relationship between David and Saul."[79]

Finally, there is another famine. "Yahweh's anger again flared against Israel, and he incited David against them: 'Go count Israel and Judah'" (24:1). If the earlier famine was Saul's fault, this one is David's, but Yahweh is angry with Israel as a whole. Although it is David who makes the mistake of commissioning the census, it is the people who are already destined to be Yahweh's victims.[80] Perhaps there was a reason, as on the previous occasion when Yahweh's anger flared (6:7), or the previous famine (21:1), though that story did not refer to Yahweh being angry. Perhaps the event was even more mysterious than that previous occasion (cf. the great wrath in 2 Kgs 3:27). "I do not know why," says Rashi.[81] If there was a reason, Samuel does not reveal it (once again, who says

[76] J. Cheryl Exum, "Rizpah," *Word & World* 17 (1997): 260–68 (264).
[77] Cf. West, "Reading on the Boundaries," 530.
[78] Exum, *Tragedy and Biblical Narrative*, 109.
[79] Morrison, *2 Samuel*, 185.
[80] Auld, *I & II Samuel*, 605.
[81] In *miqrā'ôt gədôlôt*, on the verse.

narrators are omniscient?). "Honest readers of the Bible spend much of their time scratching their heads" and need to be content to stay that way rather than inventing answers to their questions.[82] Or perhaps the anger followed on the census, as 1 Chronicles 21 infers.

David himself has already spoken of Yahweh "inciting" someone (*sût* hiphil). On the earlier occasion, Yahweh had incited Saul to pursue him (1 Sam 26:19). Inciting suggests putting into someone else's head the idea of doing something that is at least surprising and quite likely dire in some way (e.g., Deut 13:6[7]; Josh 15:18; 1 Kgs 21:25; 2 Kgs 18:32; Jer 38:22). Elsewhere, Yahweh speaks of an adversary (a *śāṭān*) inciting him to send trouble to Job for no reason (2:3), and 1 Chronicles 21:1 sees such an adversary behind the inciting of David here. "There is less theological distance between these two forms of the introduction to this narrative than most commentators suggest"; the adversary was not independent of Yahweh.[83] Inciting overlaps with the idea of toughening someone's mind ("hardening their heart") in Exodus, encouraging them to do something dire.

Everyone knows that counting things is a bad idea: It suggests pride,[84] and/or reliance on resources rather than Yahweh,[85] and/or it facilitates collection of taxes or conscription into the military. Even Joab, bless him, knows it, but he cannot dissuade David. David's insistence, the narrative assumes, shows that on this occasion Yahweh must be mysteriously at work. But afterwards, David's conscience (literally, his heart) struck him down, as happened

[82] Peterson, *First and Second Samuel*, 262.
[83] Auld, *I & II Samuel*, 605.
[84] John Mayer, *Many Commentaries in One* [on Joshua through Esther] (London: William, 1647), 466.
[85] So Gersonides and Abravanel, according to Moshe C. Sosevsky, *Samuel II* (New York: Judaica, 1989), 444.

once before (1 Sam 24:5[6]). He acknowledged it to Yahweh in terms that featured in connection with Nathan and Uriah, "I have done very wrong.… Please make your servant's waywardness pass on," and terms that featured in connection with Samuel and Saul, "I have been stupid" (1 Sam 13:13). Once again Yahweh will not simply make the waywardness go away, but he allows David to choose the consequence: famine, defeat, or epidemic. "Let us please fall into/by [*bə*] Yahweh's hand, because his compassion is plenteous" (2 Sam 24:14). It is a brave choice, because Yahweh's hand is the means whereby Yahweh brings calamity (cf. 24:16–17); it is not in itself a safe place (compare the hands in 21:9, 22). "It is a fearful thing to fall into the hands of the living God" (Heb 10:31).[86] An epidemic follows in which thousands die. Yahweh's aide threatens to destroy Jerusalem, until Yahweh says, "Stop." It is the only appearance of such an aide (*mal'āk*) in Samuel; such figures are members of Yahweh's supernatural entourage and workforce. Like the adversary in Job and Chronicles, they implement decisions of the heavenly cabinet.

David is standing by a Jebusite threshing floor, and Yahweh bids him erect an altar there for the offering of sacrifice. A Middle Eastern king cannot simply appropriate land, so David buys it from Araunah.[87] And this location is where Solomon will build the temple. That is another story, but here the motif means the narrative is an apt close to Samuel and teaser for Kings, as 1 Chronicles 22:1 makes explicit. Once again, Yahweh "let himself be petitioned for the country" (cf. 2 Sam 21:14), and the action of Araunah and David leads to Yahweh's answering prayer, as the action of David and Rizpah led to it previously. In a sense, then, Araunah plays

---

[86] Willet, *An Harmonie upon the First Booke of Samuel*, 143.

[87] See Stephen C. Russell, *The King and the Land: A Geography of Royal Power in the Biblical World* (Oxford: Oxford University Press, 2016), 16–38.

Rizpah's role.[88] As Hannah's psalm almost began Samuel with some unrealistic declarations about Yahweh's involvement with ordinary people, the stories of Rizpah and Araunah almost end Samuel with stories that illustrate Hannah's theology. The nature of narrative is not to say that God always acts that way but to say that he sometimes does, and that these acts are clues to the true nature of his relationship with his people and with the world.

THE GOD OF DAVID

Whereas Yahweh acts in unpredictable ways in the two stories in 2 Samuel 21–24,[89] the two poems in between these chapters affirm the logic and consistency of his acts. They, too, link with Hannah's psalm of thanksgiving, which almost started Samuel. That psalm did not relate very specifically to Hannah's own life but to Yahweh's relationship with Israel and his commitment to "his anointed." Samuel almost ends with a psalm of thanksgiving on the lips of David. It does not relate very specifically to his life but to Yahweh's relationship with Israel, though also to his commitment to "his anointed" (2 Sam 22:1–51, a variant of Ps 18). It is a testimony to put on the lips of a king, like other such testimonies in the Psalms. As a more general affirmation about Yahweh's dealings with Israel it might be an encouragement (e.g., after 587 BC) for people to trust that Yahweh will deliver them if they start being faithful people. Readers might welcome such an affirmation of "the traditional theological system."[90] Or, "'while your experience of God may be as capricious as the events in this book, your

---

[88] Peterson, *First and Second Samuel*, 261.
[89] Van Wijk-Bos, *A People and a Land 2*, in her introduction to 2 Sam 21–24.
[90] Cartledge, *1 & 2 Samuel*, 658.

hope, however, must be grounded in the God of these Songs of Hannah and David.'"[91] It works well as a synagogue lection during Passover, when one could view the reference to the sea as an allusion to the deliverance at the Red Sea, view faithfulness as Israel's faithfulness in the wilderness, and view the refractory person as Pharaoh (2 Sam 22:16, 27).[92]

The psalm could be interpreted as evidence that David was self-deceived, with the implication that it needs to be read ironically. Heard on David's lips, it does raise questions parallel to the hearing of Psalm 51 on his lips, or of Psalm 72 on Solomon's. Really, David? As David's testimony, summing up his experience of Yahweh's faithfulness and deliverance, its statements about his own unwavering faithfulness might be taken as antedating the wrongdoing with Bathsheba and Uriah. It would make sense coming from the time just after Saul's death, and it does refer to his being rescued from Saul (2 Sam 22:1) and his faithfulness in that context (1 Sam 24–26).[93] Or it might imply that the wrongdoing was the great exception that does not disprove the psalm's general statements (cf. 1 Kgs 15:5).[94]

The psalm begins plausibly in this connection, in testifying to Yahweh's delivering David from all his enemies, and specifically from Saul. Yahweh is a cliff, a fastness, a means of escape, a crag, a refuge, a peak, a means of deliverance, a haven, a refuge, a deliverer from violence (2 Sam 22:2–3). The complex of images (parallel to but much more extensive than Hannah's) suggests that David or Israel is a bird that needs to escape from

---

[91] Randall C. Bailey, "The Redemption of Yhwh: A Literary Critical Function of the Songs of Hannah and David," *BibInt* 3 (1995): 213–31 (231)

[92] So Rashi, in *miqrā'ôt gədôlôt* on the passage.

[93] Firth, *1 & 2 Samuel*, 519.

[94] See Noll, *The Faces of David*, 118–51.

a hunter or from a wild animal, and that Yahweh is a high ledge in a rock face onto which it can flit and find safety. No hunter or animal can reach it there. Thus, one can call on Yahweh and find deliverance.

This psalm is more overtly a thanksgiving or testimony than Hannah's, and it now makes a transition to speaking in the past tense of what Yahweh has done. Its opening praise is the truth about Yahweh that Samuel has illustrated in connection with Israel and with David. The psalm also switches to another metaphor to describe a predicament: "I was drowning and about to be overwhelmed by death's torrents." Complicating matters further, the psalm then alternates the use of *qatal* and *wayyiqtol* or *yiqtol* verbs, so that one cannot be sure when a past event is in view and when a statement is a generalization. At this point, however, the psalm does seem to declare (to paraphrase) that "threatened by death, I called out from the depths of the sea, and Yahweh listened from his palace in the heavens." He took action, which the psalm describes as thundering from the heavens. "He plucked me out of the overwhelming water and deposited me on land."

It is at this point, too, that the psalm makes its move to the statements that raise eyebrows about David (or Israel), so that the transition to *yiqtol* verbs is fortuitous. Subsequent positive comments about David (e.g., 2 Kgs 18:3; 22:2) may consider David to be a model of faithfulness to Yahweh even if he was not a model of righteousness. Here, David claims ṣədāqâ, which English translations regularly render as "righteousness." But the word denotes something more like doing the right thing by the people in whom one lives in a committed relationship, so that it means something closer to faithfulness than righteousness (see the comments on

"Government" in Chapter 6). David could perhaps more plausibly have claimed to have lived that way with Yahweh. So:

> Yahweh recompenses/will recompense me in accordance with my faithfulness,
>> in accordance with the cleanness of my hands he makes/ will make things return for me.
> Because I have kept Yahweh's ways
>> and not been faithless (*rāšaʿ*) in relation to my God....
> With the committed (*ḥāsîd*) you show yourself committed
>> with the upright (*tāmîm*) warrior you show yourself upright.
> With the pure you show yourself pure,
>> with the refractory you show refractoriness. (22:21–22, 26–27)

It is also just possible to take David's "because" statements as meaning something like "insofar as" and not quite claiming to have been obedient, faithful, and so on. One would have to make the same assumption about Israel, in a way that fitted the promises and warnings of the Torah and the arguments of the Psalms. It would still make for a tension with Samuel as a whole, where there has been no tight relationship between Israel's faithfulness or David's faithfulness and Yahweh's faithfulness. While Yahweh sometimes brings calamity on David or on Israel resulting from their faithlessness, over the long haul Yahweh continues to be faithful despite their faithlessness. His commitment to Israel and to David continues because of who he is, not because of who they are, and because of his purpose, not because of their cooperation with his purpose.

The apparent implausibility of the statements about David increases as a result of the Septuagint's use of a word meaning "blameless" for the word translated "upright" earlier, which English translations traditionally follow. But the word *tāmim* more literally means "whole" with the implication of "wholly committed," as some English translations recognize. Integrity of commitment means that "all is in order between God and man."[95] In contrast, "blameless" suggests the absence of any failure, which is more than the word claims. The word in question recurs in the psalm as a description of Yahweh:

> God is upright in his way,
>> Yahweh's word is [silver] refined.
> He is a shield to everyone,
>> people who take refuge in him.
> Because who is God apart from Yahweh,
>> and who is a crag except our God? (22:31–32)

"David's last words" (23:1) restate this understanding of Yahweh, David, and Israel. They also describe David in words that recall Hannah's, as "the anointed of the God of Jacob" (cf. 1 Sam 2:10). And like Hannah, David speaks like a prophet (2 Sam 23:2–3). It is the only passage apart from the account of David's original anointing (1 Sam 16:13) that associates the spirit of Yahweh with David. Either David himself, or someone on his behalf, affirms what he needs to be committed to being, in a way that recalls the vision for kingship in Psalm 72.

> One who rules over people as a faithful person,
>> rules in awe of God,
> And is like the light of morning when the sun rises,
>> a morning that has no clouds:
> From sunshine and from rain
>> there is growth from the earth.
> My household is like this with God, isn't it,
>> because he has set up a pledge for all time for me....
> But the scoundrel is like a thistle,
>> thrown away, all of them. (2 Sam 23:3–6)

---

[95] Hertzberg, *I & II Samuel*, 396.

As Karl Barth puts it: "The election of a man is that in spite of himself God makes this kind of man a witness to His will, the will of His grace. Election stands or falls with that which God purposes and will effect and accomplish with him, and on this very account it can only stand and not fall."[96] So it is with Israel, and with David.

---

[96] Karl Barth, *Church Dogmatics II/2* (reprinted London: T&T Clark, 2010), 190.

CHAPTER 8

Samuel in Its Theological Context in the Scriptures

The theology of Samuel is set in a series of contexts within the Scriptures. The works with which one can see points of comparison and contrast share the assumption that Yahweh is the only God and that lesser deities do not really deserve the designation God, and that Yahweh has made a distinctive commitment to Israel. Some of the points of comparison and contrast point to possible ongoing significances of Samuel.

Samuel leads into Kings, and both works assume that kings are integral to the life of Israel and to Yahweh's working with it, though Kings is less ambiguous about the propriety of kingship than Samuel. Both assume in particular that Yahweh made a commitment to the royal line of David and will be faithful to it. But both assume that kings go wrong in their relationship with Yahweh and in their lives. Both assume that Yahweh occasionally intervenes to keep Israel's story on track. Both assume that prophets stand alongside kings, often in confrontation with them. Both see a particular sanctuary as integral to the nation's life. Kings puts some emphasis on Moses's Torah, which Samuel does not mention. Kings emphasizes the building of the temple in Jerusalem and its role as (ideally) the central or sole location for the nation's corporate worship. It emphasizes the importance of serving Yahweh rather than the traditional deities of Canaan, which is less of an issue in Samuel. Kings is more ambiguous about the relationship of Judah and Ephraim. Indeed, here Ephraim has a theological significance a little like that of Saul's monarchy in Samuel: It ought never to have existed, but Yahweh is prepared to stay with it if it will submit itself to him. It does not do so.

Samuel links retrospectively with Joshua and Judges, and along with Kings it is thus part of the "Former Prophets." Prophets make hardly any appearance in Joshua or Judges, but Joshua to Kings as a whole offers a prophetic perspective on Israel's story. As well as challenging Israel about its commitment to Yahweh, it promises Yahweh's involvement in taking it to the destiny he has in mind, even though much of the time Yahweh stays in the background and lets events take their course. Joshua and Judges, like Samuel and Kings, follow on from Deuteronomy, and this entire sequence has been seen as part of a Deuteronomistic History. Like Kings, Deuteronomy and Joshua emphasize the importance of Moses's Torah, which we have noted Samuel does not mention. Deuteronomy 17:14–20 makes brief mention of kingship, speaking of Yahweh choosing Israel's king as Samuel does, but it focuses more on Yahweh's choosing a place of worship and choosing Israel as his people. Joshua, Judges, and Samuel have no equivalent to Deuteronomy's stress on worship at the place Yahweh will choose to settle his name there. Judges compares with Samuel in suggesting some ambiguous reflection on kingship. A hero like Gideon refuses to rule over the people, and one of his sons dismisses the idea of kings, while another of his sons who aspires to be king is a murderer who pays for his wrongdoing with his life. On the other hand, Judges makes a link between there being no king in Israel and the moral, social, and religious disorder of the period it covers, and it lets this judgment lead into Samuel. LXX's order has Ruth between Judges and Samuel, providing on one hand an alternative contrast and on the other an anticipatory parallel to the opening chapters of Samuel. The two books both present instructively realistic visions of family, which provides an anticipatory contrast to the grim portrayal of Saul's and David's families in Samuel.

Samuel then forms part of the broader work from Genesis to Kings, Israel's "First History." While Yahweh does not speak of making a pledge or covenant to David as he does to Abraham, there are parallels in the relationship between God and Abraham and between God and David. God makes a commitment to both of them that emerges from his grace and purpose, and not from some deserving of theirs. But God expects a responsive commitment from them, so that the relationship becomes a mutual commitment. Conversely, the dynamics of the relationship in Exodus 32–34 between Yahweh's commitment, his chastisement, and his relenting compare and contrast with the dynamics in Saul's story and David's story. Further, the dynamics of Yahweh's delivering Israel from the Egyptians reappear in his delivering Israel from the Philistines. And Yahweh looks back positively to the subsequent time when he lived among the Israelites on the move.

Israel's "Second History" comprises Chronicles–Ezra–Nehemiah, with Chronicles going over the entire story covered by the First History. In particular, 1 Chronicles 10–29 retells the story in 1 Samuel 31 to 1 Kings 2, from the death of Saul through David's life. If Joshua to Kings is a prophetic history, one might call Chronicles a priestly history, in the sense that it focuses on the importance of the temple. In connection with David, it thus focuses on his role in planning and providing for its building. Whereas the Samuel narrative centers on David's activity in the world of battle, politics, and family life, in Chronicles such stories do not feature because the narrative centers on his activity in relation to the temple. This concentration also means it lacks reference to some of his wrongdoings and failures, though it does not exactly whitewash him. The census features (1 Chr 21) because it relates to the temple. That story illustrates how Chronicles does safeguard against some of the ambiguity in the portrait of Yahweh in Samuel. In 1 Chronicles 21, it is a supernatural adversary who gives David the idea of a census, not Yahweh himself.

The Psalms have a threefold connection with Chronicles and Samuel. The introductions to twelve psalms make links with stories in Samuel. Without Samuel, these links would be impossible. Conversely, 2 Samuel 22 is a variant on Psalm 18, while Hannah's song follows the form of a psalm. Less directly linked are David's lament over Saul and Jonathan, and his "last words" (2 Sam 1; 23). Second, the Psalms draw readers' attention to the David story as undergirding Yahweh's relationship with Israel in the present, and invite readers to take David's relationship with Yahweh as a model for their relationship with Yahweh as ordinary Israelites. Third, the Psalms and Samuel are the great repositories of First Testament references to Yahweh's Anointed, Israel's current king, as someone who is commissioned by Yahweh. Like the rest of the First Testament, individual psalms do not use the term "Anointed" to refer to a future king, though the collected Psalms may presuppose that reference. They do take up the hints in 2 Samuel 7 that Yahweh's words about David's offspring have implications for future kings, going beyond the promise that David's own son will build the temple.

The Latter Prophets hardly refer to Yahweh's Anointed, but Jeremiah 33:14–22 does speak of Yahweh's indissoluble pledge with "my servant David" that he will have someone arise to ensure the exercise of faithful authority or right decision-making [*mišpāṭ ûṣədāqâ*] in the country, and that pledge recalls 2 Samuel 7:12–16;

8:15; 23:5. And one of the two indisputable New Testament references to Samuel, in Hebrews 1:5, quotes 2 Samuel 7:14. There are also plausible allusions to that chapter in John 7:42; Acts 2:30; and 2 Corinthians 6:18. The significance of 2 Samuel 7 in itself is that Yahweh really makes a commitment to David that invites his people's response in the now and for the next generation, while Jeremiah and such New Testament references remind readers that Yahweh's promise will turn out to invite extending and reapplying.

The other indisputable New Testament quotation from Samuel comes in Acts 13:22, referring to 1 Samuel 13:14; there are also references to either 2 Samuel 22 or Psalm 18 in Romans 15:9 and Hebrews 2:13. In addition, the story of Elizabeth, Zechariah, and Mary, and of the births and early years of John the Baptizer and Jesus, follow patterns from the story of Hannah and Samuel. Hebrews 11:32 regrets not having time to tell of Samuel and David, but its omission has not hindered readers from taking David as an example for a relationship with God (and in connection with Western concern with leadership). Yet Samuel does not look as if it sets David forward as an example in either connection, and interpretations of this kind have to be selective in their reading of David, using criteria that come from elsewhere.

One further link of substance rather than of words lies with Proverbs and Qohelet. Yahweh affirms that he honors people who honor him, while people who slight him get slighted (1 Sam 2:30). Faithful people find that their lives work out well; faithless people find that they do not. Eli's family illustrates the first aspect to the principle; Nabal illustrates the second. Samuel thus affirms that "traditional theological system" that underlies Proverbs (and Deuteronomy, and most other books in both Testaments).[1] On

---

[1] Cartledge, *1 & 2 Samuel*, 658.

the other hand, the stories in Samuel also illustrate the way this principle does not work out in the lives of people such as Ahimelek, Jonathan, and Tamar (as most books in both Testaments also recognize). Things often turn out tragically for people, in a way that morally and religiously one cannot understand. This aspect of the reality of life underlies Qohelet, though it does not trouble the Samuel narrative as it does Qohelet. But like Qohelet, Samuel lets the moviegoers leave the theater with a little encouragement, after presenting its tough story. David sets up an altar where the temple will be built, and offers whole offerings and well-being offerings. Yahweh lets himself be petitioned for the country, and the epidemic ceases from Israel.

Further Reading

I completed this work in 2020 during the COVID-19 lockdown when I did not have access to some books on Samuel, and omission of a book from this list may reflect those circumstances rather than my deliberately omitting it. Actually, Samuel parallels Job in being such a rich work that it is hard to write a bad book on its literary and theological potential, so many other works on Samuel are worth consulting.

Alter, Robert. *The David Story: A Translation with Commentary of 1 and 2 Samuel*. New York: Norton, 1999. Independent translation by a Jewish literary scholar, with substantial notes.

Auld, A. Graeme. *I & II Samuel: A Commentary*. OTL. Louisville, KY: Westminster John Knox, 2011. Exegesis with a text-critical and redaction-critical focus.

Bodner, Keith, and Benjamin J. M. Johnson, ed. *Characters and Characterization in the Book of Samuel*. LHBOTS 669. London: T&T Clark, 2020. Studies of individual characters.

Brueggemann, Walter. *First and Second Samuel: Interpretation: A Bible Commentary for Teaching and Preaching*. Louisville, KY: John Knox, 1990. Exposition with a focus on ideology, power, and psychology.

Chapman, Stephen B. *1 Samuel as Christian Scripture: A Theological Commentary*. Grand Rapids, MI: Eerdmans, 2016.

Cooper, Derek, and Martin J. Lohrmann, ed. *1–2 Samuel, 1–2 Kings, 1–2 Chronicles*. Reformation Commentary on Scripture: Old Testament 5. Downers Grove, IL: InterVarsity, 2016. Excerpts from Reformation and post-reformation authors.

Edelman, Diana Vikander. *King Saul in the Historiography of Judah*. JSOTSup 121. Sheffield: Sheffield Academic Press, 1991. Cross between a literary and historical study.

Eslinger, Lyle. *Kingship of God in Crisis: A Close Reading of 1 Samuel 1–12*. Sheffield: JSOT Press, 1985. Literary study focusing on the characters in the narrative and their interaction.

Firth, David G. *1 & 2 Samuel*. Apollos Old Testament Commentary 8. Nottingham: Apollos, 2009. Detailed exegetical commentary paying substantial attention to the way the story works.

Fokkelman, J. P. *Narrative Art and Poetry in the Books of Samuel, Volume I: King David (II Sam. 9.–20 & 1 Kings 1–2)*. Assen: van Gorcum, 1981.

Volume II: The Crossing Fates (I Sam. 13–31 & II Sam. 1). Assen: van Gorcum, 1986.

Volume III: Throne and City (II Sam. 2–8 & 21–24). Assen: van Gorcum, 1990.

Volume IV: Vow and Desire (I Sam. 1–12). Assen: van Gorcum, 1993. Monumental detailed literary exposition.

Franke, John R. *Joshua, Judges, Ruth, 1–2 Samuel*. Ancient Christian Commentary on Scripture 4. Downers Grove, IL: InterVarsity, 2005. Excerpts from early Christian authors.

Goldingay, John. *Men Behaving Badly*. Reprinted Eugene, OR: Wipf and Stock, 2021. Exposition looking at the male characters.

Green, Barbara. *How Are the Mighty Fallen: A Dialogical Study of King Saul in 1 Samuel*. JSOTSup 365. London: Sheffield Academic Press, 2003. Application of Mikhail Bakhtin's "dialogical" approach to narrative.

Gunn, David M. *The Fate of King Saul: An Interpretation of a Biblical Story*. JSOTSup 14. Reprinted Sheffield: JSOT Press, 1989. Literary study considering Saul as a tragic figure.

Hertzberg, H. W. *I & II Samuel: A Commentary*. OTL. London: SCM, 1964. Classic theological and exegetical commentary.

Jobling, David. *1 Samuel: Berit Olam: Studies in Hebrew Narrative and Poetry*. Collegeville, MN: Liturgical Press, 1998. Thematic literary study taking a structuralist approach.

McCarter, P. Kyle. *I Samuel: A New Translation with Introduction, Notes and Commentary*. AB 8. Garden City, NY: Doubleday, 1980.

II Samuel: A New Translation with Introduction, Notes and Commentary. AB 9. Garden City, NY: Doubleday, 1984.

Substantial pair of commentaries with detailed treatment of textual and redactional questions.

Miscall, Peter D. *1 Samuel: A Literary Reading*. Bloomington: Indiana University Press, 1986. Literary study emphasizing ambiguity in the text.

Morrison, Craig E. *2 Samuel: Berit Olam: Studies in Hebrew Narrative and Poetry*. Collegeville, MN: Liturgical Press, 2013. Literary study making links with other literary works.

Murphy, Francesca Aran. *1 Samuel: Brazos Theological Commentary on the Bible*. Grand Rapids, MI: Brazos, 2010. Theological commentary making links with systematical and historical theology.

Polzin, Robert. *Samuel and the Deuteronomist: A Literary Study of the Deuteronomic History. Part Two: 1 Samuel*. Reprinted Bloomington: Indiana University Press, 1993.

David and the Deuteronomist: A Literary Study of the Deuteronomic History. Part Three: 2 Samuel. Bloomington: Indiana University Press, 1993.

Two studies focusing on the characters and teasing out ambiguities.

Rosenberg, A. J. *Samuel I*. Reprinted New York: Judaica, 1984.

Sosevsky, Moshe C., and A. J. Rosenberg. *Samuel II*. New York: Judaica, 1989.

Pair of commentaries including translations of Rashi's commentary and excerpts from other classic Jewish commentaries.

Tsumura, David Toshio. *The First Book of Samuel*. NICOT. Grand Rapids, MI: Eerdmans, 2007.

The Second Book of Samuel. NICOT. Grand Rapids, MI: Eerdmans, 2019.

Pair of exegetical and historical commentaries.

van Wijk-Bos Johanna W. H. *A People and a Land 2: The Road to Kingship*. Grand Rapids, MI: Eerdmans, 2020.

Reading Samuel: A Literary and Theological Commentary. Macon, GA: Smith and Helwys, 2011.

Two different literary and theological commentaries with feminist insights.

Scripture References Index

Subject Index

Printed in the USA
CPSIA information can be obtained
at www.ICGtesting.com
LVHW051819301124
797961LV00001B/148